HOPE RESTORED

HOPE RESTORED

How the New Deal Worked in Town and Country

EDITED WITH AN INTRODUCTION BY

Bernard Sternsher

Ivan R. Dee
CHICAGO

Grateful acknowledgment is made to the following for permission to reprint copyrighted materials: *Atlanta History* for "The New Deal in Atlanta" by Douglas L. Fleming; University of Alabama Press for "The Civilian Conservation Corps in Mobile County, Alabama" by Billy G. Hinson; *Idaho Yesterdays* for "The New Deal in Pocatello" by Merwin R. Swanson; Rhode Island Historical Society for "Impoverished Politics" by David L. Davies; *Michigan History* for "Flint and the Great Depression" by William H. Chafe; State Historical Society of North Dakota for "The Civil Works Administration in Grand Forks County, North Dakota" by Roger D. Hardaway; Florida Historical Society for "The PWA in Tampa" by Charles B. Lowry, and " 'State of Emergency' " by Garry Boulard; *Journal of Southern History* for "The Persistence of the Past" by Roger Biles; Minnesota Historical Society for "Politics and Relief in Minneapolis During the 1930s" by Raymond L. Koch; *Southern Studies* and Randy J. Sparks for " 'Heavenly Houston' or 'Hellish Houston'?" by Randy J. Sparks; *Southern California Quarterly* for " 'The N.Y.A. at the Sea-Side' " by John A. Salmond; *Tampa Bay History* for "Stitching and Striking" by James Francis Tidd, Jr.; and *Nebraska History* for "Dawson County Responds to the New Deal, 1933–1940" by Jerold Simmons.

Library of Congress Cataloging-in-Publication Data:
Hope restored : how the New Deal worked in town and country / edited
    with an introduction by Bernard Sternsher.
        p.   cm.
    Includes bibliographical references.
    ISBN 0-929587-84-7 (acid-free paper). — ISBN 1-56663-003-7 (pbk. :
acid-free paper)
    1. New Deal, 1933–1939. 2. United States—Economic conditions—
1918–1945.   3. United States—Politics and government—1933–1945.   4. United
States—Social conditions—1933–1945.   I. Sternsher, Bernard, 1925–   .
HC106.3.H654   1999
338.973'009'043—dc21   98-54093

To the members of my generation,

"The Greatest Generation,"

who survived the nation's worst depression

and, with their allies, won a global war

Contents

Introduction

*H*ope Restored is a sequel to *Hitting Home: The Great Depression in Town and Country* (1970, rev. ed. 1989), which was concerned with Americans' reaction to the Great Depression at the local level in the years 1929–1932, a time of lost hope, when extreme suffering and poverty produced for the most part apathy rather than rebellion. Many Americans were sitting around waiting for something to happen. By mid-1932, however, foreboding class resentment was evident. Fortunately it was an election year. A vote for Franklin Roosevelt expressed the desire to "let someone else have a crack at it."

The New Deal years were a time of hope restored, even though economic recovery still had a long way to go. Despite its limited gains, the New Deal was a political and psychological success. Historians of FDR's program have usually focused on developments in Washington, D.C.—in the White House, Congress, the cabinet departments, the federal agencies. But what was of first importance to people in localities across the vast, variegated United States was how the New Deal affected the way things were in the communities where they lived; and, in turn, how the New Deal's impact was affected by economic conditions, politics, personalities, and other factors in those communities. This is what the articles in *Hope Restored* describe.

The shift from relative governmental inaction in the 1920s to a spate of New Deal legislation and agencies has, since the 1960s, been the subject of a flood of research and writing about the New Deal at the local level (as well as in states and nation), partly because of a renewed emphasis on "history from the bottom up." This fresh evidence has provided a basis for distinguishing broadly between the years 1929–1932 as an era of hope lost and the years 1932–1941 as an era of hope restored. In *Hitting Home* I noted by way of introduction that historians had never attempted a systematic explanation of the lassitude that gripped many Americans after the Great Crash, and I suggested some relevant interrelated factors—

historical, intellectual, nationalistic, psychological, and political—that contributed to those tiresome times.

The historical factor that contributed to the failure of so many Americans to protest actively is implicit in the term "Great Depression." Although the depressions of the 1870s and 1890s cannot be lightly dismissed, by definition the severest—deepest, widest, and longest—economic slump in the nation's history had no precedent. People did not expect what had never happened.

The intellectual factor that contributed to Americans' failure to protest actively was partly a matter of inability to anticipate the unprecedented. If the people expected nothing really new to happen, they saw no need to revise or discard old concepts. Even when something new did happen, the inertial force of familiar ideas often resulted in adamant adherence to them. This "intellectual lag" is a psychological matter to the extent that those who cling to conventional thoughts that are inappropriate to new conditions do so out of emotional commitment to them. A principal exemplar of intellectual lag during the Great Depression was Herbert Hoover, who, Rexford Tugwell observed, exhibited "immersion in an ideology immune to events." But many farm spokesmen and union leaders also offered traditional solutions.

A nationalistic factor with paradoxical qualities also contributed to inaction. The depression, "although challenging many traditional American assumptions, nevertheless elicited responses that combined to give a new character and energy to a resurgent American nationalism"—this is the theme of Charles C. Alexander's *Nationalism in American Thought, 1910–1945* (Chicago, 1969). One might have expected amidst the throes of collapse widespread rejection of the whole American experience, but many citizens rallied around the nation as they never had before. To paraphrase the basic theme implicit in Alexander's book, "There is nothing wrong with the American Way and the American people, but they have been betrayed by a selfish, irresponsible elite." If progress was not inevitable, it was attainable through change that was essentially nonradical in its means and ends—restoration of America to "the people."

The psychological factor that contributed to inaction—the emotional impact of unemployment—is an extremely complicated matter. In the revised edition of *Hitting Home* I included an article by William R. Phillips and myself which extended the inquiry into the New Deal era. Among other sources we cited a 1939 publication of the Works Progress Administration (*The Personal Side*, edited by Jesse A. Bloodworth and Elizabeth Greenwood) based on interviews with forty-five families in Dubuque,

Iowa. This report placed the families in three categories: those who had been on relief and had returned to private employment, those who had received no relief while unemployed, and those who were still unemployed (being on relief was not considered employment). This and numerous other studies from the 1930s questioned the conventional or textbook wisdom that even during the worst economic collapse in the nation's history, most Americans blamed themselves for their plight. This attitude was thought to gibe with the American tradition of individualism: if you're down and out, it's your own fault. And it is true that only a small minority followed to its end the sequence of self-blame, non-self-blame, radical thought, radical action. Yet the interviewees in Dubuque attributed the depression to such agents as labor-saving machinery, maldistribution of wealth, overproduction, excess labor supply, stock market speculation, businessmen, and the Dubuque Chamber of Commerce. They refused individually to shoulder the blame. Dubuque, to be sure, is not the nation, and there are no data available for a comprehensive national study, but relevant literature suggests that while many Americans blamed themselves for their plight, many others did not.

Americans' sluggish response in the depths of the Great Depression contrasts with their activism after the economy bottomed out in 1932, took halting steps forward, then a step backward (the recession of 1937–1938, which historians have been accused of overlooking), and ultimately resumed its ascent through World War II and beyond. Yet there is a certain consistency in Americans' behavior before and after 1932. It is futile to demand a bigger slice of the pie when the pie is very small or when there is no pie at all. Protest is largely a recovery phenomenon, occurring when there is something to be gained. Thus, for example, the tumultuous activism of American labor in the years 1934 and 1937 occurred amidst modest economic recovery and well after the passage of the National Industrial Recovery Act of 1933 that enabled the burgeoning of union power. But the American proletariat showed no significant interest in any kind of revolution. The unions basically wanted the right to organize in order to win a bigger piece of the capitalist pie.

Meanwhile, in the agricultural sector the most formidable protest of the period 1929–1933 was the so-called farm strikes and the withholding of products from the market. Such action was encouraged by the Farmers' Holiday Association. The most famous strikes occurred in Wisconsin and near Sioux City, Iowa, where on August 12, 1932, dairy farmers spilled the milk of would-be marketers on the roads outside the city. This farmers' protest was not a movement from the social depths. It was mounted by conservative Midwestern farmers whose level of expectation had been conditioned by better times. Like industrial workers, they sought not a panacea but immediate amelioration of their condition. Their most important achievement was to publicize their plight.

For *Hope Restored* I have selected historical articles to survey the scene because their authors have a wider perspective than contemporary observers, both with respect to the availability of relevant data and the analytical vantage point afforded by the passage of time. Unlike excerpts from books, they possess a unity that derives from their being entities in themselves; and they are especially useful in the classroom because it is impractical for an instructor to assign, say, a dozen books that address just one phase of a course.

In making this selection I had numerous criteria and topics in mind. Length was a consideration: some excellent articles are too long to be included here (only three selections are longer than twenty pages). Geography had to be considered: the New Deal was active from coast to coast. Race relations, the plight of women, and aid to youth are represented. Other topics that appear in the relevant literature show that the response to the New Deal varied from one community to another and often changed over time. Some communities responded selectively, favoring only those agencies that promoted their particular interests.

Historians of the New Deal confront such other matters as dissenting Democrats and "me too" Republicans; political "bosses" and the New Deal; voter behavior and the Roosevelt coalition; relations between the New Deal and business interests (especially their initial enthusiasm, which quickly gave way to opposition to the National Recovery Administration); workers' advances in the Northeast and Midwest (to which businessmen's responses varied) and failure to advance in the South and Southwest; aid to farmers and neglect or harsh treatment of farm workers; variations in cooperation with the New Deal as well as in the local initiation of action; continuity (especially in the South and Southwest) as well as change in Americans' ideology—aspects of the New Deal experience make a long list.

New Deal relief programs receive considerable attention in historical studies treating constitutional and other constraints on the funding of relief by localities; the politics of relief; the inadequacy of relief programs; the impact of the New Deal on local standards of relief; the plight of the unemployables when the creation of the Works Progress Administration (WPA) in 1935 left their fate to the states and localities; protests by relief workers who formed the Workers' Alliance to air grievances; the changing objectives of localities even after problems of unemployment and relief had been virtually eliminated.

Together these articles seek an understanding of the New Deal by utilizing the virtues of local history commonly noted by its advocates: the illumination of national trends—the illustration of the national generalization with the local specific; the simultaneous fostering of skepticism about national generalizations—the identification of variations on the national theme; and the demonstration of the importance of the individual's role in history. The reader will encounter many unfamiliar individuals who had a significant impact on their localities. These virtues, I believe, afford the student a more focused view of life in the thirties than the many noteworthy state studies that have appeared. For most students, a locality is a more comprehensible entity than a state. To be sure, localities exhibit variations in individual and group experiences, but the differences between, say, northern and southern Illinois, and all the communities within those sections, make it difficult to conceptualize that state as an entity.

At the same time, studies of localities frequently illustrate a historiographical development launched by Samuel P. Hays and others more than thirty years ago: the "community-society continuum." Hays asserted in 1967 that a "community-society" dimension provided a framework "which will account for different levels of political behavior and the interaction between them . . . political life at one level is of an entirely different order from that at another. They are linked not by logical similarity but by human interaction." There is no attempt here to apply or analyze Hays's theme. It is cited as part of the framework that characterized New Deal action in localities as the nation moved from a period of relative inaction to action in many ways through many agencies. What is striking about the pre–New Deal phase of the Great Depression is that the American people demanded so little. What is striking about the New Deal phase is how little action was needed to restore Americans' hope about the nation's future.

To apply the word "little" to New Deal action suggests controversy over the New Deal's accomplishments. Its achievements are often depreciated by the statement that it took World War II to get the country out of the Great Depression. This statement is inaccurate if it is meant to imply that there was virtually no economic recovery under the New Deal, just as it is misleading to assert that the New Deal moved Americans all the way out of the Great Depression. On the eve of the severe recession of 1937–1938, the Gross National Product was approximately what it had been on the eve of the Great Depression in 1929, though unemployment was still over 15 percent and higher until war production got under way in 1941. Movement and direction are vital: some recovery is better than none or continued decline.

A basic shift in the nation's mood is evident in accounts of the New Deal. In *The Failure of the NRA* (New York, 1975) Bernard Bellush writes:

> When FDR visited Portland, Oregon, in August 1934, on his way to dedicate a nearby dam, thousands of men and women jammed the streets to bid him welcome. Even workers on strike, and the unemployed who lined the route, seemed to have hope reinstalled by the mere presence of the President. A knowledgeable, independent-minded reporter commented, "The people worship him. He is their idol." This same newsman reflected sadly on the fact that FDR, who could have done so much for them, had done so little.

The reporter's remarks were especially apt at a time when federal work-relief programs were scant—between the end of the Civil Works Administration on March 31, 1934, and the beginning of the Works Progress Administration on May 6, 1935.

Yet this president, with his infectious optimism, is ranked second—in one instance first—in the "great" presidents category in various polls of historians. Can Roosevelt's detractors persuasively argue that you do not have to be very effective to be great? At present the prevailing judgment of the New Deal among historians is expressed by Anthony Badger in *The New Deal: The Depression Years, 1933–1940* (New York, 1989): "Traditional values survived the Depression and the New Deal with great resilience. The New Deal was essentially a holding operation for American society because in the democratic, capitalist United States that was what most Americans wanted it to be." In the selection on the CWA in Grand Forks County, North Dakota, the author's conclusion illustrates Badger's judgment: "Critics charge that the CWA did virtually nothing to get the country out of the Depression, but that was never its intent. What it did was simply to help the people of Grand Forks County (and every other county in the country) survive one of the harshest winters of the worst economic crisis in the history of the United States." Even such limited relief contributed to the restoration of hope.

ATLANTA, GEORGIA

The New Deal in Atlanta: A Review of the Major Programs

DOUGLAS L. FLEMING

This introductory selection catalogs New Deal activities and reactions to them—mostly favorable—at a time when Atlanta and Georgia were part of the pre–Civil War Democratic Solid South. The majority of Atlantans' views, however, were not shared by Governor Eugene Talmadge, who adamantly opposed the New Deal. Over time, beginning with the issuance in 1947 of a pro–civil rights report ("To Share These Rights") to President Truman, whites steadily departed from the Democratic party. The Democrats' adoption of a strong civil rights program in 1948, Barry Goldwater's penetration of the Solid South in 1964, and the Republicans' adoption of a "Southern strategy" in 1968 hastened this shift in party preference. Today Georgia is solidly Republican in many localities and in state and national elections. To be sure, race relations are not the sole source of this change in whites' voter behavior. What is relevant here is hindsight: Atlantans and many other Southerners accepted or tolerated the New Deal in the emergency of the Great Depression even though it did not gibe with their traditional views of the role of government. The author does not intend here to place the New Deal in a long-run context. His useful summary of major New Deal programs, however, tells us by implication, particularly in the area of civil rights, that the 1930s were not the 1960s.

From the *Atlanta Historical Journal*, 30 (Spring 1986), 23–45.

THE 1932 presidential election brought hope to Atlanta as it did to most of the nation. Her citizens' vote of support for Franklin D. Roosevelt by a ten-to-one margin signified both desire for change and admiration of a popular Georgia part-time resident. As FDR developed New Deal programs from 1933 to 1939, Atlanta reacted with great enthusiasm. The New Deal offered a means of combatting the depression, a task beyond the resources of Atlanta's private charities and city government. It also provided an opportunity to build long-needed community facilities, including a sewer system, public housing, and improved streets, schools, and hospitals.

Years before his presidency Georgians thought of FDR as their adopted "favorite son" because of his active involvement in Warm Springs. Some leading citizens even urged him to seek the Georgia governorship in 1926.[1] During the early years of the depression, the Atlanta newspapers followed Roosevelt's political career closely, especially after his presidential nomination. In late October 1932 when FDR visited Atlanta, 25,000 citizens thronged Peachtree Street to watch the candidate pass by in an open car, and the Atlanta Constitution's headline read "Next President Made Welcome by Vast Throng. Expresses Appreciation for Georgia's Welcome, Delight at Returning to 'Other Home.'"[2] No one was surprised when traditionally Democratic Fulton County cast 19,044 votes for Roosevelt and only 1,940 for Hoover. When the following March FDR said in his inaugural address, "We have nothing to fear but fear itself," hope for long-needed solutions to the city's ills surged in the hearts of her people.

The solutions soon came. The "Hundred Days" began an amazing list of programs to be enlarged during the rest of the decade. All in varying degrees affected Atlanta. In spring 1933, according to Rich's Department Store executive Frank Neely, the retail heart of the city, Five Points, lay deserted.[3] New Deal relief and construction agencies made the greatest impact. Through direct relief, they distributed necessities and funds; and through work relief and construction projects, they created jobs. Roosevelt described the New Deal as "bold, persistent experimentation." Though sometimes chaotic, it bolstered the morale of millions, including thousands of Atlantans.[4]

Plans came forth for the new administration's programs during spring and summer of 1933. On March 15, Secretary of the Interior and former Bull Mooser Harold L. Ickes announced that $3.3 billion would be spent on public works, part of a "full" New Deal to be underway by May 1 which would also include farm and unemployment programs.[5] The Constitution reported that Atlanta Mayor James L. Key and the Fulton County Commission planned "immediate steps to get the city's and county's share of the $3,300,000,000 fund." Gov. Eugene Talmadge remained silent, an early indication of his hostility toward Roosevelt's New Deal. Most local businessmen, politicians, and citizens welcomed the new federal intervention in Atlanta's economy, which gave genuine hope for the first significant economic improvement since fall 1929.[6]

Before implementing New Deal programs, FDR faced the nationwide banking crisis. On March 3, the day before Roosevelt's inauguration, with banks already closed in thirty states, Governor Talmadge ordered a three-day holiday for Georgia banks.[7] Since state and local governments could not resolve the crisis, FDR declared a nationwide banking holiday on March 6, and four days later Congress passed the Emergency Banking Bill which provided for federal aid in the reorganization and reopening of sound banks. Soon an additional federal banking reform included the Federal Deposit Insurance Corporation (FDIC). Citizens and Southern National, First National, Fulton National, and Trust Company of Georgia, strong supporters of the administration's banking policies, reopened on March 13, with deposits outnumbering withdrawals by more than three to one. By May 15, 14,000 of 18,000 banks had reopened throughout the nation, including all those in Atlanta.[8]

FEDERAL EMERGENCY RELIEF ADMINISTRATION

With the resolution of the banking crisis, attention turned to other New Deal activities, and in July 1933 the Federal Emergency Relief Administration (FERA) began direct relief and work relief. FERA programs remained the major source of relief until the arrival of Works Progress Administration (WPA) programs in fall 1935. The exception was during the winter of 1933–34 when the Civil Works Administration (CWA) provided work relief. Frank Neely described the Atlanta FERA office during its early days of operation. Located in the state capitol building in three small rooms, it filled daily with "samples of the human material to be saved." The unfortunates "sat slumped in the waiting rooms, grey faced, timid, patient." In marked contrast, the FERA's staff of "bright fresh-colored college girls troop[ed] in at the end of the day's work like beings of a different breed of heralds, as perhaps they are, of a new social order."[9] The FERA operated through the state's Georgia Emergency Relief Administration (GERA), which oversaw county relief organizations, which in turn directed local projects.

In preparation for the implementation of the FERA, the Special (Emergency) Relief Committee of Atlanta and Fulton County prepared the "Report of Past and Future Activities on Work Relief Projects" describing the diversity of work projects conducted with Reconstruction Finance Corporation (RFC) and private funds before the creation of the FERA. These ranged from 250 men employed in terracing the grounds behind Girls' High School to 20 men employed repairing shoes.[10] Unfortunately pre-FERA funds had not come close to providing for the needs of the unemployed. In the spring of 1933 cases averaged over 12,000 per month, and the limited funds provided only $10.02 per month for the average case.[11] Such a low level of support resulted in severe hardships such as those described by former FERA social worker Augusta Dunbar who, upon entering the home of a relief applicant, found that all the furniture had been reclaimed and all that remained was a plaque on the wall which said, "Home Sweet Home." Dunbar said, "The thing the woman objected [to] the most was [that] they took the stove out and put the dinner on the floor." In July the FERA increased the level of relief as much as its funds allowed, but still the average recipient was given only about two-thirds of the minimum amount of money necessary to maintain health.[12]

Gay B. Shepperson, formerly head of the state department of public welfare, directed the Georgia Relief Commission which administered the GERA. In preparation for her responsibilities, Shepperson traveled to Washington and conferred with FERA director Harry Hopkins, who also had been her boss during the 1920s when they worked together in the Red Cross.[13] The FERA took on the immense task of providing for the approximately 60,000 Atlantans on the welfare rolls in late summer 1933. From the beginning it spent the bulk of its funds in work relief projects which employed unskilled workers. In a typical project, sixty men cleared ditches and repaired roads for 123 days at Fort McPherson.[14] These projects distributed aid to the greatest number of people possible and received strong community support.

The FERA encountered major administrative difficulties in its first year in Georgia. When Hopkins appointed Shepperson and her immediate staff, he obliterated the jobs of several Georgia politicians, including that of Talmadge's stepson, John A. Peterson. Even more objectionable to Talmadge, the amount of money sent to each county by the FERA far exceeded the amount that he controlled personally in each county. This threatened his political power. It particularly irritated him that the money was controlled by a woman. The fact that the federal money was being spent at all went against his belief that frugality was the best means of combatting the depression. It also irritated the agrarian Talmadge that cities, especially Atlanta, received the bulk of FERA funds. L. Alan Johnstone, FERA field representative, sent his evaluation of the Georgia governor to Hopkins:

> Mr. Talmadge says that people in Atlanta who are on relief are all bums and loafers and that they will "out-smart" you. While walking down the street the other day with Dave Shaltz of Fla. a bum asked Shaltz for a quarter to get a shave. Talmadge said that all people on relief are like that.
>
> Talmadge insists that the people on the farms need help, but the people in the cities are chiseling. Talmadge was elected by the people on the farms.

Johnstone praised Shepperson and the professional staff, but severely criticized Talmadge and his appointees on the Georgia Relief Commission, which approved GERA projects and expenditures, but did not control daily administration or the source of funds.[15] In January 1934, Hopkins sacked the Talmadge-dominated Georgia Relief Commission and appointed Shepperson relief administrator of Georgia. At the same time, he replaced the original Georgia CWA administrator, Atlanta banker Ronald Ransom, with Shepperson. This eviscerated Talmadge's influence and made Atlanta one of the first U.S. cities to have a federally operated relief program.[16]

CIVIL WORKS ADMINISTRATION

Hopkins feared in fall 1933 that the coming winter would produce tremendous suffering since the economy remained severely depressed. The CWA was therefore created in November 1933. The FERA relinquished its work relief functions to the CWA at the same time that the federal government took over complete administrative authority for both agencies. Placing the CWA totally in federal hands throughout the nation meant that relief could be implemented more quickly. To maintain continuity with the FERA, GERA staff and programs remained in place.

The organization of the CWA in Fulton County in November took only two days because it had the highest percentage of skilled workers of any Georgia county. This allowed 9,957 workers to be transferred immediately from FERA relief rolls to CWA projects. Additional hiring resulted in a peak level of 14,407 CWA workers in Fulton County. Two departments existed, one for skilled jobs and one for unskilled. Building repairs,

TABLE 1

Selected Atlanta Art Works of the CWA Public Works of Art Project

TYPE OF WORK	ARTIST(S)
Portraits of	
Dr. Joshua Gilbert	Ralph M. Britt
Bernard Mallon	Joseph N. Colgan
Sidney Lanier	Harold T. Phillips
Hon. Allen D. Candler	Ernest M. Seagle
Paintings of	
Kennesaw Mountain	Douglas B. Wright
Historic House, St. Elmo	Henry C. Biggers
Vann House, Spring Place	Richard W. McDade
Old Crawford House, Crawford	Alfred F. Plate
Bulloch Hall, Roswell	Ms. Frances L. Turner
Jarrett Manor, Tugalo	Virginia Woolley
Drawings of	
University of Georgia	Cornelia Cunningham
Sculpture	
Bust of Joel Chandler Harris	Steffen W. Thomas
Ornament and frieze for Girls'	Fritz P. Zimmer
High School Dome	John Steinichen, Sr.
	Robert B. Logan
	Wallace Steinichen
Statues and scenery for Cyclorama	Joseph V. Llorens
	Weis C. Snell
	John Steinichen, Jr.
Corbels for Georgia Tech	Julian H. Harris
Mural panels for	
Grady Hospital	Ms. A. Farnsworth Drew
Bass Junior High School	Anna R. Alsobrook
	Ernestine Tinsley
English Avenue School	Athos Menaboni
Joel Chandler Harris School	Mignon Breitenbucher
	Bessie Mitchell
D. T. Howard School	Hale A. Woodruff
Booker T. Washington High School	Wilmer A. Jennings

Source: "Names and Addresses of Artists Employed in the Fifth Region ... until noon of the 20th of January, 1934"; untitled list of CWA Art Projects; Edgar C. Long to W. O. Bowman, Jr., 9 May 1934; J. J. Haverty to Bowman, 4 June 1934, Wilbur G. Kurtz, Sr., Papers, Atlanta Historical Society, Atlanta.

making up the largest number of Fulton County projects, included those at about 200 Atlanta and Fulton County public schools, in addition to Grady Hospital and Georgia Tech. New construction projects included the start of a new Atlanta sewer system, with a trunk sewer line laid. The largest unskilled undertaking employed workers to level and grade runways at Candler Field. Additionally, the CWA paved roads, surveyed social relief agencies, maintained a transient shelter, organized a forty-five-member symphony orchestra, provided clerical help at the state library, and staffed professional positions in the public schools in Fulton County. Also, the Division of Women's Work operated a variety of service ventures including sewing projects, nursing projects, and nursery schools.[17]

The federal government administered other CWA projects, including the Public Works of Art Project, directly from Washington. Sculptor Gutzon Borglum, original designer of the Stone Mountain carving of Confederate leaders, claimed credit for the idea and enthusiastically described his plans for Texas:

> I'm on my way out there now. Every unemployed man is going to have a job; a real job. . . . I'm going to illustrate fairy tales and paint historical paintings. . . . What we need in this country is a creative spirit—the creative urge—a development of the artistic appreciation—application of that appreciation in the public schools. . . . We can feed a tramp and put a dry shirt on his back and give him a bed and when he leaves the next morning he is still a tramp. We have been a tramp country too long. Why, I gave this school decoration idea to Harry Hopkins two months ago. He is all for it. . . . Things are going to be done now. But say, you watch Texas![18]

The fifth regional district of the art project, headquartered in Atlanta, included Georgia, Florida, North Carolina, South Carolina, and Tennessee. Regional director J. J. Haverty, founder of Haverty Furniture and an early supporter of the High Museum, was assisted by Wilbur G. Kurtz, Sr., an Atlanta artist. Haverty described the project as "designed to give employment to professional artists who have superior ability, and have years of experience in their profession, and who have no employment." Artists painted and sculpted various Georgia subjects. Kurtz's knowledge of Civil War and Atlanta history proved to be a great help in work on the Battle of Atlanta Cyclorama in Grant Park.[19]

Most CWA workers greatly appreciated their jobs, but as happens in most large organizations, there were a small number of unproductive workers. Some of these did not wish to exchange the dole for work. One Atlantan of this type whose family had accepted relief for two generations refused to work as a janitor, a maintenance man, or a delivery man and faced being denied further relief aid. His wife pleaded to CWA administrative assistant Jane Van de Vrede for help and attributed her husband's uncooperativeness to the agency's failure to find him a job "suited to his talents." Van de Vrede assigned him to the Cyclorama Art Project where she explained "they were using all grades of labor from ditch digger to the most skilled professional painter." Later she inquired how the hesitant worker was performing, and the project superintendent said, "He's doing OK. He is posing as a dead soldier." Van de Vrede replied, "At last he had a job 'suited to his talents.'"[20]

Created to last only through the winter of 1933–34, the CWA's dismantlement began in February 1934, under the efficient direction of Gay B. Shepperson, and was completed by the end of April. Many Atlantans failed to accept the CWA's temporariness. Even during the phase-out months, numerous applications for long-term projects arrived on Shepperson's desk. In response to a request by the Chamblee Public School Board for a new school construction project in March, Shepperson replied:

> The drastic curtailment of CWA activities in Georgia makes it problematical as to whether any new projects will be approved and absolutely prohibits the approval of the purchase of any material with CWA funds.[21]

Projects unfinished by the end of April presented a difficult problem. These included several school murals and work at the Cyclorama and Girls' High School. From its inception the CWA had provided wages and administration with the understanding that local authorities would provide materials. When the city failed to adopt a budget in early 1934, many art projects faced a lack of materials. Since the city's delays helped create the problem, it made sense to give the responsibility for unfinished projects to municipal government. In June, Shepperson hoped to persuade the city to take over the Cyclorama restoration project. She reasoned that because Cyclorama admission fees produced revenue, the city should be able to afford the expense of completing the project. In the end the FERA and the PWA took over the 507 unfinished projects in Georgia, including the Atlanta art projects.[22]

With the FERA again in control of both work relief and direct relief, its operations grew to their greatest levels during the last half of 1934 and first half of 1935. Programs developed during the period from the termination of the CWA until the initiation of the WPA in summer 1935 resembled those of the CWA. Some projects were transferred from the FERA in 1933 to the CWA back to the FERA and then to the WPA. One of these, the Atlanta Transient Bureau, served the urgent function of caring for the thousands of jobless drifters who traveled through Atlanta.

PWA AND PUBLIC HOUSING

At the same time the FERA and CWA combatted unemployment with re-lief programs, the Public Works Administration (PWA) undertook a tremen-dous construction program employing thousands of Atlantans, mainly on sewer and public housing projects. The PWA directed these with only a state engineer and an advisory board, with construction work done by pri-vate contractors on a bid basis. The PWA's three-zone labor scale placed the South in the lowest wage zone, which provided a minimum wage of $.40 per hour for unskilled workers and $1.00 per hour for skilled work-ers.[23]

Atlanta applied in July 1933 for $8 million worth of sewer construction projects. PWA director Harold L. Ickes announced plans to pay 30 percent of the cost. If Atlanta could not pay its small $25,000 per month to the FERA, it surely had no way to raise its required share of the sewer proj-ect, especially since Georgia's constitutional limitations on municipal in-debtedness forbade the city from borrowing additional funds. In October 1933, Atlanta leaders and the Georgia PWA advisory board unsuccessfully appealed directly to FDR for a reduction of the local share of project costs to 10 percent. By November several PWA road projects were underway in Georgia, but Atlanta still had no sewer projects. Ickes said, "Georgia has not benefited as much as some other states"; therefore, the PWA "will try to start some projects there." The first major Atlanta project, a new $346,000 city jail to accommodate 430 prisoners, received approval shortly afterwards. The sewer request remained unapproved, and at the end of 1933 the PWA transferred it to the CWA.[24]

Giving the sewer application to the CWA meant that the project could start with no additional local funds expended. It also would lead to the PWA and FERA's carrying on sewer work begun by the CWA upon its closing in spring 1934. In early 1934 the CWA reported that Atlanta had

> greatly outgrown its sewer disposal plant, over half the city sewage has been dumped in a raw condition into the various streams of water flowing into the Chattahoochee River. The citizens of the city have long realized that this condition must be remedied, but the means by which a better-ment of conditions could be brought about were not available.[25]

Atlanta's sewer construction, the CWA's largest Georgia project, cost over $1 million from January to April 1934.[26]

Atlanta's flamboyant pro–New Deal mayor, James L. Key, flew to Wash-ington in 1935 to push for approval of $6.8 million in PWA sewer work. In

TABLE 2

Some FERA Projects in Atlanta and Fulton County, 1933–36

Atlanta Orchestra
Atlanta Traffic Survey
Candler Field Construction
College Aid Program
Dental Clinic
Food Distribution Program
Fort McPherson Building and Landscaping
Fulton County Government Clerical Assistance
Georgia Department of Public Health Professional Help
Grady Hospital Building Improvement and Landscaping
Libraries Staffing and Book Repairs
National Relief Census
Nursing Projects
Public School Buildings Repair and Construction
Public Work of Art Project
Sewer System Construction
Sewing Program
Social Relief Agencies Survey
Teachers for Adult Education
Transient Bureau

Source: FERA State Files, 1933–36, Georgia, FERA, RG 69, NA.

late 1935, the new WPA and the PWA agreed to hold the city's portion of the cost to $1.5 million. In January 1936 the approved comprehensive plans for sewers and storm sewers called for PWA expenditures of $4.5 million and WPA expenditures of $2 million. At last Atlantans would have a sewage system.[27]

The PWA continued construction projects in Atlanta in 1935–36 which provided useful community facilities including buildings, roads, sewers, and water works. Georgia received the largest share of PWA works in the Southeast, and Atlanta got more than its share of these. Operating through private contractors in an effort to stimulate the economy, the PWA paid employees at rates equivalent to those found in private industry. The PWA built many school facilities in Atlanta. At Georgia Tech it erected a combination auditorium and gymnasium, a 105-by-159-foot concrete building able to seat 3,000 spectators, at a cost of $92,911. Built mainly in 1936, it was first used in January 1937.[28]

The PWA also constructed in Atlanta the nation's first federal housing projects—Techwood and University Homes. Atlanta businessman Charles F. Palmer initiated the idea. He saw the New Deal as the means for eliminating some of the city's slums while at the same time building decent housing for deserving low-income workers. At the time of his death in 1973 the *Constitution* described Palmer as "an incongruous figure to have devoted his life to the problems of the slum-dweller. Turned out in banker's grey or bureaucratic black, he looked far less the crusader than the man of affairs or a functionary of government." Nevertheless, this real estate promoter, who originally conceived Techwood Homes as a money maker for himself and other slum owners who sold the site for the project to the government, ended up crusading for public housing the rest of his life.[29]

A WPA study of the Techwood neighborhood described the former slums of "Techwood Flats" as an area that "had steadily disintegrated. Never a better class residential section, it had reached the nadir of poverty, wretchedness, and dilapidation." Close to the Georgia Tech campus and busy Peachtree Street, the slum area was a civic eyesore. The University Homes site, a rough, impoverished neighborhood known as Beaver Slide, lay in close proximity to Atlanta University and Clark, Morehouse, Morris Brown, and Spelman Colleges. Palmer and Atlanta University President John Hope took their cause to FDR in Washington, and in October 1933 the PWA approved Techwood Homes for whites and University Homes for blacks.

Not all Atlantans supported Palmer's idea. A few days after the Techwood project was announced, about 100 real estate owners met at the Ansley Hotel and organized to protest the idea on the grounds that it represented unfair competition. In the end they lost their fight, and on September 30, 1934, Harold Ickes began slum clearance for Techwood and University Homes by detonating dynamite charges at both sites.[30]

J. A. Jones Construction Co. of Charlotte, the lowest bidder, received a contract in December 1934 for $2,096,000 to build Techwood's twenty-three brick and concrete buildings to house 604 families and 308 Georgia Tech students. The Atlanta University Homes cost $1,900,000 for forty-two concrete buildings with 677 apartments. Palmer praised FDR for his role in assuring the approval of the two projects:

> President Roosevelt's part-time home state is indeed fortunate to be the first in the South to have completed plans for such outstanding housing developments. We hope the work will be well under way when President Roosevelt, whom I consider one of the greatest leaders the world has ever produced, is in the South this fall.

FDR dedicated Techwood Homes on November 29, 1935, at Grant Field on the Georgia Tech campus with over 50,000 people cheering him. The first residents moved into their new homes on August 15, 1936.[31] By that time community support had produced applications for several other Atlanta housing projects.

NATIONAL RECOVERY ADMINISTRATION

In addition to establishing the PWA, the National Industrial Recovery Act of June 1933 created the National Recovery Administration (NRA) headed by Gen. Hugh S. Johnson. The NRA planned to create a million jobs in capital goods industries by October 1933. Johnson said this would be accomplished by the

> shortening of hours and increase of wages with the repression of prices to only such increases as would accommodate increased out-of-pocket costs due to improved hours and wages, relying on profit on increased volume rather than increased price.[32]

To implement this, representatives from management, labor, and the federal government established codes of fair competition for each type of business and industry. After signing code agreements, participating businesses could display the NRA's symbol, the Blue Eagle, and its slogan, "We do our part." The NRA then enforced the codes. Establishing the many codes took much time, so FDR created the President's Reemployment Agreement which allowed the NRA to set up temporary wage and hour levels.

In the summer of 1933 Atlanta enthusiastically backed the NRA. Leading businesses announced full cooperation and the creation of hundreds of new jobs. The *Constitution* reported that because of an industry-wide textile code, "hundreds of Atlanta's unemployed will join the great procession back to work this week and thousands more will find increased sums in their pay envelopes." Atlanta's numerous retail employees received a minimum salary of $14.50 for a 40-hour week, when 140 retail companies agreed to a retail wage code at a meeting organized by the Atlanta Retail Merchants Association led by Frank Neely of Rich's and J. P. Allen of J. P. Allen Co. On August 2 the *Constitution* declared: "The wings of the Blue Eagle of the NRA spread over Atlanta Tuesday" when "more than 1,000 window signs proclaimed the fact that thousands of workers will find awaiting them shorter hours and larger pay envelopes." Businessmen stood in line at the crowded Federal Building to sign compliance slips and receive Blue Eagle signs. Many businesses publicized their support. Lane Drug Stores advertised: "Lane's has signed and intends to back the President's plan which we all hope will mean 'curtains' to the grave question of unemployment and will result in saner business conditions for all." Volunteer Food Stores told the public: "Mr. President, WE DO OUR PART is the pledge of every Atlanta Volunteer." Enthusiasm for the NRA in Atlanta brought an atmosphere similar to that at the time of the declaration of World War I. Even the Ku Klux Klan voiced support and printed a Blue Eagle on their official publication, the *Kourier*.[33]

Throughout August and September 1933 reports showed business increases, and in mid-August banks reported a 5.6 percent increase in deposits. The Chamber of Commerce, local organizer for the NRA, reported 4,325 Blue Eagle supporters by August 23, or about half of all firms in Atlanta. The Jaycees began a house-to-house and business-to-business canvass to gain pledges of support from all citizens. On September 1 the NRA announced its goal to "hike local pay rolls here $5,000,000." By September 15, 6,156 firms had signed pledges, and 170,528 employees were under the Blue Eagle. A week later the *Constitution* announced the "NRA program [is] being placed on [a] permanent foundation." NRA organizing efforts culminated in the largest parade in Atlanta history in early October when over 100,000 people lined Peachtree Street to cheer the NRA.[34]

Hugh S. Johnson visited the city November 23 to address 3,500 people in the packed City Auditorium. He praised FDR and Georgia which "he calls his adopted state." Johnson attacked the "grouches" who refused to support the NRA and compared the fight to end the depression to other wars waged in America's past.[35] At the time of Johnson's visit, Atlanta remained a site of strong pro-NRA sentiment, but throughout the nation problems existed. In the rural South employers often disliked the wage scales which far exceeded wages previously paid. Also, many white Southerners resented the lack of separate provisions for the races even though it was obvious that wages for jobs held mainly by blacks were fixed by codes to be below wages for jobs held mainly by whites. Union leaders complained that their right to organize as provided for under section 7A of the NRA was not being adequately protected. Code enforcement displeased small businesses and labor who felt that big business dominated the NRA. Additionally, many Americans thought the NRA smacked of socialism.

In Atlanta, some code violations took place, but these did not produce widespread anti-NRA sentiment. The only well-known local critic was Governor Talmadge whose opinions many Atlantans disdained anyway. Regional NRA director W. L. Mitchell oversaw investigations into complaints made by individuals against alleged code violators. Of all codes, those for the construction industry and retail food and grocery trade re-

ceived the largest number of complaints. If found guilty of noncompliance
a business could be required to make restitution to employees and could
be stripped of its Blue Eagle. NRA code adjusters investigated complaints
and filed reports. If evidence against a business existed, either the NRA
field adjuster could work out an agreement satisfactory to worker and employer, or litigation could be undertaken to force the business to make
restitution to workers.

A typical case involved DeLameter's Pharmacy, a small Atlanta concern with two retail stores, one at 719 Ponce de Leon Avenue and another
at 260 Boulevard, N.E. After receiving complaints from employees, NRA
adjuster I. C. Evans interviewed employer and workers. The employer,
store manager Freeman DeLameter, admitted to code violations pertain-
ing to requiring employees to work split shifts but excused himself by saying he had misinterpreted the code. He assured the adjuster that code
violations would not happen again. The adjuster wrote that the employee
involved, a soda and curb boy, claimed that the manager "permits employees to leave one establishment only to report for work at another of his
stores," and ordered workers whose "hours are finished, to remain in the
store with their hats and coats on so as to give the impression that they are
not on duty, although (these) employees are required to work." Further investigation revealed that a soda and curb boy was only fourteen years old,
though he had told DeLameter he was sixteen. After collecting evidence,
the NRA attorney decided not to pursue the case since the "respondent is
a small concern, and the violations claimed would not have any effect
upon interstate commerce which would support litigation."[36]

This case illustrates the types of problems encountered by the NRA in
Atlanta. Overall, the public liked the NRA's purpose, but when applied in
such a wide range of businesses the NRA became unenforceable. Even so,
after the U.S. Supreme Court declared the NRA unconstitutional in May
1935, numerous Atlanta businesses continued to display the Blue Eagle for
several months, and the *Constitution* reported that "Atlanta employers
[are] generally expected to make no changes in wages or hours."[37]

In addition to the FERA, CWA, PWA, and NRA, other New Deal programs, though less directly involved in Atlanta affairs or smaller in scope,
were also significant. The Home Owners Loan Corporation (HOLC) refi-
nanced thousands of Atlanta homes at low interest rates for long terms.
The Federal Housing Authority (FHA) financed thousands of new
dwellings in Atlanta. The Civilian Conservation Corps (CCC) created
camps throughout Georgia including one at Warm Springs. Eager youths
immediately filled Fulton County's quota of 692 men for the CCC in

April 1934. The Tennessee Valley Authority (TVA), though not operating in the immediate Atlanta area, brought great economic improvements to north Georgia, a part of Atlanta's economic hinterland. The Agricultural Adjustment Administration (AAA) acreage-reduction program benefited cotton farmers, thus helping Georgia's overall economic condition. The value of cotton produced in Georgia reached the century's low of $29,782,000 in 1932, but after AAA programs got underway in 1933 it increased to $58,628,000 in 1935.[38]

Beginning in January 1934, Atlantans celebrated FDR's birthday annually with an elaborate ball which raised funds for Warm Springs. The well-supported event characterized the close feeling between FDR and his adopted state. When she addressed the President's Club at the Biltmore Hotel in December 1933, U.S. Secretary of Labor Frances Perkins predicted to Atlantans the

> creation of a new civilization in which every American citizen, whether high or low, will have a better standard of living, enjoying leisure to develop a wholesome social and cultural life, as the result of the Roosevelt recovery program.[39]

If skeptics were in attendance they did not speak out in Atlanta. Atlantans remembered the chronic municipal fiscal crises and the inadequate community services before the New Deal. They also remembered the anguish of hopeless unemployment and knew that Atlanta's economic indicators had improved since FDR's inauguration. From 1933 to 1936 most segments of Atlanta's economy grew. Only privately financed real estate transactions and privately financed construction lagged far behind 1929 levels, mainly because of the extremely inflated 1929 real estate prices. New Deal construction reduced the negative impact of depressed privately financed construction on the overall economy.

WPA AND NYA

Though commerce and industry improved after 1933, relief rolls remained long in America's cities, including Atlanta, where the number of public relief cases declined only 0.9 percent in 1935 from the 1934 level.[40] When FDR took office in 1933, the federal government began temporary relief programs, chiefly the FERA. The persistence of high unemployment, New Dealers' preference for work relief over the dole, and their desire to establish permanent public assistance programs resulted in changes in federal policy. The administration implemented an expanded, less temporary

TABLE 3

Selected WPA Service Projects in Atlanta,
1935 and 1936

TYPE OF PROJECT	SPONSOR
Clerical Work	City of Atlanta
Clerical Work	DeKalb County Consumers Council
Clerical Work	State Dept. of Geology
Supplemental Teachers	State Board of Education
Tax Records Indexing	City of Decatur
Library Assistance	State Supreme Court
Library Book Rebinding	Atlanta Public Library
Library Book Rebinding	Atlanta Public Schools
Medical Laboratory Work	City of Atlanta
Nursing	Fulton County Board of Health
Sewing Rooms	State Dept. of Public Welfare
Relief Statistics Survey	State Dept. of Public Welfare
Surplus Food Distribution	WPA

work relief program when it established the Works Progress Administration
in summer 1935. Renamed the Work Projects Administration in 1937, the
popular WPA took over and expanded the FERA's work projects. The
FERA began phasing out direct relief funding, and local welfare agencies
took over unemployable direct relief cases. Also in the summer of 1935,
FDR signed the Social Security Act, which created a permanent program
of public assistance to support the most unemployable, indigent citizens.
This formed a major part of the modified welfare state created during the
New Deal years. These changes caught Atlanta in the middle between federal and state government policies. Participation in Social Security programs required state welfare reforms. The phase-out of the FERA caused
the city to need state help to fund direct relief for unemployables. Unfortunately for Atlanta, anti–New Deal Gov. Eugene Talmadge blocked both
welfare reforms and relief funding in 1935 and 1936.

In late 1934, the FERA took steps toward transferring relief cases of unemployables whose hardships had not resulted from the loss of work to
local and state authorities. Atlanta had not accepted the fact that the federal government had never intended for the FERA to support unemployable citizens indefinitely, and the city and county had insufficient funds to
support the unemployables. Therefore, they reacted slowly to federal demands that local government assume responsibilities for direct relief.[41] In
June 1935 when state government still offered no help to its unemployable

citizens and even failed to pay thousands of its own employees, the *Constitution* indicated that Shepperson and Hopkins "blasted" state government for its failure to meet its obligations.[42]

Summer 1935 proved to be a nightmare for Atlanta's unemployables. With FERA dismantlement underway, WPA projects not yet begun, and an inadequate state welfare system, thousands went without means of support. Citizens deluged Washington with requests for help. Since Fulton County lacked the resources to support its unemployables, the FERA reluctantly provided some funding through June 1937.[43] The uncooperative Talmadge administration made certain that state government would not fund relief or carry out welfare program reforms. Only after the inauguration of Gov. E. D. Rivers in January 1937 would state government support New Deal welfare policies.

When planning the WPA, Hopkins and FDR did not intend to abandon the unemployed who lost FERA benefits. Rather, they sought to create a comprehensive work relief program which would uplift the participants while it provided worthwhile services and facilities. FDR wanted to end direct relief, for as he told Atlanta businessman Chip Robert, the head of the U.S. Wage and Price Administration's Wage Commission, "We don't want a dole system. It's been the damnation of England."[44] FDR, Hopkins, and most professional social workers strongly advocated work relief which replaced a feeling of uselessness and futility with a sense of self-respect. The GERA stated in its September 1935 *Monthly Review of Relief Statistics* that

> the system of continuous employment on their new jobs will do much to restore the habit of regular and sustained industry which has been weakened during the past years of sporadic business activity.[45]

The WPA put first priority on helping unemployed workers. It required at least 90 percent of the workers on any project to come from relief rolls. With FERA relief diminishing, the WPA in Atlanta attempted to put hundreds to work as quickly as possible. Georgia WPA assistant administrator Robert MacDougall's wife, Margaret, later recalled those days to have been "like a war. I've heard him [MacDougall] scream out in a nightmare, 'I'm so sorry, I'm so sorry,' and I'd wake him up and he would have been talking to starving people."[46]

Hopkins appointed Shepperson as Georgia WPA administrator with as complete control over federal relief efforts as she had held in the FERA. The Atlanta-based Georgia FERA staff formed the majority of the WPA staff, which numbered 396 in 1936. In 1935 the WPA created three divi-

sions in Georgia to administer and execute its programs: Intake and Certification, Finance, and Work Projects. The WPA added four other divisions by 1940: Women's Work (later changed to Women's and Professional,
then to Professional and Service, and finally to Community Service),
Labor Management, Office Management, and Safety. All operated from
Atlanta with most offices in the then-recently built Thornton, or Ten Pryor
Street, Building.[47]

The first WPA projects approved in summer 1935 closely resembled
those of their predecessors, the FERA and CWA. In May it became known
that the federal work relief bill provided for nearly $4.9 billion to be spent,
and Atlanta's civic leaders hoped to capture a large share of the bonanza.
They rapidly drew up a $2.5 million dream list of projects including a
completed sewer system, new highways, a northside airport, a stadium, a
market, a fire department headquarters, and many school improvements.
Their hopes for funds were soundly rewarded in July when the WPA approved $7,350,000 for over $10 million worth of projects for Georgia's District 5, comprised of Atlanta, Fulton, and DeKalb counties. The list
included sewer and water system, hospital, road, school, recreation, airport, library, and public building projects.[48] The WPA required the local
government to pay about 20 percent of project costs. Harold Ickes told
Hopkins that Atlanta should and could pay a greater share, nearer the 55
percent that Buffalo, New York, and other cities had paid for PWA sewer
work. Fortunately for Atlanta, Hopkins did not increase the city's share of
expenses, but most projects could not begin until the city paid its part.
Shepperson and others spoke to community groups in the campaign seeking approval of a $1,775,000 bond issue to enable the city to raise the
matching funds. Shepperson particularly stressed the need for the $6 mil-
lion sewer system:

> Since the bond issue of 1910 the city has issued no bonds and made no
> appropriation for sewage disposal. In other words, the city, for a quarter of
> a century has stood still.
>
> Atlanta has escaped an epidemic of typhoid fever by the grace of God
> and nothing else.
>
> Atlanta is polluting every stream in every Atlanta watershed, every hour
> of the day and every night. This condition creates a menace to the public
> health which is frightful to contemplate.
>
> We have the opportunity at this time to build 54 miles of trunk sewers
> and five sewage disposal plants with the federal government furnishing 80
> percent of the money as an outright gift.

Citizens responded by approving the bond issue on September 18, 1935, thus assuring the completion of thirty projects already underway.[49]

Project selection proved to be a tough job. Robert MacDougall, a Georgia Tech–educated engineer, directed construction projects as head of Georgia's WPA Operations Division. To gain approval, a public agency sponsoring a construction or service project submitted a proposal with a complete set of plans and an estimated cost. The sponsor, often the city of Atlanta, furnished most materials and any necessary skilled labor not found on the WPA's rolls. Immediately after the Georgia WPA approved a project, it supplied labor and any materials it agreed to furnish, and it administered the project.[50] Engineers supervised construction projects, and professionals with appropriate training supervised service projects. The Georgia WPA had little trouble finding well-qualified supervisors because of the widespread unemployment of engineers and social workers. Many years after the depression when he worked for a privately owned company, MacDougall said that the dedicated WPA supervisors worked "twice as hard as those in private industry."[51]

The Roosevelt administration considered the WPA to be a temporary agency as the CWA and the FERA had been. When private business picked up in Atlanta in spring 1936, the government reduced the number of WPA workers in Atlanta to about 7,500 by the end of April. During 1936 the WPA approved mainly projects requiring unskilled workers who had little hope of finding work elsewhere. The largest WPA project in the entire South at the time, actually a combination of many projects, was the Atlanta sewer system. It provided thousands of jobs for unskilled workers who could not find employment in the improving private sector.[52] The Women's Work Division, directed by Jane Van de Vrede, administered the many service projects. The Georgia State Department of Public Welfare sponsored fifteen service projects in mid-1936, several wholly or primarily in Atlanta. Also, the Public Arts Project's music and visual arts programs reached Atlanta in late 1935 and early 1936. WPA musicians formed three groups of nonprofessionals and professionals. They performed at the Erlanger Theater and in local high schools. Atlanta's Carnegie Library and other public buildings received WPA murals.[53]

In 1935 and 1936 the WPA established itself as the major New Deal agency in Atlanta, but others also made significant contributions. One of these, the National Youth Administration (NYA), established under the WPA on June 26, 1935, operated programs for people from sixteen to twenty-four years of age. In January 1936, Fulton and DeKalb County NYA projects reached 346 youths.[54] Like the WPA, the NYA required a local sponsor for each project. For example, the city of Decatur sponsored a park project for boys, and the city of Atlanta sponsored a hand sewing and millinery training project for girls. Schools administered tuition aid programs for their students. In March 1936 Atlanta School of Social Work director Forrester B. Washington wrote that the NYA "Student Aid Program has been a virtual 'life-saver' for the students in our school this year." All accredited colleges and universities in the Atlanta area participated in the NYA tuition aid program with funds distributed in proportion to total enrollment without regard for the race of the students.[55]

The PWA worked with the WPA to construct the sewer system, though the two agencies disagreed over the amount of money the city should contribute. Since the PWA projects cost the city much more, the WPA built most of the system, with the PWA constructing only three disposal tanks in the period 1935–36. The city paid $750,000 or 50 percent of the cost of these, a smaller portion than the PWA's average non-federal project share of 71 percent. The city's release of funds for the PWA disposal plants caused it to come up short on its WPA contribution. The WPA made up the city's shortage, which reduced Atlanta's share of the nearly $6,000,000 WPA sewer work from a projected 23 percent to only 14 percent.[56]

THE SOCIAL SECURITY ACT

Not all New Deal programs which directly affected thousands of Atlantans were temporary like the FERA, CWA, WPA, NYA, and PWA. The most significant permanent programs for working Atlantans were part of the Social Security Act signed into law by FDR in 1935. It did not begin in Georgia until 1937. To participate in the federal-state welfare programs authorized by the act, Georgia had to pass state constitutional amendments. Unfortunately, Governor Talmadge blocked all efforts to pass the necessary amendments during 1935 and 1936. No Social Security amendments were enacted until after Gov. E. D. Rivers took office in January 1937. Without the amendments Georgians did not receive federal aid to the aged, dependent children, crippled children, and needy blind or for insurance against unemployment.[57] This produced a major campaign issue in the 1936 gubernatorial race and had much to do with the election of E. D. Rivers, who promised full support of the New Deal and a "Little New Deal" for Georgia.

The Social Security issue resembled the earlier conflict between Talmadge and federal officials over relief funds. Atlanta and its residents benefited from federal programs while Talmadge's ideas of less government and fewer programs represented an obstacle to progress. Even traditionally conservative businessmen realized the value of millions of federal dollars to the Atlanta economy, and none of Talmadge's attacks diminished FDR's popularity in Georgia. On election day 1936 FDR swept Fulton County by 27,003 to Landon's 3,515 votes. All economic levels supported him with the wealthy Buckhead district voting for Roosevelt by a margin of 1,135 to 349.[58] Prior to his presidency, FDR had made strong friendships in Georgia, and the policies of his first administration reinforced the affection of the people of Atlanta for their adopted son.

The 1937–38 recession necessitated increases in federal spending, mainly by the WPA and the Social Security Administration. In 1939, with economic recovery again underway, federal relief programs became less important, and dismantlement of the WPA began. As war spread through Europe in late 1939 and in 1940, prosperity and war preparedness took the attention of FDR and the American people away from the depression.

Though much remained unchanged, Atlanta in 1940 was a more modern, stronger city than she had been before the depression. Modern businesses stood ready to alter the face of the city and region. As a result of positive changes brought by the New Deal, the city possessed strengths and a foundation for future growth far superior to that found in 1929. By 1940 Atlanta had the best infrastructure of any Southern city. Its sewage and water system, highways and bridges, and airport improvements provided the requisite facilities needed to support plant expansions, transportation growth, and new construction during and after World War II. Additionally, new public housing developments, school and health care improvements, recreational facilities, and public assistance programs provided thousands of Atlantans with a better urban environment with substantially improved living conditions. The business elite had shrewdly adapted to the times. They had set aside their laissez-faire economic ideas and had accepted the New Deal's approaches to solving pressing community problems. They had gained a large list of urban amenities for Atlanta without losing their influence over local government or giving up Atlanta's low taxes as an inducement to potential investors. The city-federal partnership stood firmly established in 1940. Created during the difficult years of the depression, this partnership recognized the fact that the United States by the 1930s was no longer a nation of self-sufficient farmers and that the nation's cities served as its economic centers.

In U.S. cities outside the Southeast, states provided a large part of funds for schools, public works, and public assistance. Since Atlanta received little help from the state, the arrival of federal aid meant even more than it did to cities in other regions. Also, because of the business leadership's acceptance of New Deal programs, Atlanta benefited from federal spending in the 1930s more than most American cities. In a sense, she provided a willing laboratory for New Deal experimentation. Atlanta had one of the earliest completely federally administered relief programs under the FERA because of Gov. Eugene Talmadge's unwillingness to cooperate with federal policies. Atlanta received the first federally financed public housing, Techwood and University Homes, and the largest WPA project undertaken in the South, the Atlanta sewer system. FDR, Harry Hopkins, and Gay Shepperson had seen Southern poverty and realized its impact upon Southern cities. They had a personal commitment to help the city. The farsightedness and pragmatism of federal and local leaders, the honest administration of the programs, and their tremendous accomplishments permanently altered the city physically. Because of the New Deal, Atlanta survived the ordeal of the depression and entered the 1940s in better shape than ever before.

NOTES

1. Frank B. Freidel, *FDR and the South* (Baton Rouge: Louisiana State University Press, 1965), pp. 7–9, 20; *The Little White House, Warm Springs, Georgia* (New York: Raymond K. Martin, 1948), n.p.; John Earl Allen, "The Governor and the Strike; Eugene Talmadge and the General Strike, 1934" (M.A. thesis, Georgia State University, 1977), p. 98.

2. *Atlanta Constitution*, October 24, 1932.

3. U.S. Work Projects Administration of Georgia, *Occupational Characteristics of Negro Workers of Atlanta Georgia* (Atlanta: U.S. Work Projects Administration, 1937), pp. 70–71; Gilbert H. Boggs, Jr., ed., *A History of the Georgia Civil Works Administration in Georgia, 1933–1934* (Atlanta: U.S. Civil Works Administration, 1934), p. 19, bound copy in Jane Van de Vrede Collection, Georgia Department of Archives and History (hereafter cited as Van de Vrede Collection).

4. Richard F. Hofstadter, *The Age of Reform from Bryan to F.D.R.* (New York: Vintage Books, 1955), p. 316; William E. Leuchtenburg, radio interview, "ABC News Nightline," December 22, 1982.

5. *Atlanta Constitution*, March 15, 16, 18, April 30, 1933.

6. Ibid., May 18, 21, June 23, July 3–6, August 8, 10, 1933.

7. *Atlanta Journal*, March 3, 1933.

8. *Atlanta Constitution*, March 10–16, May 2, 15, 1933.

9. U.S. Work Projects Administration of Georgia, *A Report of the Social Security Survey of Georgia* (Atlanta: U.S. Work Projects Administration, 1937), p. 11; Boggs, ed., *Civil Works Administration in Georgia*, p. 19.

10. Special Relief Committee of Atlanta and Fulton County, "Report of Past and Future Activities on Work Relief Projects, May 1, 1933," File "Georgia General A–C," FERA State Series, March, 1933–36, Records of the Federal Emergency Relief Administration, Record Group 69, National Archives Building, Washington, D.C. (hereafter cited as FERA, RG 69, NA).

11. Special Relief Committee of Atlanta and Fulton County, "Report for April 1933," "Report for May 1933," File "Georgia General A–C," FERA State Series, March 1933–36, FERA, RG 69, NA.

12. Radio Free Georgia, "The Great Depression, Part II: Relief and Welfare Efforts," Living Atlanta Series, tape 36 (Atlanta: Radio Free Georgia Broadcasting Foundation, Inc., 1981).

13. *Atlanta Constitution*, June 21, August 25, 1933, January 6, 1934.

14. Brig. Gen. L. H. Bach to Hopkins, August 11, 1933, File "FERA State Files, 1933–36, Georgia 450, Work Relief," FERA State Series, 1933–36, FERA, RG 69, NA; Shepperson to Jacob Baker, Director of FERA Work Relief and Special Projects, Washington, D.C., August 31, 1933, File "FERA State Files, 1933–36, Georgia 450, Work Relief," FERA State Series, 1933–36, FERA, RG 69, NA.

15. Johnstone to Hopkins, September 18, 1933, File "FERA State Files, 1933–36, Georgia 406, Field Reports," FERA State Series, 1933–36, FERA, RG 69, NA; *Atlanta Constitution*, June 23, 1933.

16. Johnstone to Hopkins, January 19, 1934, File "FERA State Files, 1933–36, Georgia 400, Field Reports," FERA State Series, 1933–36, FERA, RG 69, NA; *Atlanta Constitution*, January 6, 7, 9, 1934. By the end of March 1935, the federal government had assumed direct control of FERA operations in Georgia, Louisiana, Massachusetts, North Dakota, Ohio, and Oklahoma.

17. Boggs, ed., *Civil Works Administration in Georgia*, pp. 61–66, 109, 112, 123, 172–73.

18. *Atlanta Constitution*, December 30, 1933.

19. J. J. Haverty to Doris Simmons, art teacher, January 8, 1934, Wilbur G. Kurtz, Sr., Papers, Atlanta Historical Society, Atlanta (hereafter cited as Kurtz Papers); Meta Barker to Wilbur Kurtz, July 23, 1930, Kurtz Papers.

20. Jane Van de Vrede, personal notes, File "Cyclorama," Van de Vrede Collection.

21. Boggs, ed., *Civil Works Administration in Georgia*, p. 30; *Atlanta Constitution*, February 18, 1934; Edgar C. Long, Chief Clerk, CWA of Georgia, to Weis C. Snell, April 28, 1934, Kurtz Papers; Shepperson to Moody E. Smith, principal, Chamblee Public Schools, March 3, 1934; File "Georgia Projects A–K," General Administrative Correspondence, November 1933–May 1934, Central Files of the Civil Works Administration, Records of the Civil Works Administration, Record Group 69, National Archives Building, Washington, D.C. (hereafter cited as CWA, RG 69, NA).

22. Willis A. Sutton, superintendent, Atlanta Public Schools, to Haverty, February 24, 1934, Kurtz Papers; Haverty to Sutton, March 2, 6, 14, April 2, 1934, Kurtz Papers; Long to Ada M. Barker, Fulton County CWA administrator, and T. J. Durrett, Jr., Fulton County CWA engineer, May 18, 19, 1934, Kurtz Papers; Shepperson to Barker, June 22, 1934, Kurtz Papers; *Atlanta Constitution*, March 24, 1934; Boggs, ed., *Civil Works Administration in Georgia*, p. 29.

23. *Atlanta Constitution*, July 23, 27, 30, August 14, 18, 1933.

24. Ibid., July 30, August 27, 29, September 21, 24, 27, 28, October 9, 19, November 15, 23, December 16, 29, 30, 1933, October 8, November 8, 1934. The PWA's small staff left few records, and most of those were lost before they could be sent to the National Archives. There are no significant PWA records there for Atlanta.

25. Ibid., January 5, 6, 1934; Boggs, ed., *Civil Works Administration in Georgia*, p. 64.

26. *Atlanta Constitution*, January 30, February 5, 6, March 23, 24, 1934.

27. Ibid., October 30, November 2, 1935, January 30, 1936.

28. "The PWA and Georgia," *Newsweek* 12 (December 1938): 12; PWA, *Public Buildings: A Survey of Architecture of Projects Constructed by Federal and Other Governmental Bodies between the years 1933 and 1939 with the Assistance of the PWA* (Washington, D.C.: U.S. Federal Works Agency, 1939), p. 320; U.S. Federal Emergency Administration of Public Works, *The Story of the PWA in Pictures* (Washington, D.C.: U.S. Federal Emergency Administration of Public Works, 1936), p. 1.

29. *Atlanta Constitution*, October 13, 15, 1933, June 19, 1973; David B. Jenks, "Charles Palmer and the Division of Defense Housing Coordination, 1940–1942" (M.A. thesis, Emory University, 1972), p. 17; Charles F. Palmer, *You and Your City* (Atlanta: Church and Community Press, 1963), pp. 6–9.

30. *Atlanta Constitution*, October 19, 1933, April 15, May 5, July 1, 3, September 30, 1934; U.S. Work Projects Administration of Georgia, *Techwood Neighborhood* (Atlanta: U.S. Work

Projects Administration, Georgia, 1939), p. 7; Radio Free Georgia, "Techwood and University Homes, Part I: The Nation's First Federal Public Housing Projects," Living Atlanta Series, tape 45 (Atlanta: Radio Free Georgia Broadcasting Foundation, Inc., 1981).

31. *Atlanta Constitution*, July 21, 23, November 25, December 21, 1934, November 29, 30, 1935, September 2, 1936.

32. Hugh S. Johnson, *The Blue Eagle from Egg to Earth* (1935; reprint ed., New York: Greenwood Press, 1968), pp. 196–97.

33. *Atlanta Constitution*, July 30, 31, August 1, 2, 4, 1933; Michael S. Holmes, *The New Deal in Georgia: An Administrative History* (Westport, Connecticut: Greenwood Press, 1975), p. 186.

34. *Atlanta Constitution*, August 13, 15, 21, 24, 25, September 1, 15, 22, October 5, 1933.

35. Ibid., November 24, 1933, February 14, April 15, June 29, 1934.

36. John I. Hynds, special assistant to NRA regional director, to W. L. Mitchell, regional and state director, NRA, November 16, 1935, File "Analyses of State Offices, Docketed Cases," General Correspondence, January 1, 1935–January 1, 1936, Georgia–Kentucky, Records of the National Recovery Administration, Record Group 9, Federal Records Center, East Point, Georgia (hereafter cited as NRA, RG 9, FRC E.P.); File "Blue Eagle Removal Information," General Correspondence, January 1, 1935–January 1, 1936, Georgia–Kentucky, NRA, RG 9, FRC E.P.; D. B. Lasseter, executive assistant, Atlanta State Office, NRA, to W. M. Galvin, assistant field division administrator, NRA, Washington, D.C., November 15, 1935, File "Code Authority Administration," Atlanta Administration Records, January 1935–January 1936, Restitution to Negroes, NRA, RG 9, FRC E.P.; File "NRA Code Violation: DeLameter's Pharmacy, Atlanta, Georgia," April 2, 3, 9, 1934, NRA, RG 9, FRC E.P.

37. *Atlanta Constitution*, May 30, 31, 1935.

38. Ibid., March 10, April 8, 21, 24, July 3, 6, 14, 18, 1933, June 29, 1934; U.S. Department of Agriculture, *United States Cotton Statistics, 1909–1949* (Washington, D.C.: Government Printing Office, 1951), p. 12.

39. *Atlanta Constitution*, December 13, 1933.

40. Atlanta Social Welfare Council, *Relief and Service*, p. 2, Atlanta Lung Association Collection, Atlanta Historical Society.

41. U.S. Work Projects Administration, *Final Statistical Report of the Federal Emergency Relief Administration* (Washington, D.C.: U.S. Work Projects Administration, 1942), p. 7; WPA, *Occupational Characteristics*, pp. 70–71; State of Georgia, *Report of Georgia Department of Public Welfare, January 1, 1937–June 30, 1938*, pp. 17–18.

42. *Atlanta Constitution*, June 1, 3–5, 7, 23, 1935.

43. Russell to Hopkins, July 25, 1935, File "FERA State Files, 1933–36, Georgia 400," FERA State Series, FERA, RG 69, NA; Harrington to Russell, July 25, 1935, File "FERA State Files, 1933–36, Georgia 400," FERA State Series, FERA, RG 69, NA; Stauffer to Russell, July 26, 1935, File "FERA State Files, 1933–36, Georgia 400," FERA State Series, FERA, RG 69, NA; WPA, *FERA Final Statistical Report*, p. 7; Hopkins to Robert F. Maddox, Atlanta Community Chest president, November 1, 1935, File "Georgia Public Relations," WPA State Series, 1935–43, WPA, RG 69, NA.

44. William Anderson, *The Wild Man from Sugar Creek: The Political Career of Eugene Talmadge* (Baton Rouge: Louisiana State University Press, 1975), p. 172.

45. FERA of Georgia, *Monthly Review of Relief Statistics* 1, no. 11 (September 1935): 1.

46. *Atlanta Constitution*, July 6, 1935; Radio Free Georgia, "The Great Depression, Part III: Unemployment and the New Deal Welfare Projects," Living Atlanta Series, tape 37.

47. Shepperson to Col. Lawrence Westbrook, U.S. WPA assistant administrator, July 22, 1935, File "Georgia, Correspondence with State Administrator, 1935–44," WPA State Series, 1935–44, WPA, RG 69, NA; Emerson Ross, Director of WPA of Georgia Division of Research, Statistics, and Records, to Ramspeck, October 24, 1936, File "Georgia, Correspondence with State Administrator, 1935–44," WPA State Series, 1935–44, WPA, RG 69, NA; Holmes, *New Deal in Georgia*, pp. 95–96.

48. "Condensed Report of Miss Gay B. Shepperson to Federal Agencies Conference, Atlanta, Georgia, April 10, 1936, 'Summary of Relief Activities in Georgia,'" Jane Van de Vrede Papers; *Atlanta Constitution*, May 12, June 6, July 6, 1935.

49. Horatio B. Hacket, FERA assistant administrator, to Hopkins, August 23, 1935, File "Georgia, Correspondence with State Administrator, 1935–44," WPA State Series, 1935–44, WPA, RG 69, NA; *Atlanta Constitution*, September 19, 1935; Ickes to Hopkins, August 5, 1935, "Georgia Specific Projects, 1935–43: Sewers, Drainage, and Sanitation Facilities," WPA State Series, 1935–44, WPA, RG 69, NA; U.S. Works Progress Administration of Georgia, "Semi-monthly Narrative Report, September 1, 1935, to September 15, 1935, District 5, Atlanta, Georgia," File "Georgia Projects (General), 1935–43," WPA State Series, 1935–44, WPA, RG 69, NA; David L. Browne to J. C. Capt, October 1, 1935, "from the files of the Project Control Division," File "Sewer, Drainage, and Sanitation Facilities," WPA State Series, 1935–44, WPA, RG 69, NA.

50. WPA "Radio Talk, WSB, Atlanta, Georgia, 5:00 P.M., July 13, 1936," typed script, Margaret L. MacDougall Collection, Atlanta Historical Society (hereafter cited as MacDougall Collection); Radio Free Georgia, "The Great Depression, Part III."

51. Radio Free Georgia, "The Great Depression, Part III."

52. WPA "Radio Talk," MacDougall Collection; U.S. Works Progress Administration, Division of Social Research, *Survey of Cases for Works Program Employment in 13 Cities*, Research Bulletin, series 4, no. 2 (Washington, D.C.: U.S. Works Progress Administration, 1937), p. 16; *Atlanta Constitution*, March 18, 1936.

53. State of Georgia, Board of Control, Eleemosynary Institutions, *Georgia Board of Control Eleemosynary Institutions Report for 1936* (Atlanta: State of Georgia, 1937), n.p.; Harry A. Glaser, supervisor, Federal Music Project to Georgia, to Nicolai Sokoloff, director, Federal Music Project, February 1, 1936, File "Georgia Specific Projects, 1935–43: Music Program," WPA State Series, 1935–44, WPA, RG 69, NA; Glaser to Sokoloff, February 24, 1936, File "Georgia Specific Projects, 1935–43: Music Program," WPA State Series, 1935–44, WPA, RG 69, NA; L. P. Skidmore, director, Federal Art Project of Georgia, to Thomas C. Parker, assistant director, Federal Art Project, File "Georgia Specific Projects, 1935–43: Art Program," WPA State Series, 1935–44, WPA, RG 69, NA.

54. U.S. Federal Security Agency, War Manpower Commission, *Final Report of the National Youth Administration, Fiscal Years 1936–43* (Washington, D.C.: Government Printing Office, 1944), pp. v–viii; U.S. National Youth Administration of Georgia, "Report on the National Youth Administration of Georgia, June 26, 1935, to December 31, 1938" (Atlanta: U.S. National Youth Administration, January 1939), pp. 1–7; *Atlanta Constitution*, October 9, 1936; "Report on State Activities, March 9, 1936," File "Georgia Administrative Reports, September 1935–April 1936," NYA Administrative Reports, 1935–38, NYA, RG 119, NA.

55. "Report of State Activities, April 9, 1936," File "Georgia Administrative Reports, September 1935–April 1936," NYA Administrative Reports, 1935–38, NYA, RG 119, NA; Forrester B. Washington to R. R. Paty, Georgia NYA Director, March 11, 1936, File "Georgia Administrative Reports, September 1935–April 1936," NYA Administrative Reports, 1935–38, NYA, RG 119, NA.

56. L. C. Benedict to Malcom J. Miller, U.S. WPA field representative, July 26, 1937, File "Georgia Specific Projects, 1935–43: Sewer, Drainage, and Sanitation Facilities," WPA State Series, 1935–44, WPA, RG 69, NA.

57. *State of Georgia, Report of Georgia Department of Public Welfare*, 1937–38, p. 19; *Atlanta Constitution*, March 20, 1935. The old-age pensions generally called "Social Security" did not require any state participation.

58. *Atlanta Journal*, November 4, 1936.

The Civilian Conservation Corps in Mobile County, Alabama

BILLY G. HINSON

The Civilian Conservation Corps recruited urban men, ages eighteen to twenty-five (the age qualifications were later modified twice), for work relief in the form of useful projects in the countryside, especially in the conservation of natural resources. The simple assumption behind the CCC—still valid—was that young men who were neither in school nor working were likely to get into trouble, emotionally and otherwise. CCC participants also benefited from education, improvement of health, and attainment of self-respect. A special component of this relief program was the requirement that all but a few dollars of the enrollees' pay be sent to their dependents. A pet program of President Roosevelt, the CCC was probably the most popular New Deal program. It expired, along with other work-relief agencies, during World War II.

THE United States was in the throes of the Great Depression when Franklin D. Roosevelt became president. In response to this crisis his administration established several work relief agencies. One was the Civilian Conservation Corps, created on March 31, 1933, to provide work for unemployed young men, promote conservation of forests, control plant disease and pests, and prevent forest fires, floods, and erosion.[1] The

From the *Alabama Review*, 45 (October 1992), 243–256.

conservation work of the CCC benefited the nation by providing many permanent improvements, and CCC workers found the organization left a lasting effect on their lives.

Four executive departments cooperated with the corps. The Department of Labor selected and certified the enrollees. The War Department gave them physical examinations, officially enrolled them, and supervised the men while they were in the camps. When the enrollees left the camp to work, they were supervised by the Department of Agriculture if the project was on state and/or private land (except state parks) or by the Department of the Interior if the project was in state parks.[2]

The Civilian Conservation Corps was established officially as the Emergency Conservation Work with Robert Fechner as the national director. The secretaries of each of the cooperating executive departments appointed a representative to an advisory council to assist the director.[3] The council decided to enroll unemployed single men, ages eighteen to twenty-five, who were willing to allow $22 to $25 of their $30 monthly pay to be sent to their dependents. Subsequently, the age range was changed twice; in September 1936 the range was seventeen to twenty-eight years of age and in April 1937, seventeen to twenty-three.[4]

On April 20, 1933, the U.S. Department of Labor authorized the Relief Administration of Alabama to select young men for the CCC in the state. Later, in February 1936 the Alabama Department of Public Welfare assumed this selection responsibility. Approximately 5,291 young men from Alabama were hired during the first enrollment period between May and July 1933.[5]

The CCC developed two camps in Mobile County to be occupied only by Caucasians. The first camp was Camp Rendell, opened on June 14, 1933, on public and private lands.[6] The nearest railroad station and telegraph office were located at Rendell, and the post office was at Chunchula.[7] The second camp was established near Citronelle on August 31, 1935. This camp was confined to state land, Cedar Creek Park, consisting of 640 acres.[8]

The first enrollees for Camp Rendell assembled at Fort Barrancas, Florida, to be conditioned for CCC work. After two weeks the young men boarded a train that took them to Rendell.[9] On June 14, shortly after noon, 188 men arrived at the campsite located at the old Patterson brickyard on a hillside near the Mobile and Ohio Railroad and Chickasabogue Creek. They immediately began preparing food and sleeping quarters for the night, clearing away debris, pitching tents, and digging drainage ditches. They unloaded mattresses, groceries, and other supplies from a railroad

car. The commanding officer was Captain E. G. Walsh of the Mobile
army reserve corps. Walsh planned to use the tents as sleeping quarters
until the men could renovate the oblong brick kilns, a job that would require approximately two weeks.[10]

In time the young men erected four barracks, two large houses, and
four small houses and reconstructed a brick shed to serve as a mess hall.
The latter structure later was moved to another location in the camp and
was used as a combination mess hall and recreational hall. In January 1934
the camp completed construction of a washroom and a bathhouse with
twelve showers.[11]

Young men enrolled in the CCC for a variety of reasons. Some had to
serve as family breadwinners when their fathers were too ill or earned too
little income to support their families. Others joined because no jobs were
available after graduation from high school. The scene at one center for
physical exams reflected the economic desperation of the times. As Edgar
A. Bowles of Mobile underwent his physical examination, a short man
named Thomas stood ahead of Bowles in the examination line. After one
look at Thomas, the doctor pronounced "You're too short," stamped "rejected" on his papers, and told Thomas to "move over there." Bowles remembered that "Thomas stood over there and then came up when I was
getting checked and said 'Doctor, I want to tell you something. Us little
folks get just as hungry as those big ones.'" The doctor looked up at him
and stamped "passed" on his papers.[12]

Enrollees worked on state-owned or privately owned lands. By April
1934 the camp at Rendell had access to 40,000 acres of state-owned land
and 195,000 acres of privately owned land.[13] By 1938 the amount of privately owned land on which the CCC worked was 92,304 acres, and the
major contributing cooperatives were C. C. Huxford, Ray Sawmill Company, Alabama Property Company, Creola Lumber Company, T. A. Hat-
ter and Company, Taylor Lowenstein and Company, Stover Manufacturing
Company, and Conservation Land Company.[14]

The men in this camp participated in a variety of work: constructing
truck trails to facilitate fire fighting and fire prevention activities, cutting
firebreaks, erecting telephone lines, building lookout towers and vehicle
bridges, clearing roadsides, collecting seeds, controlling insects, planting
fields, building pump houses and latrines, drilling wells at tower sites, and
constructing various buildings to be used by the enrollees, such as bath-
houses and recreational rooms.[15] One junior forester said he must have supervised the cutting of a thousand miles of truck trails, and official reports
substantiate that impression.[16]

These truck trails facilitated fighting forest fires, but sometimes the men at the camp were summoned to fight fires outside of those areas. Such was the occasion in 1938 when nearly every camp enrollee participated in fighting a fire in Wragg Swamp in Mobile (where the malls are now located on Airport Boulevard, east of Interstate 65).[17]

Food for the enrollees was plentiful, palatable, and nourishing. Before the men left camp for work, they had a hearty breakfast. For example, on March 26, 1934, they had cornflakes, fresh milk, pork sausage, hominy grits, bread, syrup, and coffee. For lunch in the field they had pork and beans, bread, apples, and iced tea. After returning to camp at the end of the day, their evening meal consisted of spareribs, sauerkraut, french baked potatoes, turnip greens, bread, butter, fruit cup, oranges, apples, cocoa, and milk. The Mobile County economy benefited from the CCC purchases of food and other products from local companies.[18]

Camp Rendell workers praised the quality of their meals as "wonderful," "the best food" prepared by the "best cooks," and "hard to beat today." One worker recalled that the young men had "plenty good things to eat. They didn't misfeed us."[19] These glowing comments must be understood as the reactions of young men from impoverished homes who found such meals to be especially appealing.

When the camp at Rendell first opened, the young men ate all meals from mess kits that they were responsible for washing. They took these kits to the fields where lunch was served. Camp trucks brought food to the work area where the workers filed into a line to be served. After the meal the young men soaped and washed their mess kits in a vat of hot water. Later, the enrollees used china plates while in camp but continued using their mess kits in the field.[20]

The Roosevelt administration planned to provide enrollees with educational opportunities after they completed regular work hours. Each camp was to offer an educational program suited to the needs of its particular enrollees. In addition, the young men learned useful skills by on-the-job training.[21]

The educational program for CCC workers developed slowly. After nine months in operation the camp was unable to adhere to a regular instructional schedule because fire fighting consumed so much time. Some of the men took correspondence courses, and officers assisted them.[22] By the end of 1934, however, significant progress had been made, with regular classes held in spelling, arithmetic, English, algebra, agriculture, penmanship, business law, first aid, estimations, and typing. The classes averaged an attendance of twenty. The best-attended classes were three spelling classes averaging seventy-one students and three arithmetic classes averaging fifty-three students. The poorly attended classes were those in penmanship, with an average attendance of three, and typing, four.[23]

Camp leaders expanded the educational program by May 1935 to include vocational classes in auto mechanics, accounting, craftsmanship, journalism, lifesaving, personal development, and scout-master training.[24] By the end of the year additional classes were offered. Each Wednesday night the commanding officer or camp educational adviser lectured on citizenship, and the camp surgeon addressed the issues of health. Classes were held in a variety of places in the camp: the library, shop room, mess hall, recreational hall, officers' mess, and the old educational office.[25]

By October 1938 subjects were organized on a quarterly basis so that progress could be regularly checked and proficiency certificates granted. Almost half of the classes represented academic-subject content, and enrollees could take regular examinations at local schools to earn full credit for the classes.[26]

The camp also had a library, which was located originally at the southern end of the mess hall. Later the library was housed in a building 40 by 20 feet, and by October 1938 it included "approximately 700 books and pamphlets, and fifty magazines, together with eight daily newspapers." A "traveling library" was available also, and enrollees borrowed more books from that source than from the camp library.[27]

After work the enrollees enjoyed various recreational activities, including basketball, volleyball, baseball, football, boxing, tennis, and horseshoe pitching. The recreational hall held a piano, radio, ping-pong game, and miniature pool tables. Occasionally, the camp held dances.[28] To supply partners for the CCC workers the company commander dispatched army trucks to Mobile to bring young ladies to the dance. A young man could take a lady outside the dance hall, perhaps for a smoke, but the couple could not wander around the camp. A watchman was responsible for ensuring proper behavior. The camp baseball team was a popular activity and played other teams, including one from the nearby state prison at Atmore.[29]

CCC officials were concerned not only about education but also about health and sanitation. A camp doctor was headquartered at Rendell to attend to sick or injured men. Enrollees were examined monthly for venereal disease. Occasionally, positive cases were reported. The camp report of January 2, 1935, showed that four cases of gonorrhea had been detected in the previous nine months.[30] In late 1937 the camp received an allotment of $1,000 to repair buildings and to erect an outside sterilizer shed to treat those men infected with head lice.[31]

An artesian well supplied abundant water. Kitchen and bath water was piped out 150 yards from the camp area and emptied into an open ditch. Sewage went through septic tanks into cesspools, out through laterals, and into the ground.[32]

In spite of abundant water, occasionally an enrollee failed to bathe frequently. Coworkers would warn the negligent person and, if the warning did not achieve a satisfactory response, would give him a thorough scrubbing with a firm brush. The soap and brush treatment did not have to be repeated.[33]

The CCC emphasized safety and had a safety committee, weekly fire drills, and fire protection facilities such as extinguishers, water barrels, buckets, fire axes, ladders, sand barrels, water tank, and water faucets for fires only. Trucks had guardrails, seats, and governors. The camp provided instructions on first aid and on fighting forest fires.[34]

The men in the corps had opportunities to attend religious services. The Mobile Ministerial Association supplied ministers who visited the camp once or twice a week. By late 1935 a Sunday school with a superintendent and three teachers was organized in the camp. A monthly report of religious services showed that as of September 28, 1936, Camp Rendell had 173 Protestants and 7 Catholics. The enrollees also attended the church of their choice outside of the camp.[35]

Most CCC workers received $30 a month, and those who became leaders earned $36 and $45. The company commander and camp superintendent selected the leaders. The purpose of the additional pay was to reward outstanding leadership, hard work, and special skills. No more than 5 percent of the authorized strength of the company could be paid $45, and no more than 8 percent could receive $36.[36]

Enrollees wore blue-denim work clothes or fatigues and out-of-date regular army uniforms with plain buttons instead of army ones. President Roosevelt approved special CCC uniforms of spruce green with special CCC insignia in 1939, but by that time Camp Rendell had been abandoned.[37]

Camp Rendell closed on May 1, 1939, and thereafter the rigid buildings were transferred to the U.S. Army, which released them to the National Park Service. The portable buildings were transferred to the CCC camp at Citronelle.[38]

Although less information is available for the second CCC camp in Mobile County than for Camp Rendell, reports reflect that such camp activities as food, education, health, recreation, safety, and pay resembled those of Camp Rendell.[39] Nevertheless the work projects of the two camps differed markedly. The primary work project for the Citronelle camp was the construction of a twenty-three-acre recreational lake with trails, bathing beach, picnic area, and roads. By mid-March 1937 the young men had completed 90 percent of a dam and a caretaker's house, constructed roads and foot trails, planted the area with 40,000 young trees and shrubs, and fenced the area.[40]

After the CCC completed the project, the camp was abandoned in late 1937. Another camp was established there on August 1, 1939, to maintain the recreational facilities at Cedar Creek State Park. The enrollees were involved in general park improvement such as constructing and servicing roads and enhancing the beach.[41] The Citronelle camp closed on August 15, 1941.[42] By this time the federal government was phasing out the Civilian Conservation Corps.

The CCC significantly contributed in Mobile County to the conservation of natural resources and the development of a recreational area in a state park. It provided discipline and training that benefited the armed forces in World War II and assisted the enrollees when they sought employment in the private sector. CCC volunteers continue to be proud of their accomplishments and grateful for the opportunity to have been members of the Civilian Conservation Corps.

NOTES

1. XLVIII, *United States Statutes at Large*, 22–23. For general information on the activities of the CCC during the Depression see Leslie Alexander Lacy, *The Soil Soldiers: The Civilian Conservation Corps in the Great Depression* (Radnor, Pa., 1976); for information on the Alabama CCC camps see Robert D. Gunnels, "The Civilian Conservation Corps in Alabama" (M.A. thesis, Auburn University, 1990).

2. Dean Snyder to Loula Dunn, August 25, 1938. Snyder sent Dunn copies of the *Public Welfare Manual*, published by the Alabama State Department of Public Welfare, July 1, 1938, pp. 1–2, Folder—"Alabama," Box 2, *State Procedures: Records, 1933–1942*, Records of the Civilian Conservation Corps, Record Group 35, National Archives, Washington, D.C.

3. U.S., President, Executive Order, "Relief of Unemployment Through the Performance of Useful Public Work," Appendix 2, in *Chronology, CCC-Labor Department, April–September, 1933*, Folder—"Cooperation 779," Box 1, *Documents Relating to the Organization and Operations of the CCC, 1933–1942*, CCC, RG 35.

4. John A. Salmond, *The Civilian Conservation Corps, 1933–1942: A New Deal Case Study* (Durham, 1967), 30, 59; W. Frank Persons, "Letter to All State Directors of Selection of Men to be Enrolled for Emergency Conservation Work," Series Four, Letter of Instruction N. 53, April 23, 1937, p. 1, Folder—"Al. Forecast, July 1937–April 1938," Box 1, *Statistical Report on Enrollees, 1933–1942*, CCC, RG 35; L, *United States Statutes at Large*, 320.

5. Dean Snyder to Loula Dunn, August 25, 1938, *Public Welfare Manual*, pp. 1–2. Although hired from Alabama, CCC enrollees could be sent to another state.

6. Neil M. Coney, Jr., Special Investigator, report to the Director of Emergency Conservation Work, "Camp Report," April 5, 1934, p. 1, Box—"Begin Series 715," *Camp Inspection Reports, 1933–1942*, CCC, RG 35. All references from the *Camp Inspection Reports* are found in this box.

7. Station and Strength Report of the CCC, August 31, 1934, p. 2, Folder—"August 31, 1934," Box 2, *Station and Strength Reports, August 31, 1934–December 31, 1935*, CCC, RG 35.

8. Reddoch, "Camp Report," January 10, 1936, p. 1, and Reddoch, "Supplementary Report," October 6, 1939, p. 1, *Camp Inspection Reports*; "Station and Strength Report of the CCC," June 30, 1935, p. 61, Folder—"June 30, 1935," Box 2, *Station and Strength Reports, August 31, 1934–December 31, 1935*, say that the camp was established on June 17, 1935.

9. Goodman G. Griffin, "History of Company 1485," Folder—"Civilian Conservation Corps," p. 1, Mobile Public Library, Mobile.

10. Mobile *Register*, June 15, 1933.

11. Griffin, "History of Company 1485," p. 1.

12. Personal interview with Carl Edward Bates in Eight Mile, Alabama, March 9, 1990; personal interview with Hillry E. Faulkenberry in Mobile, Alabama, September 11, 1990; personal interview with Connie B. Johnson in Citronelle, Alabama, March 6, 1990; personal interview with Edgar A. Bowles in Theodore, Alabama, September 28, 1990.

13. Coney, "Camp Report," April 5, 1934, p. 1, *Camp Inspection Reports*.

14. The companies are listed in order from the greatest to the least amount of land made available to the CCC. No records of leases have been found in the Mobile County Courthouse, and the author is inclined to believe one source who said that oral agreements were made for land use. U.S., Department of Agriculture, Forest Service, *Alabama: State CCC Maintenance Report, May 31–June 11, 1938* (Washington, D.C., 1938), 34. This report is located in Folder—"Inspection," *CCC Administrative Files, 1937–1947*, SG 6194, Division of Forestry, Alabama Department of Conservation, Alabama Department of Archives and History, Montgomery.

15. The various work projects are documented in numerous reports found in Folder—"CCC Work Plans, Camp S-52," *CCC Administrative Files, 1939–1947*, SG 6195. For information on the forestry work of the CCC see Robert Fechner, *Forests Protected by the CCC* (Washington, D.C., 1939), and Perry H. Merrill, *Roosevelt's Forest Army: A History of the Civilian Conservation Corps* (Montpelier, 1981).

16. Telephone interview with Alex M. Fuqua of Brewton, Alabama, November 20, 1990; C. F. Attaway, "Monthly Work Progress Report, Supplemental Report," May 31, 1936, p. 1, Microfilm, Reel Box 39, *Monthly Work Progress Reports, 1933–1942*, CCC, RG 35.

17. Personal interview with Lewis Prescott Lisenba in Mobile, Alabama, September 13, 1990.

18. Coney, "Camp Report," April 5, 1934, and Ivan C. DuBois, "Camp Exchange Statement," October 25, 1936, p. 1, *Camp Inspection Reports*.

19. Faulkenberry interview; personal interview with Fred Boothe, Jr., in Citronelle, Alabama, September 25, 1990; personal interview with John David Turner in Citronelle, Alabama, September 25, 1990.

20. Faulenberry interview; Lisenba interview; Bowles interview.

21. Dean Snyder to Loula Dunn, August 25, 1938, *Public Welfare Manual*, p. 5. For general information on the educational activities of the CCC see Frank Ernest Hill, *The School in the Camps: The Educational Program of the Civilian Conservation Corps* (New York, 1935).

22. Coney, "Camp Report," April 5, 1934, p. 5, *Camp Inspection Reports, 1933–1942*.

23. Obie R. Cottle, Camp Educational Advisor, "Monthly Educational Report," December 30, 1934, p. 1, ibid.

24. Ibid., May 1935, p. 1.

25. Charles H. Wilkinson, Company Commander, "Resume of classes for December 1935," January 10, 1936, p. 1, ibid.

26. Obie R. Cottle, "Civilian Conservation Corps Educational Report to Director of CCC," October 12, 1938, p. 1, ibid.

27. Office of the Company Commander to the Director of Emergency Conservation Work, October 27, 1936, p. 2, Cottle, "Educational Report," October 12, 1938, p. 1, and Cottle, "Monthly Educational Report," December 1934, p. 2, all in ibid.

28. Coney to Director of Emergency Conservation Work, "Supplementary Camp Report," April 5, 1934, p. 1, Office of the Company Commander, 1485 Company, "Recreational Equipment, January 10, 1936," p. 1, and Reddoch, "Supplementary Report to Director of Emergency Conservation Work," January 2, 1935, p. 2, all in ibid.

29. Bowles interview; Faulkenberry interview; Lisenba interview.

30. Coney, "Camp Report," April 5, 1934, p. 2, and Reddoch, "Supplementary Report," January 2, 1935, p. 2, *Camp Inspection Reports*. The names of doctors are found in the camp reports of Reddoch, January 2, 1935, p. 2, January 10, 1936, p. 1, October 27, 1936, p. 1, December 10, 1937, p. 1, October 12, 1938, p. 1, ibid. The physicians who served the camp during its six years of existence included Frank Vinson, Alex B. Calder, C. M. Hogan, Dave Berman, Walter H. Minor, and Edwin C. Corcoran.

31. J. H. Burke, Captain, to Commanding Officer, Company 1485, Camp S-52, December 22, 1937, p. 1, ibid.; Lisenba interview.

32. Reddoch, "Camp Report," October 27, 1936, p. 1, *Camp Inspection Reports*.

33. Faulkenberry interview.

34. J. Billups, "Camp Report to Director of Emergency Conservation Work," June 14, 1935, p. 2, and Reddoch, "Camp Report," October 27, 1936, p. 2, *Camp Inspection Reports*; Fuqua interview.

35. Coney, "Camp Report," April 5, 1934, p. 1, Reddoch, "Supplementary Report," January 10, 1936, p. 1, and Ivan C. DuBois, "Monthly Religious Services Report," September 28, 1936, p. 1, *Camp Inspection Reports*; Faulkenberry interview.

36. Office of the Director of Emergency Conservation Work, Release for Monday Morning Newspaper, June 12, 1933, Folder—"Cooperation 779, Chronology: Civilian Conservation Corps and Labor Department, April–September, 1933," Appendix 33, and Franklin D. Roosevelt, Executive Order, June 7, 1933, "Administration of the Emergency Conservation Work," Appendix 27, both in Box 1, *Documents Relating to . . . CCC.*

37. "Special Enrollee Uniforms," pp. 1–2, Folder—"Document 781: Dept. of Agriculture, CCC Chronological Reference Material by Subjects," Box 1, *Documents Relating to . . . CCC.*

38. Federal Security Agency, CCC, *Fiscal Control, CCC Camps by Corps Areas: Status Record of CCC Camps Authorized Since Inception of Program Up to and Including Dec. 31, 1941,* Vol. 1, Table III, p. 63, Box 1, *Corps Area Camp Status Reports, 1939–1941,* CCC, RG 35; J. S. Carmack, "Civilian Conservation Corps: Camp Disposition Completion Report, August 16, 1939," p. 1, Folder—"Agriculture-Forest Service-Alabama," Box 1, *Records of the Liquidation Unit, 1933–53: Correspondence Relating to the Disposal of Buildings, 1935–1942;* J. S. Billups, "Camp Report," March 15, 1937, p. 1, *Camp Inspection Reports.*

39. Federal Security Agency, CCC, "Status Record of the CCC Camps Authorized Since the Inception of the Program up to and Including December 31, 1941," Manual Vol. 1, p. 46, Box 1, *Corps Area . . . Reports.*

40. Billups, "Camp Report," March 15, 1937, *Camp Inspection Reports.*

41. Reddoch, "Camp Inspection Report," October 6, 1939, p. 1, ibid.

42. Federal Security Agency, CCC, "Status Record of the CCC Camps Authorized Since the Inception of the Program up to and Including December 31, 1941," Manual Vol. 1, p. 46, Box 1, *Corps Area . . . Reports.*

The New Deal in Pocatello

MERWIN R. SWANSON

New Deal programs and reactions to them were as varied in this remote lo-cality in the Rockies as they were in larger cities that have been the subject of numerous studies. The second part of this selection explores the attitudes of local businessmen toward the New Deal. At the national level, Roosevelt had suffered considerable loss of favor in the business community by 1935, and he turned to labor for compensating support. Meanwhile, Pocatello businessmen exhibited sophisticated selectivity, favoring programs that pro-moted their own particular interests. This stance was characteristic of the "broker state" under which well-organized, well-financed, and articulate in-terest groups sought federal aid without regard for other interest groups. It is sometimes assumed that the "broker state" mediated between various inter-est groups, but it was more like the spokes of a wheel without a rim, each spoke moving toward the center, Washington, independently of the other spokes.

AMERICANS properly remember the 1930s as a decade of poverty from the Depression and a decade of reform under the New Deal. Memories of the period focus on important people and events—Franklin Roosevelt, strikes, the unemployed at the soup kitchens. These national memories are en-tirely appropriate, but the experiences of the cities and small towns of America, such as Pocatello, Idaho, sometimes differed from national pat-terns. Politics, labor relations, and programs to give help to the unem-

From *Idaho Yesterdays*, 23 (Summer 1979), 53–57, and 21 (Fall 1977), 9–15. Two articles are here combined.

ployed were inevitably a part of the life of every American city during the 1930s. A description of the conditions existing at the national level, a close look at what happened in Pocatello, and some analysis of the similarities and differences between the two provide an example of how national and local patterns varied.

The 1930s created our modern political world. From the 1890s through 1932 Republicans in the United States were the dominant political party. Beginning in the late 1920s and culminating with Franklin Roosevelt's victory in 1936, the Democratic party built a winning coalition that remains a central political force. Though politics in Pocatello did change during the 1930s, what happened here differed from what happened nationally.

Pocatello Democrats dominated politics in the city during the 1920s. C. Ben Ross served as Pocatello's mayor before becoming governor of Idaho in 1930. Ross was a Pocatello businessman and represented the faction of local Democrats, including men such as Ben Davis, that the press labelled pro-business. This group dominated local politics until Ross went to Boise, and then a fight erupted for control of the town's Democratic organization.

Thomas Coffin, a local attorney, led the Democrats opposed to Governor Ross. In 1931 Coffin challenged the Ross faction at the Democratic convention in the city. When Coffin overcame the opposition of those such as Ben Davis, who argued Coffin would split the party and make efficient government impossible, local politicians said the victory was an upset and a major realignment of Pocatello's political make-up.[1] What the realignment meant in terms of the administration of government in Pocatello is unclear, and perhaps the issues were ones of personality rather than substance. But a group around Coffin, identified as pro-labor, had won the city.

The municipal elections of 1933 saw the Democrats split and run two candidates for mayor. The division brought both Boise and Washington, D.C., into Pocatello politics. On election eve Parker Carver, Ross's personal secretary, came to Pocatello to boost the Ross candidate, while newly elected Congressman Thomas Coffin broadcast a speech to local supporters by phone from the national capital strongly implying that Franklin Roosevelt was vitally interested in a victory for Coffin's man. Both factions lost as the Republicans elected a mayor for the first time in a decade.[2]

The local Republicans were in a potentially awkward position in the 1930s. On the face of it, they could not normally expect to win local elections, given the popularity of Roosevelt, the New Deal, and the local

Democrats. They therefore attempted to avoid opposing the New Deal and stressed the separate character of local and national issues. In the municipal elections of 1933, for example, the Republicans knew that they stood an excellent chance for victory. One appeal that the chairman of the Republican Central Committee made sought to steal some of the popularity of the national New Deal—he called for a *Republican* "New Deal for Pocatello." With the tradition of Democratic victories in the city, the Republicans argued that a "new deal" for Pocatello meant replacing Democrats with Republicans.[3] In fact, the victory of the Republicans in the local election of 1933, like the victory of Coffin two years earlier, produced no perceptible change in city policies. The only apparent theme running through the political news of the period was that of competition between labor and management.

Coffin's further career deserves note. He had political ambitions beyond Pocatello. In 1932 he won the Democratic nomination and the general election to Congress from Idaho's Second Congressional District. His nomination and victory were both surprises because the seat had been held for two decades by Republicans. Coffin went to Washington, loyally supported Franklin Roosevelt and the New Deal, and had a bright future as long as the New Deal remained popular in Idaho. Unfortunately, Coffin died when he stepped in front of an automobile in Washington, D.C., in June, 1934.[4]

National politics changed as much during the 1930s as at any time in this century; but while local politics and elections were lively, no changes similar to those on the national level occurred. Pocatello was a Democratic stronghold at the beginning of the period and, despite the 1933 elections, remained so throughout. National issues did not directly intrude into the local scene, except insofar as the popularity of the national Democrats and Franklin Roosevelt contributed in a general way to victories for local Democrats.

Organized labor transformed itself in the United States during the 1930s. At the beginning of the Depression the American Federation of Labor (AFL), composed of unions representing only skilled workers, dominated organized labor. Following a decade that saw changes in laws and public attitudes, the appearance of the Committee for (later Congress of) Industrial Organization (CIO), major strikes, and a jump in union membership, organized labor assumed its contemporary position in American society. The experiences of organized labor in Pocatello, however, were very different.

The number of union members, the number of unions, and other obvious measures of labor's strength in Pocatello are not readily available.
But stories in the press variously stated that Pocatello was the strongest
union town in the West or the strongest in the nation.[5] Even allowing for
exaggeration, the Pocatello Central Labor Union (AFL) enjoyed an unusual position in the local community during the 1930s. A labor representative was a requirement on any committee claiming to represent the
"community interest." When the National Recovery Administration set up
a local board to monitor wages and prices in Pocatello, labor nominated
one of the three men to serve on the body.[6] The labor leaders of Pocatello,
especially C. V. Lund and August Rosqvist, were able to create problems
for the local Community Chest when the Chest appeared to insult organized labor. During the 1930s the Bannock Hotel used nonunion workers.
When the Community Chest chose to hold a banquet at the hotel, the
Central Labor Union reacted swiftly. Lund and Rosqvist promised no support from labor for the 1935 campaign. The following year the Community Chest agreed to hold future banquets and other activities on neutral
ground; in return, labor pledged full cooperation.[7]

Other, more conventional labor disputes also occurred in Pocatello.
There were several strikes in the city and an apparent campaign to bring
the open shop to the city. The Retail Clerks Union and local five-and-ten-
cent stores—Woolworth's, Kress's, and Newberry's—repeatedly had trouble
coming to terms. In 1933 the union and the stores argued over the forty-
four- versus the forty-hour week; another dispute led to a union boycott in
early 1935.[8] In late 1935 a group of employers identified only as the Associated Employers of Pocatello fought efforts of the Retail Clerks to expand;
the union identified Safeway and Pay 'n Takit as the principal targets and
a boycott followed.[9] In 1932 the building trades faced a deadline from the
Master Builders Association to agree to a wage cut or have Pocatello adopt
the "American Plan"—that is, the open shop. But the two sides negotiated
their differences.[10]

More typical of labor relations in the city, however, were the negotiations in 1933 between the local teamsters and the Coal Dealers Committee. The union local and dealers' representatives deadlocked and then
quickly reached an agreement.[11] Negotiations, strikes, and boycotts, such
as those in Pocatello in the 1930s, are the normal pattern of labor-
management relations today; but for the 1930s, Pocatello was unusual. No
strikes paralyzed the city or any important local industry; strikes were, by
the standards of the 1930s, placid. With minor exceptions the businessmen
of Pocatello accepted the legitimacy of unions. Pocatello already had

achieved the modern relationship between labor and management that most of the nation was still seeking in the decade.

Pocatello was easily the most important center for union activity in the state. The State Federation of Labor routinely elected its local leaders to state offices, but the leaders, especially August Rosqvist, were not from the traditional AFL mold. Labor historians describe the AFL of the 1920s and 1930s as a tradition-bound group of craft unions unable or unwilling to organize the mass-production industries or to see beyond the narrow interests of its members. Rosqvist was a very different sort of person. He immigrated to the United States from Sweden, worked as a carpenter in Pocatello, involved himself in the local building trades, and quickly became a spokesman for the Pocatello Central Labor Union. Perhaps because of his experiences in Sweden, he put the influence of the local unions behind several causes that were as radical as reasonably imaginable in a small western city. The Central Labor Union, for example, supported efforts to establish consumer co-ops in the city as an alternative to free-enterprise retailers; regular columns in the weekly *Idaho Labor* justified the co-ops in openly Socialist terms. Further, the Central Labor Union supported a series of Socialist speakers in Pocatello with a cash donation and by providing a hall for the talks.[12]

The Pocatello Central Labor Union and its weekly paper, *Idaho Labor*, did not always support the national AFL in the crucial dispute of the decade within organized labor. John L. Lewis and others created the Committee for Industrial Organization (CIO) in 1935–1936 with the aim of organizing the mass-production industries—autos, steel, rubber, etc.—that the AFL had overlooked. The AFL resented the new organization, but *Idaho Labor* carried stories favorable to the CIO and the major strikes that the CIO unions were winning in the later 1930s. On occasion, to be sure, the national leaders of the AFL received a good press, too; but the hostility of the national offices of the AFL toward the CIO did not pervade the Pocatello Central Labor Union.[13] Clearly, national patterns of behavior within organized labor did not always occur in Pocatello.

The most nearly universal problem facing the United States in the 1930s was providing jobs for the unemployed—approximately one fourth of the work force in the spring of 1933. Pocatello's experience in this regard did not appreciably differ from that of the rest of the nation. Under the New Deal the federal government spent lavishly to create jobs for people who were out of work. The Civil Works Administration (CWA), the Federal Emergency Relief Administration (FERA), the Works Progress Ad-

ministration (WPA), and other such agencies differed—sometimes importantly—in goal and operation. But most people remember them collec-
tively and most commonly as the WPA.

The work relief programs received wide criticism during and after the
1930s. Critics, especially Republicans, argued that Democrats used them
for political purposes—rewarding friends and punishing enemies—and
that the projects wasted money and promoted laziness. Both of these criticisms were heard in Pocatello; and the disappointed candidate for mayor
in 1941 claimed that local Democrats scared voters with the claim that a
Republican city government would mean an end to work projects in the
city.[14]

Criticisms of inefficiency and loafing were less specifically directed toward Pocatello. Harry Hopkins suggested that the loafing and inefficiency
usually happened in the next town or another state; local residents and
leaders almost invariably supported the projects in their area. In fact, not
one Pocatello city council member voted against a single work project in
the 1930s, nor did any individual or group speak out publicly against work
relief projects in Pocatello, nor did the Washington offices of the programs
receive complaints against WPA or related projects.[15] To the contrary,
Pocatellans consistently cried for more money, more projects, and more
jobs for the city.

No figures exist for the total number of jobs, hours of work, or money
expended to provide jobs on work relief in Pocatello. The effect on the
local economy, if the reports of local businessmen were accurate, was substantial. The number of projects undertaken and the lasting benefits of
those projects to the community is still impressive. Though some of the
projects now need replacement, their long years of service belie the charge
that the WPA was only make-work. The major projects in Pocatello included several important sewers, a park, two overpasses, a viaduct, a city
hall, and several buildings on the campus of the University of Idaho Southern Branch. Besides these projects the WPA sponsored other kinds of work
that were by nature transient and less visible. These included sewing
clothes and canning food for the unemployed, binding books in the library, school lunches, puppet shows in the parks, a city band, and a nursery on the local campus.[16]

Another important type of work project in the Pocatello area did not
provide work for local people. The Civilian Conservation Corps (CCC)
was the most popular program providing work for the unemployed to
come out of the 1930s. The CCC took unemployed youths and put them
to work on conservation projects on public land. Pocatello was the site of

a CCC camp from 1935 until 1942. The camp had from 80 to 150 young men who worked on a variety of conservation and recreation projects in the vicinity. The main camp, according to CCC records, was five miles south of Pocatello, and there was an auxiliary camp near the ranger station on Mink Creek Road.[17]

The view of camp life shown in the reports was a weekly round of work, education, recreation, and weekend activities. The projects that the local camp worked on included road work in the national forests, park facilities on Scout Mountain, and the terraces still visible on the benches surrounding Pocatello. In addition to the work projects, the CCC provided extensive educational and recreational activities for the young men. The recruits enrolled in courses of study ranging from basic literacy to work at the University of Idaho Southern Branch. Sports activities were common within the camp and with other camps in the area. Frequent visits by townspeople to the camps and vice versa and a weekly radio show on KSEI demonstrated the good feeling between the community and the CCC. The positive view of the CCC locally was common throughout the nation.[18]

The New Deal in Pocatello brought some changes to Pocatello but left much of the life of the city unchanged. Political alignments were shuffled but did not drastically alter the city's political complexion, and in any case the type of change differed substantially from that occurring at the national level. Likewise, labor relations in the city did not drastically alter in the city nor did they follow the national pattern, largely because the labor unions in Pocatello had already won an important position in the economic and political make-up of the city. The most dramatic change that occurred was the physical change that came with the many public works projects throughout the city. If the New Deal was a major turning point in American history, it did not have similar importance for Pocatello.

POCATELLO'S BUSINESS COMMUNITY AND THE NEW DEAL

A conventional view of businessmen during the 1930s shows a Republican world of business opposing the expansion of the power of the federal government under the Democratic New Deal. This interpretation is partially valid and explains why the National Association of Manufacturers and U.S. Chamber of Commerce were prominent critics of many programs associated with Franklin D. Roosevelt. But national spokesmen for business did not necessarily speak for the businessmen on Main Street. When the businessmen of Pocatello realized the severity of the Depression, they supported many programs of the New Deal because those programs promised direct economic benefits to their city. At the same time, the business community of Pocatello opposed the political implications of an enlarged role for the federal government.

The crash on Wall Street in October of 1929 had little immediate effect on the economy of Pocatello. Before the crash, the *Pocatello Tribune* buried the problems of the stock market in the financial pages. The crash did appear on page one, but the story was secondary to the big news of the day: the conviction of Secretary of the Interior Albert Fall as the receiver of bribes in the Teapot Dome scandals. Even two months later the paper seemed not to have realized the importance of the crash and praised the advice given in a pamphlet from the First Security Bank. The pamphlet stated that some hardships did result from the collapse of stock prices but concluded that in ending a speculative splurge, "The recent stock market debacle . . . should be regarded as necessary in order to protect legitimate business." The attitude that the problems were temporary was understandable. No prolonged depression had soured the national economy since the 1890s, and businessmen had come to believe in the "permanent plateau of prosperity." The businessmen of Pocatello would only slowly recognize the severity of the economic crunch.[19]

The local press minimized the approach of hard times by featuring stories illustrating the most optimistic aspects of the economy. When the number of boxcars of wheat and potatoes shipped from Pocatello rose in the fall of 1930, the event was a story for page one. The *Tribune* gave special attention to stories about employment on the Oregon Short Line, a crucial factor in the economic health of Pocatello. Layoffs inevitably either appeared as small items in the paper or did not appear at all; the recalls of those laid off were banner stories. A common editorial theme of 1930–1931 was "Keep Everything in Perspective." The older and wiser business leaders, wrote the *Tribune*, "calmly interpret present deflation as a cyclical phenomenon and as just another necessary adjustment toward a normal relationship among classes and industries, toward better stabilization and co-ordination, toward a new period of expansive prosperity."[20]

During the first years of the Depression the newspaper and the business community emphasized regaining national and local self-confidence. Modern economists of all political persuasions agree that the Depression occurred for valid reasons—too little money in circulation, a maldistribution of income, or an international economic crisis. But the business community in Pocatello as elsewhere tried to persuade itself that the problem was one of confidence. "Boosting" could end the Depression: "[W]e have reached the trough of the wave and are now preparing for another rise. . . . [If] the great bulk of the people adopt a cheerful and optimistic attitude and go ahead doing business as usual, the chances are overwhelming in favor of a good business year in 1930. . . ." The local paper criticized the pessimism of Americans. After observing that the United States had an abundant share of the world's resources, the editor lamented, "[We] would seem . . . to have about 1 percent of the courage, three-quarters of a percent of the nerve . . . of almost any one country. . . ." And even if times were hard elsewhere, Pocatello could escape. Mayor C. Ben Ross argued in November, 1929, that depression would bypass Pocatello—even with a fifty percent decline in housing construction in the city—because street construction and the Oregon Short Line were still strong. As late as December, 1930, the *Tribune*'s editor could assert, "Here the depression is a myth. . . ." Periodically the paper ran a column called "Plus Signs," a syndicated list of the most optimistic news about the economy. "Plus Signs" for September 23, 1931, ran on the page opposite a story detailing the collapse of a Pocatello bank.[21]

The closing of the Citizens Bank and Trust Company in Pocatello was a major blow to the confidence of the business community. Heavy withdrawals had pressured the bank for several months. The directors of the bank, fearing a run that the bank could not survive, did not open on September 23 in order to equalize losses among the remaining depositors. The failure was the third largest in the history of the state, and by 1938 the bank had repaid only half its liabilities of $708,000. The bank's problems came from agricultural loans that had, in the language of the State Banking Commission, "poor prospects for repayment." The local officers of the First Security Bank, the other major bank in Pocatello, probably received warning about the imminent collapse of the Citizens Bank and Trust and in any case could draw upon the resources of the First Security Bank system to withstand a local panic. But a run on the local First Security Bank did not occur. The same paper that announced the closing of the Citizens Bank and Trust carried a full-page advertisement from First Security detailing its assets and liabilities and giving an important promise to the local economy. The First Security Bank offered to allow individuals to borrow from the bank and use deposits frozen in the Citizens Bank and Trust as collateral. This assurance avoided any local contraction of business for want of cash and affirmed the confidence of the First Security Bank in the health of the local economy. The Citizens Bank and Trust even "borrowed" some of the prestige of the First Security when a former director of the bank supervised the liquidation of the defunct institution. The action of First Security avoided further trauma in the financial community of Pocatello, and the creation of the Idaho Bank and Trust Company in late 1933 filled the void left by the failure of the Citizens Bank and Trust.[22]

Of the multitude of New Deal agencies that touched Pocatello in the 'thirties, the business community of the city reacted to none with greater enthusiasm than to the National Recovery Administration, or NRA. The spirit of attack and the military rhetoric associated with General Hugh Johnson at the national level carried down to Pocatello. A front-page editorial in a local paper in early August, 1933, "Place Your Bets on America," marked the beginning of a month of public meetings, pledges, and door-to-door visits to get all of Pocatello behind the new organization. The NRA hoped to create jobs and bring prosperity by limiting the number of hours per worker per week to forty—thus passing the available work around—and by maintaining purchasing power through a minimum wage of forty cents per hour. Employers and businessmen agreed to end "unfair" competition and to adopt common policies on prices and services. National business leaders wrote NRA codes for the major industries, and local communities added details. Throughout August and September committees of representatives of businesses—groceries, wholesale houses, auto dealers, gas stations, furniture dealers, to name only a few—met to work out practices for these businesses in Pocatello. Where appropriate the committees coordinated their efforts with other local committees in northern Utah and southern Idaho. One small businessman objected to the NRA codes because the guarantees of forty cents per hour and a forty-hour week, standard in all NRA codes, would drive people such as himself out of business. The head of the Pocatello Chamber of Commerce responded without sympathy: "Any person who stands apart from [the NRA] is likely to be uncomfortable in the eyes of his neighbors and even under the law."[23] Small operators in Pocatello received no special consideration.

The Pocatello Chamber of Commerce directed the activities of the NRA in the city. The Chamber established a pseudo-military structure of organization with a "General," a "Lieutenant General" (required to be a woman), and three "Colonels." One "colonel" oversaw a survey of the unemployed and of jobs available; another took charge of publicity and education; and the third ran a speakers bureau. Each "colonel" appointed "majors," who in turn appointed "captains," each of whom coordinated eight individuals in his or her "company." A door-to-door campaign sought pledges from private individuals to patronize only those businesses supporting the NRA. By early September local businesses had so rallied behind the program that almost all advertisements in the *Pocatello Tribune* displayed the Blue Eagle, symbol of the NRA.[24]

The enforcement of the NRA codes in Pocatello rested in the hands of a local Compliance Board and a local "police force." The "police force," the result of a suggestion of President William Green of the American Federation of Labor, was a self-appointed group headed by the president of the Pocatello Central Labor Union. The group planned to monitor the compliance of local businesses with the code, but the effectiveness of the "force" was minimal. No examples of successful enforcement appear, even in the pages of the local AFL newspaper. The Compliance Board was the official enforcement agency of the local NRA. The board consisted of the president of the Chamber of Commerce; one representative each from the retail, the wholesale, and the industrial trades; representatives from labor and from consumers; and a lawyer.[25] The ability of the board to function was severely limited, however, by the unwillingness of the NRA to resort to legal force—a justified fear given the eventual fate of the NRA. Only one employer, a firm constructing sewers in the area, was prosecuted for violations of the NRA codes, and the case was dismissed. Instead of legal steps, the Compliance Board relied on what now seems a naive faith in the power of community pressure. The president of the local Chamber of Commerce and of the Compliance Board stated: "[T]he board is not a council of inquisition. . . . The job of these boards is to secure compliance. If an employer willfully persists in non-compliance with the agreement after being fully informed of his obligations [Stop and ask yourself, what will happen? Prosecution? Jail? Fines? Tar and feathers? Social ostracism? No.] he is no longer entitled to the blue eagle and the federal government will take it away."[26]

The NRA had little impact on the local economy. The local "General" claimed the NRA found 178 new jobs; the *Pocatello Tribune*, for example, fashioned twelve new paper routes in the city. But the effect was minimal, and Pocatellans welcomed the spurt of new jobs that came with the Civil Works Administration in the late fall of 1933. After the enthusiasm of August, little notice of the NRA appeared in the *Pocatello Tribune*, the weekly paper of the local AFL, or the records of the Chamber of Commerce. The Blue Eagle slowly disappeared from the pages of the local paper, and by May, 1935, the only one remaining was that carried by the paper itself on its masthead. When the Supreme Court ruled the NRA unconstitutional the daily paper made no comment.[27]

The trauma of the collapse of the Citizens Bank and Trust and enthusiasm for the NRA were of short duration. The effect of unemployment on Pocatello businesses, however, was continuous, and Pocatello's businessmen were in the forefront of efforts to provide work and paychecks for the unemployed. When President Hoover made loans available to states for relief, Pocatello's mayor appointed a committee chaired by a local attorney to oversee the use of the funds. The same committee became the local Relief Board under the Federal and State Emergency Relief Administration and the local board for the Civil Works Administration and the Works Progress Administration (WPA).

Pocatello aggressively sought its share of the money from the various agencies of the New Deal to create jobs for local men and women. The city government, the Chamber of Commerce, and the Relief Board used the federal programs to accomplish a variety of projects long sought for the city. Easy travel between the east and west sides of Pocatello was a perennial problem. The main link in the 'twenties was an antiquated bridge over the yards of the Oregon Short Line. The replacement of the overpass with a viaduct—still a principal connection in the city—added $250,000 in wages to the local economy.[28]

The New Deal made possible projects of a new character for the city. The WPA, for example, provided small sums to make comforters for families on relief, to mend books in the public library, to provide band concerts in the city park, to sponsor a public forum for controversial speakers, to pay for hot lunches at several public schools, and to give puppet shows for children. But the great majority of the money went for projects traditionally associated with public works: sewers, riprap for the Portneuf River, new surfaces for streets, an overpass (in addition to the viaduct) for the railroad yards, several buildings and an athletic field at the University of Idaho Southern Branch, a public swimming pool, and a police station.[29]

At no time did anyone in the city of Pocatello—inside or outside the business community—express reservations about the federal money coming into the city. The minutes of the city council, the local newspaper, the records of the Pocatello Chamber of Commerce, and correspondence from Pocatello to agencies such as the WPA in Washington, D.C., revealed the enthusiasm of the business community for the fruits of this expanded role of the federal government. The Pocatello City Council was the main sponsor of federal projects in the city; from 1930 until 1940 not a single vote by an individual council member was cast against the authorization of a project funded by the federal government. The amount of

money that came into Pocatello under federal works programs during the
New Deal is not known. The PWA spent $1,260,000 in Bannock County
between 1933 and 1935; the WPA spent more than $300,000 in its first year
of operation, 1935–1936; and the CWA spent $480,000 in the winter of
1933–1934.[30] The effect of the payrolls of these projects on the local economy can only be guessed. But certainly the businessmen felt that public
works programs were important in maintaining purchasing power.

The desire of Pocatello businessmen for federal money to create jobs
in Pocatello did not mean that the businessmen endorsed an enlarged role
for the federal government in national economic planning. The business
community viewed the federal grants in the most pragmatic way possible:
agencies like the WPA and Civil Works Administration were sources of
money for the Pocatello economy—nothing else. Unless Pocatello directly
benefited from a new agency and an enlarged role of the government, the
business community of Pocatello would oppose the expansion of power.

The articulate leaders of the business community in Pocatello, perhaps
sharing doubts with businessmen everywhere, feared that the economic
crisis of the 'thirties might lead to an undesirable restructuring of the
American economy. Change might mean that private businesses would
play a less important role than in earlier decades. Such a threat might
have come from the movement to create several consumer cooperatives in
Pocatello under the sponsorship of the local AFL. The Pocatello Chamber of Commerce vigorously opposed the movement, protested against a
class at the University of Idaho Southern Branch on the virtues of consumer co-ops, and fought a bill in the state legislature to encourage cooperative stores. One president of the Pocatello Chamber used his
inaugural address to denounce the possibility of governmental ownership
of railroads or any form of transportation.

But when compromises with private enterprise promised economic
benefits for Pocatello, such objections to governmental involvement ended
quickly. In 1931 the United States Department of the Interior had established a plant in Pocatello to manufacture poison bait for rodents. The law
under which the plant operated prohibited governmental ownership of the
plant, so the Interior Department ran the plant in cooperation with a private partner. The Farm Bureau worked with the Department of the Interior for four years, but by 1935 that group was locally moribund. The
Department of the Interior approached the Chamber of Commerce in
Pocatello and asked if it would serve as sponsor. The Chamber of Commerce, noting that the plant employed fourteen people and involved no

financial commitment from the Chamber, gladly cooperated with the Interior Department. The direct benefit of the plant's operation to Pocatello overrode any doubts of the Chamber about the Socialist overtones of the project.[31]

The business community also approved other expansions in the power of the federal government whenever direct benefits came to Pocatello businesses. When the Idaho Bank and Trust Company received a loan of $100,000 from the Reconstruction Finance Corporation, no one in Pocatello criticized the governmental aid. Similarly, when the Stockgrowers Loan Company was awarded loans totaling $43,500 from the RFC no objections to governmental intrusion into the private economy arose. The Pocatello business community also appreciated the role of the Home Owners Loan Corporation in underwriting 650 homes in Bannock County.[32]

The last example of the pragmatic (or perhaps self-serving) attitude of the business community toward expansion of the role of the federal government involved the question of public power and regional planning in the Northwest. The apparent success of the Tennessee Valley Authority in bringing electricity and a measure of economic progress to the Upper South inspired discussion about many "little TVAs," and the Columbia and Snake river system was an obvious candidate for a program for regional development. The leaders of the business community in the Northwest believed that some kind of power project would come to their region. These leaders, however, wanted to limit the involvement of government to the construction of dams and the production of power for sale to private utilities. This type of power project contrasted with the broad economic and social planning of the early years of the TVA. The Pacific Northwest Regional Planning Commission spoke for the business community and maintained contact with groups, such as the Pocatello Chamber of Commerce, that opposed programs for the Northwest modeled on the TVA.

The Chamber of Commerce created a Pocatello Planning Commission in part to help channel any planning for the region in acceptable directions. The Pocatello Planning Commission agreed with the regional body that planning in the Northwest was inevitable but hoped that "constructive thinking and planning" would be the rule. The businessmen of the region, in other words, wished to circumscribe whom the thinkers and planners would be. The Regional Planning Commission scheduled a series of hearings in the Northwest to—so the Commission announced— gauge popular opinion on what kind of planning should occur, what territory should be included, and what role the federal and state governments should play. When the hearings came to Pocatello the Regional

Commission and the Pocatello Planning Commission discreetly worked to limit the "public opinion" expressed to those who agreed with the approach of the business community. A regional leader confided to the secretary of the Pocatello Chamber, "[A] general mass meeting would not produce the results desired. However, certain publicity will be necessary and I would appreciate it if you and Hugh [McCosham, President of the Chamber of Commerce] would get together and see that the *proper* publicity is forthcoming." And of course the local Chamber did provide the appropriate audience and recommendations.[33]

By the late 'thirties the response of the business community in Pocatello to the New Deal—encouraging programs directly beneficial to the city and quietly derailing those not favored—was much more sophisticated than the response of the months following the Crash in 1929. The business community in Pocatello had not immediately recognized the magnitude of the economic problems that it would face during the 1930s and tried to wish away the Depression. When the failure of the Citizens Bank and Trust Company and the presence of the unemployed made clear the seriousness of the situation, businessmen were eager to look to the federal government for solutions to the problems. The desire for federal relief money and for help for business through the NRA and loans to some businesses from the Reconstruction Finance Corporation belied any principles against an expanded role for the federal government. Where benefits to Pocatello businessmen were unclear, however, or did not exist, the business community opposed enlargement of the powers of the federal government. The businessmen of Pocatello accepted limited adjustments in the American economy so long as the businessmen remained central to the economic life of their community.

NOTES

1. *Pocatello Tribune*, April 9, 1931, 1, April 29, 1931, 1.

2. *Ibid.*, April 12, 1933, 1.

3. *Ibid.*, April 17, 1933.

4. *Ibid.*, June 10, 1934, 1, November 6, 1932, 1.

5. [Thomas Coffin] to George W. Hunt, May 15, 1932. 1932 Wage Agreement file, Box 20, Rosqvist Papers, Idaho State Historical Society, Boise: *Pocatello Tribune*. August 3, 1936, 1.

6. Lockwood to C. Ben Ross, November 3, 1934, NRA file, Box 38, Ross Papers, Governors' Files, Idaho State Archives, Boise.

7. *Idaho Labor* (Pocatello), March 21, 1936, 1, May 11, 1935, 1, May 25, 1935, 1: *Pocatello Tribune*, June 23, 1935, 8.

8. *Idaho Labor*, December 9, 1933, 2: *Idaho Examiner* (Pocatello), December 16, 1933, 1.

9. *Idaho Labor*, February 16, 1935, 1; November 23, 1935, 1; *Pocatello Tribune*, November 24, 1935, 3.

10. *Ibid.*, April 22, 1932, 3.

11. C file, Box 1, Rosqvist Papers.

12. *Idaho Labor*, September 8, 1933, 1; December 5, 1936, 1; March 20, 1937, 1; undesignated box of pamphlets and papers, Rosqvist Papers.

13. *Idaho Labor*, November 21, 1936; 4; February 13, 1937, 1; July 25, 1936, 1.

14. Miller to Colwell and attachments, May 12, 1941, Idaho 610.2 A–Z file, Box Idaho 610–611 (1935–1936), Records of the Work Projects Administration, Record Group 69, National Archives (hereafter cited WPA Records).

15. WPA Records. Complaints received in Washington criticized details of a project but not projects as wholes. Most complaints came from workers.

16. "WPA To Be Started" file, 1931–1936, Ross Papers; WPA Records. Both lists of projects are taken from longer incomplete inventories of projects in the city.

17. *Pocatello Tribune*, June 27, 1935, 10; October 25, 1935, 1.

18. File F-101, Records of the Civilian Conservation Corps, Record Group 35, National Archives; *Pocatello Chieftain*, November, 1936, 1, February, 1936, 3, March, 1936, 1, November, 1937, 7.

19. *Pocatello Tribune*, October 25, 1929, 1; January 6, 1930, 4.

20. *Pocatello Tribune*, September 24, 1930, 1; December 2, 1931, 4; April 26, 1932, 1; November 18, 1931, 1.

21. *Pocatello Tribune*, January 18, 1930, 4; October 7, 1930, 4; November 27, 1929, 10; December 12, 1930, 4.

22. *Pocatello Tribune*, September 23, 1931, 1, 7; December 31, 1933, 1; Clara Elizabeth Aldrich, *The History of Banking in Idaho* (Boise: Syms-York Company, 1940); Citizens Bank and Trust Company Papers, Idaho State Historical Society, Boise.

23. *Idaho Examiner*, August 5, 1933, 1; Notebook, "Minutes, Various Committees, Pocatello Chamber of Commerce," Chamber of Commerce Papers, Idaho State University Archives (hereafter cited as C of C); *Pocatello Tribune*, July 25, 1933, 8; August 1, 1933, 1; August 2, 1933, 2; August 8, 1933, 2; August 13, 1933, 1.

24. *Pocatello Tribune*, August 28, 1933, 1; August 14, 1933, 2.

25. *Pocatello Tribune*, September 29, 1934, 1; August 14, 1933, 1; October 13, 1933, 2; October 19, 1934, 1; October 25, 1934, 1.

26. *Pocatello Tribune*, September 8, 1933, 1; *Idaho Labor*, 1934–1935, *passim*.

27. *Pocatello Tribune*, May, 1935, *passim*. The Supreme Court's decision was based on the unconstitutional delegation of powers by Congress (the codes being viewed essentially as laws) and on unconstitutional regulation of intrastate commerce.

28. *Pocatello Tribune*, July 24, 1933, 1; August 1, 1933, 1; September 25, 1933, 1.

29. *Pocatello Tribune*, July 24, 1933, 1; September 25, 1933, 1.

30. "Minutes, Various Committees, Pocatello Chamber of Commerce," C of C; "Minutes," City Council of Pocatello, 1930s, City Hall, Pocatello, *passim*; state reports for various agencies, Records of the Work Projects Administration, National Archives, Washington, D.C., *passim*. (hereinafter cited as WPA Records); Federal Projects in Idaho file, C. Ben Ross Papers, Idaho State Archives, Boise. Like most of the Western states, Idaho received well above average funds per capita from the federal government during the New Deal; indeed, the state ranked eighth in the nation in federal per capita expenditures between 1933 and 1939. See Leonard J. Arrington, "Idaho and the Great Depression," *Idaho Yesterdays* (Summer, 1969), 13/2: 2–8.

31. President Manson—1936 file, Historical File II, C of C; Robert L. Wrigley, "Poison Bait Plant Unique . . . ," *Pocatello Tribune*, January 29, 1941, 3.

32. Table 1, p. 28, Reconstruction Finance Corporation Monthly Reports, July–December, 1932, WPA Records.

33. Pacific Northwest Regional Planning Commission file, Historical File II, C of C; Wood to Nash, September 4, 1935, *ibid.*; Herman C. Voelta, "Genesis and Development of a Regional Power Agency in the Pacific Northwest, 1933–1943," *Pacific Northwest Quarterly* (April, 1962), 53:65–76.

Impoverished Politics: The New Deal's Impact on City Government in Providence, Rhode Island

DAVID L. DAVIES

In the voluminous discussion of intergovernmental relationships during the New Deal, one seldom hears the voice of a local, nonpolitical administrator. One may not wholly agree with the author's conclusions here, but he raises important hypothetical questions—how would local government in Providence have confronted the Great Depression on its own, and how would it have developed without the New Deal? He also implies a dilemma: if unusual measures seem appropriate in a crisis, do they have an inertial or persisting life that becomes no longer appropriate to the situation?

BEFORE the Great Depression, the last hope of the destitute, disabled, and unemployed in Providence was either the compassion of the City Council or private charity. Life-sustaining food, fuel, clothing, and shelter were local governmental responsibilities. Poor relief was a serious charge in ordinary times and an awesome burden as the Great Depression deepened. That burden would have surely tested the resiliency and responsiveness of municipal institutions, the level of government closest to taxpayers' daily lives. The Depression dramatically altered many institu-

From *Rhode Island History*, 42 (August 1983), 86–100.

tions of American life, and Providence city government might have evolved into something very different if local officials had directed social welfare efforts. The New Deal, by emphasizing the federal role in welfare, prevented such a test. As it happened, the similarities between the conduct and ethics of Providence government in 1929 and 1939 are more striking than the differences.

The Great Depression did not force major change in the city's governance, in large part because state and federal programs minimized the policymaking role of local officials in relief, the major issue of the decision of a larger administrative apparatus. Local officials returned, with the onset of New Deal programs, to perennial political preoccupations—ethnic and personal rivalries.

The city's officials did not protest this subordination. They did not demand primary responsibilities in looking after their poor and unemployed, or, for that matter, any new responsibility at all. Councilmen reacted to the emergency of the first years of the Depression with impassioned rhetoric and a willingness to tackle difficult economic and political issues. After the 1932 election that brought Franklin D. Roosevelt and Governor Theodore Francis Green to power, however, local officials quickly disappeared from public debate and official correspondence on welfare issues (at least they are silent in the surviving public records). City taxpayers retained a large and increasing responsibility for underwriting the local share of welfare costs throughout the 1930s. Their local elected officials, however, did not direct expenditure of those local dollars. State and federal officials assumed the responsibility for directing welfare expenditures. Local officials, moreover, delayed political accountability for relief costs by using the expedient of long-term borrowing. The poor benefited from new standards for social work administration introduced by state and federal bureaucrats and by sizable federal relief expenditures. But if every benefit has a cost, the poor family's gain was Providence's loss: the city government missed the opportunity of a century to rise above "business as usual."

Providence in 1930 was the second largest city in New England with a population of 253,000 inhabitants. The capital city of the smallest and most densely populated state, Providence contained almost 40 percent of Rhode Island's population. The city's population was far from homogeneous. About 70 percent were either foreign-born or of foreign-born parents, 26 percent of whom originated in England or Ireland and 21 percent in Italy. Other ethnic groups included Armenians, French Canadians,

Germans, Greeks, Lithuanians, Poles, Portuguese, Russians, Swedes, and Syrians, while blacks comprised 2 percent of the citizenry.

On the eve of the Depression, Providence's government was, by all appearances, already a weak and unstable institution, ill-prepared for a major crisis. A weak mayor and strong council form of government confined the mayor to presiding over council meetings and wielding occasional tie-breaking votes. A bicameral council of thirteen aldermen and thirty-nine councilmen controlled the city administration. Department heads reported to this legislative body of fifty-two members, not to a single individual. (No other American city of 200,000 to 500,000 residents had a larger council; Minneapolis was the second largest with twenty-six.) An absence of discipline within the political parties and ever-present ethnic rivalries compounded the diffusion of authority. The mayor was a Democrat; the governor and General Assembly were solidly Republican. The city's antiquated accounting system provided little control over expenditures. The city's economy relied on jewelry, metalworking, and textiles. Jewelry firms did not prosper in hard times, and textile mills had been migrating south for many years. In 1929, Providence seemed poised for disaster.

Most of Providence's councilmen were nominal Democrats. Amendment XX to the state's constitution, adopted on November 6, 1928, had finally eliminated property qualifications for city voters, and Democratic strength in power and more ethnic wards asserted itself at the next opportunity—the election held in November 1930. In that election, Democrats gained a majority for the first time in both the Board of Aldermen and the Common Council.

As in many other northeastern cities, the Irish dominated city politics. Once Democrats controlled patronage, the roster of choice city jobs became a collection of Irish surnames. Italo-Americans, however, were a more vocal and aggressive political force in Providence than in other cities in the region. Italians were active in both parties, with power concentrated in only two of the city's thirteen wards. In Wards 13 and 4, Italo-Americans controlled all offices and ward committees.

With a cumbersome government, ethnic divisions, mature economy, and unstable political parties, Providence entered the Great Depression. Almost from the beginning, city officials and private agencies spoke freely of "crisis." In September 1930, Alderman C. Walter Pabodie, chairman of the Special Committee on Conditions at Dexter Asylum, warned that a large number of "jakey" cases taxed the city's poor fund to the limit. (The limit in this case was $10,000 owed to the state for institutional care of derelicts fond of Jamaican ginger spirits.)[1] As months went by, however, the unprecedented seriousness of the crisis became apparent.

The Community Fund and Family Welfare Society received the first flood of victims; the latter delivered services to 4,000 families in 1931 as opposed to 500 to 600 in "normal times."[2] Civic leaders and private agencies formed the Providence Emergency Unemployment Committee to coordinate efforts and provide relief with jobs, funded by private subscriptions, that paid fifteen dollars a week. It was not until July 1931, however, that the committee's head publicly acknowledged the limits of private responsibility for relief. By that time, the total number of "outdoor relief" recipients had increased almost threefold from the 3,610 recipients of November 1929.

Reacting to the growing unemployment, the City Council reflected traditional approaches to charity. In December 1930, the council requested that all city employees donate 2 percent of their wages to the Milk and Fuel Fund from which the director of public aid was to purchase milk, bread, and coal for needy families.[3] Along with volunteerism, residency requirements also revealed the city's traditional approach to charity. The city sought to take care of its own, but only its own. The council found that a recent ordinance requiring all city workers to be qualified electors had thrown 100 municipal employees out of work. It struggled to retain current city employees while imposing some sort of residency requirement. Councilman William Lovett expressed concern that outsiders might have jobs while citizens were being thrown onto relief.[4]

City politicians also joined in other voluntary schemes to provide for unfortunates. The City Council formed a special Milk Fund Football Committee to oversee a benefit game between Providence College and Rhode Island State College at Brown Stadium. Reporting that tickets were selling rapidly, Sol Bromson, a Republican alderman from affluent Ward 2, encouraged fans to "attend the game—Root for your favorite—and thus make sure that the needy and unemployed of Providence will have food and fuel during the dark days of winter."[5] Cooperative efforts and charitable impulses seemed adequate remedies to some. Analysts at the Brown University Bureau of Business Research recognized in 1931, however, the growing severity of conditions: "Relief has obviously been merely supplementary; families of five do not live on $16 a month."[6]

As business did not revive, the City Council struggled with the realities of the deepening depression. The number of poor, dependent, or jobless assisted by the city almost tripled between 1930 and 1931, from 545 to 1,490. In 1932 the number more than tripled again, this time to 5,335.[7]

Providence's goal was to provide for relief needs until such time as the state could supply additional assistance. Proclaiming a "keep your self-respect policy," Mayor James E. Dunne implied that the problem was still manageable at the local level: "We are going to attempt by close supervision and through use of any additional appropriations the finance committee can make out of the reserve fund to care for our problem until more money is made available by the state."[8] By the fall of 1931, both the city and state were reassessing their respective roles. Having spent $307,000 for outdoor aid in fiscal 1930, the chairman of the city's Finance Committee, Peter F. Reilly, hoped to provide for increasing relief rolls through the conservative expedient of departmental fund transfers (shifting line items in the regular operating budget). In any event, Reilly did "not intend to let anyone go hungry in Providence," but "if it is given out that a huge sum has been appropriated for public aid, there will be crowds of people asking for help who perhaps do not really need it. The problems must be handled in [a] scientific manner."[9]

As in other states, municipal officials waited for leadership from the State House in the form of outright grants of interest-free loans. That kind of relief was not forthcoming in Rhode Island under Republican Governor Norman S. Case. Providence Democrats and Republicans, therefore, called a truce and unanimously passed a resolution for unprecedented tax-anticipation loans. Democrat Frank Duffy introduced the necessary resolution and Republican Sol Bromson moved passage. When the object was locally funded relief, the council's resolve was bipartisan.

Local politicians did disagree on the specifics of some relief issues, but they compromised as conditions worsened. In March 1931, city officials split on whether municipal departments would cooperate with efforts of private citizens to provide relief and hire the Providence Emergency Unemployment Committee's workers who were earning fifteen dollars per week. The committee had money for more than 1,000 short-term jobs, but it lacked the necessary employers. The committee asked the city to create temporary positions in municipal departments. After consulting with union representatives, a minority in the Board of Aldermen and a majority in the Common Council decided to approve jobs that paid prevailing wages, even if that meant fewer hours for each worker. Republicans and a few Democrats, including the mayor, wanted to provide jobs at the lower rate paid to those on private relief. They insisted that half a loaf was better than none. The majority Democrats, however, were sensitive to rumors of a plot to reduce wages everywhere, with city departments in the vanguard. They continued to insist on prevailing wages, and, as a result, blocked the funding of any jobs. Council President Lovett explained his insistence on prevailing wages: "We are 100 percent in favor of putting them to work, but under American hours of labor and American conditions . . . is it fair to tell men they must work 44 hours for $15? This is a progressive country. Are we going back to the days of slavery?"[10] Yet one year later, in April 1932, these same councilmen, anticipating a $1,000,000 budget deficit, joined in a unanimous vote to reduce city wages by 10 percent.[11]

By November 1931, the City Council approved its own plan for employing 550 men on public works. Rush Sturges, the Republican alderman from affluent Ward 1, insisted that the men should receive the prevailing wage—fifty-two cents per hour—for common labor. Sturges also pointed out: "These figures are not important, but the principle is. These men should not be made to feel they are working as city wards. It is the only way they can keep their self-respect. They should not be made to work with slave drivers standing over them and paying them about 20 cents an hour."[12]

Within a few months of each other, a labor Democrat and a staunch Republican had stood up for higher relief wages, both having invoked the image of wage slavery. The 550-job plan, financed entirely by city appropriations, passed both chambers unanimously. The council's evolution into a governing entity that created and implemented social policy thereby reached its zenith. Almost as if the council itself recognized that this level of responsibility was a little frightening, the relief debate—as expressed in the public record—quickly evaporated. The council routinely approved funding over the next few years, without controversy and virtually without comment in the official proceedings or in the local press.

Gradual state and federal advances into social programming prompted the city's retreat. A bipartisan consensus on relief objectives also existed at the state level. J. Howard McGrath, state chairman of the Democratic party, supported Republican Governor Case's program of 3 percent state relief loans, "reserving the right to make constructive criticism."[13] Despite some bickering, the General Assembly unanimously approved Case's program. In Ohio, a state where urban-rural conflict and entrenched conservatism hindered relief, a Cleveland newspaper commended Rhode Island: "The expeditious action evidently was made possible by political harmony and agreement as to methods. Though it might be criticized as giving the executive too much control of legislation, it certainly represents the quick work befitting emergencies."[14]

Not all of Rhode Island's local governments, however, appreciated the opportunity to borrow money from the state at 3 percent interest. The Providence City Council resolved to spurn such aid and to rely instead on the city's resources. Alderman Burke pointed out that whereas Providence, up to December 1931, had appropriated $620,000 for relief work, the state had appropriated nothing.[15] Frederick Peck, the State Finance Commissioner and a Republican, indicated in March 1932 that only ten cities and towns had taken advantage of the program and that only two more had indicated their intention to do so: "This would seem to indicate that many of the towns have no serious unemployment problem and are perfectly able to finance their own requirements without assistance from the state."[16] (Providence eventually borrowed $1,000,000 from the state in 1932, a year in which the city's unemployment climbed to over one-third of the work force.)[17]

Theodore Francis Green, running ahead of Roosevelt, unseated Case in 1932. Green promptly proposed a $6,000,000 aid plan for cities and towns to meet relief needs. The plan would cancel $2,500,000 in relief loans already extended to localities and provide an additional $3,000,000 out of state funds. The program ran counter to Republican doctrine that state aid should be business-like and well within conservative debt limitations. Doctrine or no, Republicans lined up in support of the essentials of Green's plan. The secretary of the Republican City Committee in Providence expressed support for the plan at the first public hearing. After some minor compromising, the bill sped through the General Assembly without a dissenting vote.

Economic conditions alone did not bring about these consensus, bipartisan positions, either at the state or local level. Other sections of the country had far more serious economic problems accompanied by bitter ideological and political divisions. Industrial production and employment in Rhode Island and Providence followed national trends, bottoming out earlier and deeper in 1932. The largest manufacturing decline was in textiles, and the greatest difficulties were outside of Providence in the Blackstone Valley and in Bristol County, which had unemployment rates over 50 percent in 1932.[18] Statistics from all sectors of Providence's economy show the Depression's impact, but relative to other major cities the decline was more manageable. The state and the city had some bright spots. No local government in Rhode Island, for instance, went into default. Bank failure is a standard yardstick for measuring one aspect of the Depression's impact, but Rhode Island's banks generally weathered the storm. The state began and finished the decade of the thirties with sixty-eight institutions. By the beginning of 1931, Rhode Island banks had the largest cash reserves

since 1918.[19] The mood in Rhode Island seemed to be concerned with re-
trenchment, not panic. Substantial property wealth, especially in Providence, helped cushion the shocks for institutions, although individual and
family hardship were real and pervasive.

Nevertheless, prior to Christmas 1931, businessmen sponsored Providence Day discounts to attract shoppers, and all sales volume records were
"smashed."[20] The somewhat desperate enthusiasm of 1931 receded, however, as the Depression got worse. Unemployment climbed from about 7
percent in 1929 to around 32 percent in 1932 (or about 35,000 workers).[21]
By 1933, net retail sales in Providence were half those of 1929, and 800
fewer stores existed (out of 4,036 in 1929).[22] Textile profits in some products recovered early. In 1934, Martha Gellhorn, a roaming federal investigator, reported to Harry Hopkins: "The mill owners I saw didn't seem as
cheerless as their Massachusetts colleagues though it has now become a
ritual for mill owners to weep about their impossible lives and how no
man can make a decent living any more. One of them, however, in a burst
of candor, admitted that the whole group had cleaned up in 1933 in a way
which resembled war profiteering and that any textile manufacturer who
hadn't was such a mutt that he deserved bankruptcy."[23]

The city government adjusted to the Depression; it did not confront a
real fiscal crisis at any specific time. Real property values supported city
tax revenues, and valuation losses were far less in Providence than in most
other cities. A *Providence Journal* editorial in October 1933 reported a 4.1
percent decline in real estate valuations in the city since the 1931 peak,
and concluded that "the showing is an excellent one after four years of
economic disturbance."[24] Between 1932 and 1937, assessed valuations fell
14.9 percent nationwide, 15.8 percent in nearby Massachusetts, and as
much as 34.7 percent in Ohio. Rhode Island valuations decreased only 6.2
percent in the same period.[25]

Despite this firm foundation for meeting relief costs out of current tax
revenues, Providence avoided the immediate tax hikes and voter unrest
that accompany pay-as-you-go policies. Unlike many cities, Providence
could get credit. When Mayor Dunne called for tax-anticipation notes in
November 1931 to raise $300,000 for relief, he established Providence's
long-range financing program. Between 1932 and 1938, Providence borrowed some $9,000,000 for relief. Other cities in the region financed re-
lief out of current revenues. So while Providence paid $2.14 per capita
from current revenues in 1934, Boston paid $18.25, Worcester $10.54, and
Hartford $12.03.[26] In many states, strictly enforced debt limits and over-

spending in prosperous years forced cities to rely on current revenues. Borrowing relief funds, on the other hand, delayed political accountability for higher tax bills for a few years. Without the pain of immediate higher taxes, poor relief did not require difficult choices and political controversy.

Local relief costs did not figure prominently in the review of city finances prepared in 1936 by the Providence Governmental Research Bureau (the predecessor of the Rhode Island Public Expenditure Council): "Providence seems to have weathered the usual difficulties occasioned by the depression in a manner much more satisfactory than have most other cities. Municipal services have been rendered without appreciable curtailment; interest and principal payments on the public debt have been maintained; all essential relief has been provided; and municipal revenues have been sustained so that no very serious problems have been created by tax delinquency or accumulated deficits."[27]

The City Council enthusiastically accepted federal relief money, even when the federal contribution was only one-third of total costs under Federal Emergency Relief Administration (FERA) and Public Works Administration (PWA) programs. The first inflow of federal dollars under the New Deal was through FERA, channeled through the State Unemployment Relief Program.

The state relief program was part of the administrative apparatus set up to supervise local welfare and relief programs. It conditioned Providence officials, and welfare directors in other towns, to centralize control. Federal staffer Robert Lansdale reported to Aubrey Williams in a field report: "All investigation for need is controlled by a State social work investigation force headed in the State office in Providence. This is the tightest arrangement I have discovered. It of course permits no argument. The State determines the budgetary needs and the towns must accept them (likewise all expenditures by localities are controlled in advance)."[28] While Martha Gellhorn reported to Harry Hopkins that in Massachusetts "administrative incompetence had become a menace" to poor relief, the situation in Rhode Island was different: "The unemployed themselves are getting pretty good service, as these things go."[29]

State relief aid was not absolutely crucial to Providence's ability to finance job programs, but it was more generous than in most other states. Of the $13,000,000 expended in Providence for relief between July 1933 and December 1935, only $5,000,000 was contributed by FERA (38.6 percent). The state program provided $3,200,000 (24.8 percent), leaving Providence with the balance of $4,800,000 (36.6 percent). (Contribution averages for the entire country were 71.8 percent federal, 10.1 percent state, and 18.1 percent local.)[30] Rhode Island contributed a greater percentage of state and local funds than any other state. It is important to note that despite Providence's diminished responsibility for program content and administration, the local contribution in tax-supported dollars matched the federal effort and exceeded the state's generosity.

This state and local self-reliance did not result in lower benefits for the poor: in 1935, Rhode Island ranked eighth among all states in monthly relief benefits per family. Providence in 1934–1935 provided average relief benefits per family of $35.94 per month.[31] (The average for eighty-nine cities over 100,000 population was $30.60. Boston led all with $50.93.)[32] By way of comparison, the average monthly wage for manufacturing workers in Providence was $75.58 in 1935.[33]

Conditioned to state supervision, Providence officials worked relatively smoothly with WPA administrators, most of whom were former state bureaucrats. When problems arose, inefficiency or red tape was generally at issue, as in the wholesale transfer of workers to WPA projects. Democratic party leaders censured WPA administrator J. Burleigh Cheney for "lack of cooperation." Cheney replied, "You can't play politics with empty stomachs. There are no politics in WPA and there won't be any."[34]

"Politics" in fact permeated upper echelons of state and federal programs. City officials seeking to use federal programs for political advantage had to skirt statewide supervisors well-schooled in political expediency. The first state administrator, George S. Cody, was forced out by FERA-WPA field representative R. C. Branion, with Harry Hopkins's approval, because of alleged payroll and expense account abuses. Cody had a protector in Governor Green, however, who resisted firing Cody for fear that recently ousted budget director and political foe Thomas McCoy would use the information in his public campaign against the governor. Cody quietly resigned to become a state parole officer. Roosevelt Democrats quickly tagged his successor, J. Burleigh Cheney, as politically dangerous. As Hopkins counseled Branion over the telephone: "This thing in Rhode Island is getting very hot. Here this guy Gerry [Senator Peter Gerry] walked out on us and on the President. This fellow Cheney is Gerry's henchman, and every other Democrat is raising hell because we keep a man who is tied up with Gerry."[35] They resolved to force Cheney's resignation, which occurred months later. (Gerry was an incorrigible maverick Democrat.) Cheney's successor was Farrell D. Coyle, who apparently had his political loyalties in order. On relief issues, virtually all political maneuvering was at the state and federal levels. Evidence is lacking that politics guided actual distribution of dollars and jobs. Unpredictable and complex rivalries within both parties created a kind of political stalemate that allowed state and federal social workers to maintain professional standards.

A precarious political balance at the city level owed much to Democratic infighting and ethnic rivalries. Republicans remained competitive because of the dissension in Democratic ranks and the similarity of party platforms on socio-economic issues. In 1936, Colonel Patrick H. Quinn, former state Democratic chairman, warned James Farley, a presidential aide, of upcoming Democratic setbacks in Providence municipal elections: "We are hoping that there may be such a change in the personnel of nominations for city offices in Providence that our municipal ticket will look like a 'new deal' and attract back the support of the (in my opinion) thousands of loyal Democrats who certainly will not support the present municipal officers and who might remain away from the polls altogether." Quinn held that Mayor Dunne was a "fine fellow" but had been tarred not only by political sins of the past ten years "but with those of some of the most asinine members of the Common Council who ever acted in public."[36] He concluded that Dunne would not be renominated. Dunne led the Democratic ticket, but was returned to office by a mere 791 votes. In 1932 Dunne had prevailed by 23,762 votes, in 1934 by 14,285. (The president's aides were not ordinarily interested in local elections, but Rhode Island attracted their attention after a Republican, Charles Risk, was elected to Congress in a 1935 special election, an election with implications for the New Deal's continuing appeal.) As the New Deal progressed, the Providence Republican party and independent movements grew in strength.

Ethnic rivalries also prevented formation of a unified Democratic machine that could tilt relief favors to loyalists. The anomalies of Providence ethnic politics stood out in Ward 13, the Federal Hill section of the city. Predominantly Italian and containing more relief cases than any other ward in Providence, Ward 13 displayed an independent Democracy and its own brand of competitive Republicanism. The red flag for both movements was the symbol of "Tammany Hall," opposition to which drove Italian Democrats into alliances with Republicans and created Italian Republicans. Relief was only one of many issues. Ward politicians gave it only passing notice in their election campaigns. Ethnic pride was a far greater concern.

By the 1930s the Italians of Providence had secured a durable political base in city and state politics. (The Italians of Boston had much more difficulty gaining political influence proportionate to their numbers.) Italo-Americans took over ward committees of both parties in wards 4 and 13 in Providence, beginning in the 1920s and consolidating in the 1930s. General political disunity provided opportunities to expand Italo-American power. The factions and close votes in the City Council gave elected Italo-Americans much more influence than they might have held in a government dominated by a powerful mayor or a cohesive party.

Italian Democrats controlled wards 4 and 13, but were not subservient to Irish Democratic leaders. Democratic aldermen Ventrone, Parente, and Luongo often voted with Republicans against "Tammany." Alderman Parente and Councilman D'Agnenica eventually broke with the party to build independent factions. In the election of 1934, the first since the New Deal programs had begun, former Representative Torelli, a Democrat, urged Federal Hill voters to break the back of Tammany and vote straight Republican.[37] An independent stance was also important for Italian Republicans. The best showing of Republicans on the "Hill" occurred after party insurgents took nominations away from regulars.[38]

Providence's Italian newspaper, *The Italian Echo*, strikingly reveals the complexity of political attitudes within the Italo-American community. Ethnicity, unemployment, and the New Deal did not necessarily add up to Democratic votes. Although the *Echo* honored Al Smith, it waged vitriolic warfare against Tammany, Roosevelt, and Italian Democrats ("pagnottisti" or hirelings). Prior to the New Deal it warned: "Both nationally and locally the Democratic party is controlled by elements hostile to the immigrant groups. . . . No amount of distortion and hokum can obscure the fact that only at the hands of a Republican Administration can the so-called foreign groups receive fair-play and an equal opportunity."[39] The *Echo* was not unconscious of the suffering within the community, but its suggested remedies stressed action of a European variety: "An Emergency Dictatorship that could interpret relief in terms of the country as a whole, with the dispassionate outlook of a general in war, should be established. Somebody with the forcefulness of—the comparison seems inevitable—Mussolini. . . . America may yet find that it needs a bit of fascist tonic to revive her sleepy and loose liberalism."[40] After the New Deal had established a track record, a new editor was no kinder to Roosevelt:

> The purpose of the New Deal, both national and local, is to keep the masses down, to keep them under control. The device has been effective as we see hundreds of citizens of Italian birth or extraction actually *terror-stricken* because of the threat held over them by the New Deal feudal lords who administer relief. . . . Roosevelt himself represents a group that is congenitally opposed to everything Italian. He cooperated with the League of Nations against Italy and today he clandestinely cooperates with the Span-

ish Soviet against the German and Italian fascists. Why! BECAUSE AMONG HIS ADVISORS ARE REDS WHO WANT TO SEE FASCISM DESTROYED.[41]

But, as the *Echo* observed a week later, citizens of Italian extraction in fact voted for Roosevelt in large numbers, and voters in wards 4 and 13 consistently returned Democratic candidates. Yet the strident positions of the *Echo* suggest attitudes and beliefs within the Italian community that vote totals do not explain. Many Italians consistently supported Republicans and independents, and many ethnic voters had ambivalent opinions about Roosevelt.

Italo-American Republicans like Benjamin Cianciarulo, deputy speaker of the House, rose to prominence in the state Republican party, but Cianciarulo must have found that his heritage was a liability in scaling the Yankee-dominated party hierarchy. Yet the Republican party actively sought Italian votes, and in close city and state elections a Democratic majority in Italian wards might not be as important as the size of that majority in determining the outcome in an election. In the 1934 mayoral race, Democrat Dunne beat Republican Collins in Ward 13 with 74 percent of the vote, and in Ward 4 with 66 percent. In 1938, the same two candidates competed for Italian votes, but Dunne came away with only 58 percent in Ward 13 and 51 percent in Ward 4. Republican Collins, however, was the election winner with a plurality of 4,951. In the two Italian wards, 7,471 voters supported the Republican, more than enough to put him over the top.

Despite the independence of Italian politicians, many did not seek to change the system that allowed machine control of party caucuses. Rather, they sought to take over the existing system. "Good government" reforms were suspect. In November 1935, Providence played host to the National Municipal League, which held its forty-first annual conference at the Biltmore Hotel. In the heady company of Judge Samuel Seabury ("the scourge of Tammany") and municipal expert Dr. Thomas Reed, Democratic Councilman Peter Reilly called the Providence form of government out-of-date: "Providence city government is cumbersome, antiquated, wasteful, and . . . there is no central responsibility anywhere. . . . Patronage is rife; there is practically no control over expenditures; deficits are created without anyone knowing about it and no one is responsible. And in the background is a caucus set-up perfectly adapted to perpetuating machine control."[42] The conference concluded that Providence needed a city manager and proportional representation, and over the next few years, the *Providence*

Journal, the League of Women Voters, Republican Mayor John F. Collins, and others pushed for an appropriate charter change. The city manager was seen as a nonpolitical, strong executive, and proportional representation promised an end to machine control of caucuses. But other voices encouraged Italian Democrats to see the proposed charter as a means to exclude "racial groups" from representation. In February 1939, John O. Pastore called the charter "a sugar-coated pill," forced on the people of the city by "the swanky East Side crowd."[43] Italo-Americans were sufficiently represented within the existing system to tolerate if not assist in its perpetuation. The bipartisan Italian campaign against "Tammany" did not result in a unified Italian effort to break the machine's control of nominations.

Although incumbent politicians could avoid changes in the political system, they could no longer avoid the repercussions of those years of easy borrowing at the beginning of the Depression. The long-deferred tax hikes came back to haunt officials in the late 1930s. As taxes inevitably increased, patronage and corruption became major political issues, not so much because of glaring abuses but because debt-service costs made the usual waste more visible. Occasional stories appeared in the press that encouraged citizens to question whether city officials were profiting from relief appropriations. Commissioner of Public Works Charles A. Maguire's attempt to retain his post while undertaking lucrative PWA consultancies was one example. A former Democratic alderman from Ward 4, Angelo Parente, urged voters at a Republican rally to "turn out the crooked politicians" by voting a straight ticket. "Mr. Maguire has been a decided asset to the Dunne-Ganier machine," he added.[44]

Republicans and independents prevailed in key 1938 state and city contests, and voters rejected a proposed $27,000,000 state bond issue to finance PWA projects. John F. Collins, in the Republican, Independent Citizens, and Good Government column, defeated Dunne. The Democrats lost a citywide office for the first time since the suffrage was extended to non-propertied citizens in 1928. Fusion candidates for the City Council in the low-income wards 11 and 12 defeated Democrats, including Raymond Shawcross, president of the aldermen. Democratic incumbents were not benefiting from all those years of dispensing relief.[45]

In contrast, Pawtucket voters reelected Democratic Mayor Thomas McCoy with a 69 percent plurality. A closer look at McCoy's administration might reveal how a strong city boss could make relief and patronage work to his advantage despite state and national trends to the contrary. Perhaps the ethnic differences between Providence and Pawtucket provide an answer. Yet in large heterogeneous cities like Pittsburgh, local Democrats effectively used relief dollars to expand the influence of their political organizations. Providence Democrats missed this opportunity.

Forces from without and within directed or acquiesced in the impoverishment of Providence politics. Relief administration played a central role. The federal government extended the carrot, and the state applied the stick. The easy-going anarchy of Providence political life ensured that no local official could amass power by finding loopholes in job programs. Millions of dollars spent on jobs and public works projects provided risks and opportunities. Providence took and got neither.

Providence had not been found wanting in its initial response to the economic calamity of the century. City officials generally said and did the right things, while the responsibility was theirs alone. Had the New Deal been delayed two or three years, Providence might have displayed vision and capacities far beyond expectations. This experience might have provided a base on which to develop local approaches to the welfare and revitalization problems of later decades. Mistakes would have occurred, but they would have been local mistakes, largely funded with local dollars. As it happened and has continued to happen, local government kept the onus of a disproportionate share of the cost while higher levels of government set the priorities and took the credit, either for program results or for the grudging enlightenment of local officials. It is only fair to add that if the jobless of Providence had had a choice, they would have been loath to gamble on local competence and professionalism. Under state-federal direction, the poor of Rhode Island received relatively fair and uniform assistance. But Providence government, denied issues of substance, focused instead on the insubstantial—personal and ethnic rivalries.

The conventional view of the Great Depression has fiscal necessity forcing the federal government and the nation's cities into a new partnership. Certainly many cities across the country had neither the means nor the will to provide for the Depression's victims. For these cities the New Deal was a godsend. In the specific case of Providence, however, the New Deal was less of a partnership and more of a buy-out, less a rescue from calamity and more a restructuring of federalism on terms favorable to and dictated by federal and state agencies.

NOTES

1. *Providence Journal*, Sept. 13, 1930. "Jakey" was American slang for a ginger-flavored intoxicant from the Caribbean.
2. *Ibid.*, Nov. 12, 1931.
3. *Ibid.*, Dec. 30, 1930; *Records of the Providence Board of Aldermen*, XXXIII, 254–255.

4. *Providence Journal*, Dec. 2, 1930.

5. *Providence Magazine*, Nov. 1931, 358.

6. Brown University Bureau of Business Research, *Brown Business Service*, VIII (Dec. 14, 1931), Report 5, 22. The bureau determined that families of five required $10.25 weekly for subsistence. Brown University Bureau of Business Research, Fact Finding Committee, Governor's Conference on Employment and Relief, *Employment and Unemployment in Rhode Island*, Report No. II (June 13, 1932), 1.

7. Providence Governmental Research Bureau (PGRB), *Newsletter*, Dec. 1938, No. 45.

8. *Providence Journal*, Oct. 5, 1932.

9. *Ibid.*, Sept. 28, 1931.

10. *Ibid.*, Mar. 18, 1931.

11. *Ibid.*, Apr. 17, 1932, Sept. 30, 1937.

12. *Ibid.*, Nov. 14, 1931.

13. *Ibid.*, Sept. 22, 1931.

14. *Cleveland News*, Dec. 7, 1931 (in the files of the President's Organization on Unemployment Relief, RG 73, National Archives, Washington, D.C.).

15. *Providence Journal*, Dec. 9, 1931.

16. *Ibid.*, Mar. 5, 1932.

17. Brown University Bureau of Business Research, *Employment and Unemployment in Rhode Island*, Report No. I (May 31, 1932), 26.

18. *Ibid.*

19. *Providence Magazine*, Jan. 1931, 5.

20. *Ibid.*, Dec. 1931, 385.

21. Brown University Bureau of Business Research, *Employment and Unemployment*, Report No. I, 26.

22. *Providence Journal Almanac*, 1937, 73.

23. Martha Gellhorn to Harry L. Hopkins, Dec. 19, 1934, FERA-WPA Narrative Field Reports, Harry Hopkins MSS, Box 66, Franklin D. Roosevelt Library, Hyde Park, N.Y. See also James T. Patterson, ed., "Life on Relief in Rhode Island, 1934: A Contemporary View from the Field," *Rhode Island History*, XXXIX (1980), 79–91.

24. *Providence Journal*, Oct. 1, 1933.

25. PGRB, *Newsletter*, Oct. 1937, No. 32.

26. International City Management Association (ICMA), *Municipal Yearbook*, 1937, 329.

27. PGRB, *A Financial Review of the City of Providence*, Sept. 1936, summary.

28. Robert T. Lansdale to Aubrey Williams (Memorandum on Rhode Island), June 27, 1934, Hopkins MSS, Box 59, Rhode Island Field Reports, Roosevelt Library.

29. Gellhorn to Hopkins, Dec. 19, 1934, Hopkins MSS, Box 66, Roosevelt Library. See also Patterson, ed., "Life on Relief," *R.I. History*, XXXIX (1980), 86–91.

30. ICMA, *Municipal Yearbook*, 1937, 413.

31. PGRB, *A Comparison of Public Relief Expenditures*, Oct. 1935, 25.

32. ICMA, *Municipal Yearbook*, 1937, 413.

33. Henry W. Mann, *Manufacturing in Rhode Island*, Rhode Island State Planning Board, Special Report No. XIII (Dec. 30, 1937), 63.

34. *Providence Journal*, Mar. 3, 1936.

35. Branion and Hopkins, Aug. 25, 1936, Transcripts of Telephone Conversations with State Relief Directors and Other Officials, Hopkins MSS, Box 66, Roosevelt Library.

36. P. H. Quinn to James Farley, Sept. 10, 1936, President's Official File 300, Box 90, Roosevelt Library.

37. *Providence Journal*, Nov. 2, 1934.

38. *Ibid.*, Oct. 1, 1938.

39. *The Italian Echo*, Aug. 26, 1932.

40. *Ibid.*, Nov. 13, 1931.

41. *Ibid.*, Oct. 30, 1936.

42. *Providence Journal*, Nov. 26, 1935.

43. *Ibid.*, Feb. 9, 1939.

44. *Ibid.*, Oct. 11, 1938.

45. Three letters to James Farley in President's Official File 300, Box 98, Roosevelt Library, mention the 1938 setbacks for the Democratic party. Thomas P. McCoy found the Democratic collapse in Providence astounding. See McCoy to Farley, Dec. 16, 1938, *ibid.* J. J. Cunningham cited the fraudulent actions of caucus officials and injudicious distribution of patronage as reasons why many Democrats deserted the party. Cunningham to Farley, Dec. 22, 1938, *ibid.* James H. Kiernan explained the losses as due to a number of factors: waning appeal of the New Deal, relief recipients were voting Republican, people were fearful of taxes and opposed to expensive public works bond issues, and some other reasons. Kiernan to Farley, Nov. 30, 1938, *ibid.* Dunne claimed that the amount of money spent by the Republicans in the past eighteen months was unprecedented and that the new voting machines were to blame for his own defeat. Dunne to Farley, Dec. 19, 1938, President's Official File 300, Box 90, Roosevelt Library.

Flint and the Great Depression

WILLIAM H. CHAFE

This selection illustrates the vulnerability of a one-company or one-industry city to economic decline. Flint, like other industrial boom towns of the 1920s, experienced a typical sequence: exhaustion of private relief, then local government relief, then state relief. Ultimately this resulted in requests for federal aid and—under local protest—the shift of welfare administration from city hall to Washington, D.C. This article also shows how the creation of the Works Progress Administration confirmed the fact that the devastation of the Great Depression was cutting across ethnic, occupational, and class lines.

ONE of the most fruitful areas of study open to historians of the New Deal is its effect on the cities of America. Scholars have devoted a great deal of attention to the New Deal as a national event—its politics, legislative accomplishments, and ideological conflicts. But what happened in Washington tells only part of the story. Equally important was the effect of decisions made in Washington on the lives of people across the country. Consequently, it may be important for our understanding of the Great Depression and the New Deal to measure these events from the perspective of the local community.

Flint, Michigan, was and is a company town. Its economic survival depends upon the auto industry. A manufacturing center for carriages in the

From *Michigan History*, 53 (Fall 1969), 225–239.

late nineteenth century, it became in the twentieth century a central production facility for General Motors, containing branches of Chevrolet,
Fisher Body, Buick, and AC Spark Plug. Like the auto industry, the city
expanded rapidly, growing in population from 13,103 in 1900 to 156,492 in
1930.[1] At the beginning of the Depression, more than half of Genesee
County's 83,000 employed citizens worked for GM.[2] Today the corporation
still dominates the city. The largest office building in town, the college library, the child health center, and a recreation park all bear the name of
a former vice-president of GM, and as late as 1966, when Flint purchased
public vehicles, it invited bids only from GM truck makers.[3]

Frequently, community facilities failed to keep pace with the city's
rapid growth. Housing was a major problem. In the early years of the century, GM representatives scoured the country urging unskilled workers to
journey to Flint. When the workers arrived, however, there was often no
shelter for them. Migrants who came during the boom years of 1908–1920
lived in tarpaper shacks, tents, and railroad cars, all without sanitary facilities. Neither the city nor the corporation would invest the capital to lay
water mains or sewers, and working-class areas were flooded by spring
thaws and heavy rains. In 1919 GM began to construct company housing,
but its most ambitious plan—to build a 2,759-person dormitory—was forgotten as a result of the recession which followed World War I. Although
3,200 GM homes had been built by 1933, housing remained a major problem for Flint, and a government survey taken at the beginning of the New
Deal showed that one-third of Flint's families lived in substandard housing while one-tenth lived in structures classified as "dangerous."[4]

Flint was thus not untypical of many industrial boom towns of the
1920s. It had experienced the full thrust of the decade's economic prosperity, and it offered social and economic advancement to aspiring newcomers. Yet the city also faced problems. It lacked stability and tradition.[5]
Population increases exceeded the city's capacity to provide adequate housing and sanitation. And the growth of the private sector of the economy
had outrun the growth of the public sector. Flint's experience during the
Depression and the New Deal may thus shed some light on critical variables which affected similar cities across the country.[6]

In Flint as elsewhere, voluntarism characterized the early response to
the Depression. Private agencies dispensed relief to clients whose problems
fell within their particular province, although persons who were not wid-
owed mothers or homeless children sometimes had difficulty finding a
niche for themselves. Private charity had not traditionally made provision
for those who were healthy and able, yet still unemployed. The Flint

Community Fund, an umbrella organization of sixteen agencies ranging
from the Junior League to the Salvation Army, acted as a central fund-
raiser and checked relief recipients to insure that no one got more than
his due.[7] It did little, however, to effectively mobilize new resources. An
occasional churchman, like the Rev. John E. Zoller of the Methodist
church, enlisted religious facilities in the cause of general relief (Zoller fed
as many as 1,200 a day at his tabernacle), but most churches restricted their
efforts to their own congregations.[8] The weekly potluck supper was a primary means by which the church could provide a form of relief and at the
same time bolster spirits among its congregants.

On a city-wide level, the Flint Relief Commission was established in
1931 in response to a request from the President's Organization on Unemployment. Its administration, however, was unwieldy. Consisting of twenty-
one leading citizens, the commission divided its responsibilities into
twenty-one separate parts with a commissioner in charge of each. The food
division collected donations of food, the clothing division solicited clothing, and the odd jobs division assigned six hundred men to areas of the
city where, on their own initiative, they might seek temporary employment
from local residents. Although a public body, the commission was financed by private contributions.[9] Indeed, so dedicated was Flint to the
ethic of voluntarism that even the free milk for 2,500 school children was
paid for by proceeds from a benefit band concert sponsored by the Lion's
Club.[10]

Public welfare was even less effective and served primarily as a political issue to be used by opposing sides in the faction-ridden City Commission. In the bitter 1932 campaign, two renegades from the camp of
Republican Mayor William McKeighan charged his administration with
using welfare workers to register voters for his own political machine.
When the renegades were subsequently recalled by petition, their counterattack consisted of the charge that the city was shortchanging relief recipients. For both factions, welfare employees and clients were a source of
patronage and political power.[11]

Until 1933, then, assistance to the needy in Flint was limited. Its inadequacy rested primarily in the fact that older forms and institutions were
unable to cope with a crisis as large as the Depression. In effect, the existing structure of welfare could not adapt to the new demands placed
upon it, and no new structure arose from within the local community to
assume the task. What happened in 1933 was that from without, the federal government seized the initiative and reordered the older forms and institutions of charity. By injecting an outside influence, the state usurped

local power, replaced voluntarism, forged a new structural apparatus to attack the Depression, and in the process fostered significant changes in the administration and philosophy of local relief.[12]

Money was the key instrument of change. The governmental body which held the purse strings also dictated policy. Michigan relief administrator Fred Johnson pointed out to local residents that under Hoover's Reconstruction Finance Corporation, loans were offered to local governments, and administration consequently remained in local hands. Under the Federal Emergency Relief Administration (FERA), in contrast, grants were given to states, and the disbursing agent—the federal government—retained control over their expenditure.[13] As a result, direction of the Flint welfare operation moved from City Hall to Washington.

The cause and effect of federal control were clearly revealed in a controversy surrounding the appointment of Victor S. Woodward as director of the County Emergency Relief Administration (CERA) in August, 1933. Flint politicians preferred the appointment of a local man. Woodward, however, was a former aide of Harry Hopkins in New York's relief administration and was appointed allegedly because the federal government required that every local committee be headed by a trained social worker. When Flint citizens protested such outside control, the County Emergency Relief Committee confessed it was powerless to interfere. Woodward, the Committee declared, "was recommended by the federal agents who have had to do with supplying the funds. . . . The source of support should make significant . . . how far removed . . . supervision is from local control and influences that are not constructive. We primarily are the agents of the United States government and we function virtually at its pleasure."[14] The infusion of federal funds had transformed, for the moment, the power structure of the local government, making jealous local politicians the servants of the federal establishment.

One immediate consequence of federal control was the emergence of a new welfare hierarchy. Relief ceased to be locally initiated and controlled. FERA in Washington mandated the establishment of the State Emergency Relief Administration (SERA) in Lansing, and SERA administered its grants through CERA in Flint. Significantly, two-thirds of CERA's members were chosen by the state rather than by local officials. The order of federal bureaucracy replaced the confusion of local voluntarism.[15]

Simultaneously, there occurred a substantial change in Flint's approach to relief. Prior to 1933, welfare applicants had to obtain the endorsement of two taxpayers before they could be considered for assistance. A poorly trained staff spent much of its time referring clients to the proper private agencies. The self-image of welfare employees, according to a 1933 report, was that of detectives and investigators rather than public servants whose responsibility to dependents was as great as to taxpayers.[16] Under the New Deal, in contrast, the local welfare administration recognized the universality of the Depression's impact. People of all classes and backgrounds had been stricken, and every citizen had a right to public assistance until a job became available. It was uneconomic and inhumane, Woodward insisted, to permit people to live in squalor or to provide them with only enough relief to survive. "[E]very human being," he emphasized, "is entitled to live in quarters which are decent."[17]

Under Woodward's guidance, the County Relief Committee discarded old welfare shibboleths and redefined the task of relief:

> The welfare problem is not merely one of doling out relief on the basis of the old-time poor departments; . . . we have a great problem of social rehabilitation; . . . thousands of families never have had to resort to public aid. . . . [For their sake] we are not content with mere investigation.[18]

Woodward's commission attempted to treat each case individually. Trained supervisors were added at the ratio of one for every eight caseworkers. The staff climbed from sixty-five in May, 1933, before the federal takeover, to one hundred eighty in April, 1934.[19] Equipped with more workers, outside financing, and a different conception of the task at hand, the welfare administration set out to meet the needs of Flint's unemployed with new energy and purpose.

A striking improvement in public health represented a major achievement of the new approach. Early in the Depression, Flint ranked third in infant deaths and fifth in maternal deaths in a comparative study of twenty-two cities—a consequence, the study concluded, of grossly inadequate public health services in Flint.[20] By 1936, in contrast, the maternal mortality rate among Flint relief clients had plummeted to two-thirds that of the general population, a result of intensive prenatal and postnatal care under government sponsorship. In 1935 alone, public health nurses made 8,053 prenatal and postnatal visits, encouraging patients to see the doctor, teaching personal hygiene, and stressing instructions received by expectant mothers in monthly mailings from the State Health Department.[21] A plan under which each public patient could choose his own doctor further aided the local public health program. In its first year of operation, public monies financed 13,081 office visits by relief clients.[22]

Even more impressive were the lifesaving results achieved through government support and supervision of public recreation. In the summer of

1935 Flint opened sixteen new playgrounds with sixty-nine recreation directors at a cost of $11,711. The investment paid off. Average weekly attendance at the playgrounds doubled to 54,152, while juvenile delinquency and traffic fatalities fell drastically. "We have had no children hurt playing in the streets [this summer]," reported the director of the project. Moreover, because the city had hired lifeguards, no children drowned in the swimming holes for the first time in years.[23]

Housing reforms were another major improvement. A special committee abolished rents based on property assessment and tax warrants and instead created a rent schedule geared to the size, condition, and utilities of an apartment. The housing and salvage division of the County Relief Administration made repairs which landlords could not afford and deducted the cost from rents—an interesting forerunner of city rehabilitation of private housing today.[24]

Harry Hopkins's Works Progress Administration financed and inspired most of the local improvements. Children bicycled on streets newly paved by WPA workers, while their parents joined in evening operettas performed by WPA orchestras in outdoor WPA theatres. Other federal efforts included modernizing the airport, cleaning the local lake for recreation purposes, building parks, painting schools, extending sewers, surveying traffic, and manufacturing sheets, mattresses, and shoes.[25] What Robert and Helen Lynd observed in Middletown was true of Flint also: "In 1933 the city shifted over, with the interjection of federal planning into the local scene . . . [and] was asked to state its civic desires positively, to frame a new series of axioms and to go ahead and act on them. Having no alternative, the city began to play the new game . . . and for a brief span of months . . . had the experience of pressing the buttons . . . to 'see how it works.'"[26] In both Flint and Middletown, the changed atmosphere resulted in the achievement of civic improvements which five years before would have been unthinkable.

As the Depression deepened, increasing numbers of Flint people had occasion to experience directly the benefits of the welfare state. Local unemployment oscillated constantly due to seasonal layoffs in the auto industry, but 1938 marked the nadir of the Depression in Flint. During the previous low in late 1934 and early 1935, the maximum number of families on relief had been 10,561. In the first six months of 1938 the number soared to 19,650.[27]

The backgrounds of the jobless revealed the growing universality of the Depression's impact. The percentage of native-born whites on the relief rolls increased from 68.1 in 1934 to 77.1 in 1939. Over a quarter of the 1938 total had never received relief before. Most significant, however, was the sharp rise in educational and occupational levels among relief recipients. Whereas in 1934, 28.2 percent of the people on welfare had a high school diploma, the figure leaped to 51.3 percent of new applicants and 40.4 percent of the total in 1938; 40.7 percent of the new applicants were professional men, moreover, managers, officials, white collar workers, and skilled laborers. In addition, more than half of the total applied for relief during the first month after loss of income.[28]

Clearly the day had passed when welfare was restricted to the pariahs of the community. Substantial citizens who earlier had clung to a job or escaped relief by withdrawing savings or doubling up with relatives had now exhausted their resources and were compelled to seek assistance. As a result, suffering and want ceased to be the exclusive domain of voluntary charities or the private responsibility of individual citizens. "The human care of dependents has gone past private agencies," a prominent Flint citizen observed in 1938, "and is now a public job—a big one."[29]

Significantly, the major regression in public policy toward reliefers followed the partial withdrawal of the state from direct responsibility for the welfare administration. Federal financing of direct relief ended with the passage of WPA, and the resulting burden placed on local authorities spurred deep resentment of the state's continuing domination of the welfare board. With increased appropriations from the county came insistent demands for more local control—in effect, a repetition of the federal government's argument in 1933 that money means power—and in July, 1936, a new Relief Commission took office, two-thirds of whom represented choices of the county instead of the state.[30]

Restoration of local control carried with it a reaction against many premises of the federal program. The County Board of Supervisors charged that administrative costs could be slashed by 50 percent and that many reliefers could find work easily if only they were willing to look.[31] More extreme was the response of new welfare administrator Louis J. Ludington to the recession of 1938. Beginning in April with a plan to move 12,000 "unemployables" out of the county, Ludington graduated by August to the proposal that second-generation reliefers be sterilized. Too many welfare recipients, he charged, had a "decidedly communistic attitude . . . [rooted in their] having too much time to think about themselves and their troubles." When Ludington was removed in September, he claimed to be a "Moscow trial victim" punished by the state and the auto workers union for prosecuting welfare chiselers.[32]

At first glance, it would appear that the administration of Ludington represented the undoing of all that had been accomplished under Woodward and that by the end of the Depression the leadership of Flint had returned full circle to the individualism and voluntarism of pre-New Deal days. But the statistics of the 1938 recession belie such an interpretation. The impact of the Depression experience had broadened, not narrowed, as time passed. The number of middle-class victims who sought relief almost immediately in the 1938 crisis demonstrated that the welfare state had become during the Depression an indispensable presence in Flint. However much individuals such as Ludington might berate public assistance, more and more Flint people relied upon it in time of need. Thus it seems that the Ludington episode did not signal a community-wide revulsion against relief as much as a political reaction against the New Deal. Given this fact, it might be better to seek an explanation for Ludington's actions in the framework of other conclusions which can tentatively be drawn about the Flint experience.

First, it appears that whatever change in social welfare policy occurred in Flint during the Depression owed its existence to outside intervention from state or federal authorities. In the early years of the crisis, older forms of voluntarism prevailed. New policies coincided with the structural reorganization which accompanied the establishment of the New Deal relief program. State intervention thus emerges as the critical variable in explaining the introduction of progressive welfare policies. The local community did not possess within itself the energy or imagination to forge new forms of relief adequate to the crisis.

Second, money provided the lever by which the change in welfare policy was accomplished. As long as local taxes or charities supplied the financial base for relief, local leaders retained control, and the notion that public welfare was a dole, not a right of citizenship, prevailed. When the federal government became the major source of funds, on the other hand, it insisted that its own personnel take over. Federal administration, with a new and different conception of welfare, was a quid pro quo of financial aid.

Third, the New Deal programs substantially benefited the Flint community. More and more Flint residents received public assistance directly from a welfare administration which considered such aid a right of citizenship, not a symbol of shame. Moreover, the entire community gained indirectly. Public health care and recreation facilities improved drastically. Streets were paved, parks were built, and cultural programs were developed. New Deal funds helped to renovate and modernize the city, permanently improving its physical appearance and public services. By the end of the 1930s, the people of Flint had become accustomed to a level of public services which, in the future, they would not wish to see withdrawn.[33]

Fourth, the gains registered under the New Deal took place at the cost of alienating some local leaders who had previously exercised control and who would return to power when the Depression crisis ended. The major fault of New Deal welfare policies in Flint was that they were imposed from without, with seemingly little effort made to develop a cooperative relationship with local political forces. By taking so little account of local pride—as, for example, in importing a relief administrator from New York instead of choosing one of similar views from Flint—New Deal officials generated resentment among local leaders and diminished the possibility that at a future date the community itself would carry on the programs and philosophy initiated by Washington.

Thus Ludington's attack on the welfare system and the county insistence on retaking control of the relief committee after the withdrawal of direct federal relief funds may be partially explained by the anger local leaders felt at being denied a voice in the earlier New Deal programs. It may be argued that federal authorities could achieve their goals only by imposing them on local communities. But, until evidence from other communities comes in, we may speculate that the failure to consult and respect local leaders represented a major error in the New Deal's attempt to permanently alter the values and structure of American society.

Whatever the case, the experience of Flint during the Depression suggests how dramatic were the effects on local communities of New Deal programs. By accumulating a series of such studies, we may better be able to understand the variables which determined the ultimate impact of the New Deal on the American people. Until now, scholars have concentrated on explaining the ideas and political forces which created the New Deal; in the future, perhaps a similar amount of energy will inform us of the success the New Deal had in carrying through its programs in local communities.

NOTES

1. U.S. Bureau of the Census, *Fifteenth Census of the United States: 1930, Population*, 1, 25.

2. Frank H. Landers, *Local Government in Genesee County* ("Michigan Government Studies," No. 14; Ann Arbor: University of Michigan Press, 1941), p. 5.

3. *Flint Journal*, April 20, 1967, clipping, Flint Public Library. The Mott Foundation, about which more will be said in a subsequent footnote, is a major influence in Flint.

4. Frank Rodolph, "Industrial History of Flint," MS, Flint Public Library, pp. 500–505; *Flint Journal*, March 2, 1939, clipping.

5. Geographical mobility was extraordinarily high in Flint due to the growth of the local economy. During the 1920s the population increased 73 percent. As a result of the continual flow of migrants, turnover in some plants was 200 and 300 percent in a year. Indicative of the instability of Flint's pre-Depression population is the fact that in 1934 only 36,500 Flint residents had been born in Flint. Moreover, 14,000 people in that year were under 5 and 29,000 were under 10; when the large majority of these who were Flint-born is subtracted from the previous figure, comparatively few Flint-born adults are left. The Depression had the effect of stabilizing Flint's population, and the community grew only 7.7 percent in the 1930s. See A.C. Findlay, "The Population of Flint," in Flint Institute of Research and Planning, "Compiled Studies," mimeographed MS, 1938. To my knowledge the only copy of this work is in the Flint Public Library.

6. The present paper does not qualify as a full-fledged community study because it concentrates on the narrow area of social welfare policy and leaves untouched the important experience of various ethnic, political, and economic groups. In particular, the paper does not cover the dramatic increase in political participation in Flint during the Depression (from 37 percent in the election of 1928 to 85 percent in the election of 1932), or the critical shift in economic power which accompanied the famous GM sit-down strikes of 1937. Each of these areas, however, has been previously dealt with. On the politics of Flint, see Samuel Eldersveld and J. K. Pollock, *Michigan Politics in Transition* ("Michigan Government Studies," Number 10; Ann Arbor: University of Michigan Press, 1942); Pierce F. Lewis, "Geography in the Politics of Flint" (unpublished Ph.D. dissertation, University of Michigan, 1958); and Max P. Heavenrich, "The Participation of Flint Citizens in Elections," Flint Institute of Research and Planning, "Compiled Studies." For a survey of the sit-down strikes, see Sidney Fine, "The General Motors Sit-Down Strike: A Re-examination," *American Historical Review*, LXX (April, 1965), 691–713.

7. *Flint Journal*, January 1, 1932, clipping.

8. *Ibid.*, June 24, 1931, clipping; Court Street Methodist Church, *Bulletins*, 1929–1937. Bound copies of the *Bulletins* may be found at the church.

9. *Flint Journal*, January 1, 1932, clipping.

10. *Ibid.*, October 2, 1932, clipping.

11. *Ibid.*, March 1, 1932, April 2, 1932, November 7, 1932, clippings. The issue dominated Flint politics in 1932. In six months shifts in political power resulted in four different city managers.

12. The term "state" is used to denote a government outside of and larger than the county government. It would include both the government of Michigan and that of the nation.

13. *Flint Journal*, August 30, 1933, clipping.

14. *Ibid.*, November 3, 1933, clipping.

15. Frank Landers, *The Administration and Financing of Public Relief* ("Michigan Government Studies," Number 17; Ann Arbor: University of Michigan Press, 1942), pp. 6–7.

16. Flint Public Welfare Board, "First Annual Report," May 1, 1933–April 30, 1934, mimeographed MS, p. 2.

17. Genesee County Welfare Relief Commission, "Our Needy Neighbors," Bi-annual Report, November 1, 1933–June 30, 1935, mimeographed MS, p. 3; Flint Public Welfare Board, "Second Annual Report," May 1, 1934–June 30, 1935, mimeographed MS, n.p.

18. *Flint Journal*, November 3, 1933, clipping.

19. Flint Public Welfare Board, "First Annual Report," n.p.

20. Dr. Carl E. Buck, "Genesee County's Health Facilities and Needs," Flint Institute of Research and Planning, "Compiled Studies," n.p.

21. Flint Public Welfare Board, "Third Annual Report," July 1, 1935–June 30, 1936, mimeographed MS, n.p.; Genesee County Welfare Relief Commission, "Our Needy Neighbors," Health Division, pp. 2, 4.

22. Flint Public Welfare Board, "First Annual Report," n.p.

23. Genesee County Welfare Relief Commission, "Our Needy Neighbors," Educational and Recreation Project, n.p.

24. *Ibid.*, Housing and Salvage Division, n.p.

25. *Flint Journal*, April 28, 1935, August 28, 1936, clippings.

26. Robert and Helen Lynd, *Middletown in Transition* (New York: Harcourt, Brace & Co., 1937), pp. 121, 125.

27. Erdmann D. Benyon, "Characteristics of the Relief Case Load in Genesee County," MS, Flint Public Library, p. 2. The Benyon study took place in 1938 under WPA sponsorship.

28. Approximately 45 percent of the new families were headed by persons under 30. Seniority rules made it difficult for the young to keep work during hard times, and at the same time, they had fewer credit resources because of their age. Equally important, having grown up during the Depression, they were much less reluctant to rely on public aid; *ibid.*, pp. 1, 7, 30, 41, 44, 50.

29. *Flint Journal*, November 1, 1938, clipping. The prominent citizen was E. S. Guckert, director of the Flint Institute of Research and Planning.

30. Genesee County Welfare Relief Commission, "Neighbors on Relief," Second Annual Report, July 1, 1935—June 30, 1936, mimeographed MS, n.p.

31. *Flint Journal*, July 16, 1937, clipping.

32. *Ibid.*, April 30, 1938, August 5, 1938, September 13, 1938, clippings. Less extreme than Ludington's views were those of Harold Inch, City Commissioner and chairman of a committee in charge of overseeing WPA projects. Inch, for example, knew relief was necessary but objected to what he called third-generation reliefers. Especially galling to him were welfare recipients who traded their food stamps for beer. With the end of direct funding of relief, it would seem that men like Inch gained more and more control over relief distribution; interview with Harold Inch, April 22, 1967.

33. One of the most fascinating stories in Flint history is that of the Mott Foundation. Although outside the scope of this paper, the foundation's role in Flint is worthy of mention. Founded in 1935 by the then vice-president of GM, the foundation rapidly became one of the twenty-five largest in the country. Almost all of its money is spent in Flint, most of it through the public school system where foundation and board of education officials operate interdependently. The foundation provides basic social services from child health care to vocational training, although it specializes in adult education. The foundation is devoted to individualism and free enterprise and seeks to build "strong individuals with self-reliance . . . to counteract the weakening of our nation by the ever increasing tendency to depend on government . . . and industry security programs that relieve the individual of responsibility." It would not be going too far to say that in Flint the foundation has become a surrogate for the state in providing many social services in post-New Deal days. How and why the foundation operates as it does—through public bodies—would make an excellent project for a student interested in theories of social control; see "Philosophy of the Mott Foundation," in *Mott Foundation Projects*, a 1965–66 descriptive brochure; and Peter L. Clancy, "The Contribution of the Charles Stewart Mott Foundation in the Development of the Community School Program in Flint, Michigan" (unpublished Ph.D. dissertation, Michigan State University, 1963).

The Civil Works Administration in Grand Forks County, North Dakota

ROGER D. HARDAWAY

The Civil Works Administration, a short-term work-relief program (November 1933–March 1934), was created by executive order in anticipation of a severe winter marked by grossly inadequate relief. This selection provides an example of local participation in a New Deal program. In a rural area, in an agency often called urban-oriented, seventy-three of the eighty-one projects were proposed by local governmental units. The author's conclusion suggests the broader question whether the New Deal not only should have done more but could have done more—conceivably much more—than it did to improve the lives of all Americans. In the 1960s historians emphasized the shortcomings of the New Deal; more recent literature tends, as is evident in other selections, to emphasize various obstacles to change.

WHEN Franklin D. Roosevelt became president of the United States on March 4, 1933, the country had been in an economic depression for three and a half years. Businesses that had once ridden high on the prosperity of the 1920s were bankrupt or struggling to survive. Likewise, many farmers were on the verge of financial ruin. Banks were failing daily. Perhaps the most devastating aspect of the Depression, however, was in the suffering endured by the families of the men and women who had been thrown

From *North Dakota History*, 58 (Spring 1991), 20–30.

out of work. These laborers relied upon periodic paychecks for survival, and many had seen their last ones months or even years before. One of the most pressing problems the new president faced in 1933 was to relieve the distress of the unemployed.

Much has been written about Roosevelt's New Deal program of recovery for the nation.[1] Critics, contemporary and later ones, assailed the policies of the New Deal as being socialistic, and more than one called the president a communist and a dictator. Opponents complained that the alphabet agencies Roosevelt created to combat the problems of the nation were too costly and were not designed to foster permanent economic stability. Many questioned the advisability of spending government money on "make-work" projects. Conversely, admirers lavished praise upon the progressive Democrat and credited him with rescuing the country from the conservative fiscal policies of the 1920s that had resulted in disaster and depression. Regardless of such differences of opinion, little doubt can exist that the New Deal gave the country's ailing economy a boost when it needed it most. Unemployed laborers were grateful for the chance to work and earn money again, even if the jobs were temporary and unworthy of their skills. Small business owners were delighted to see customers once again spending money. Those hurting from the Depression cared little about the philosophical debates surrounding the New Deal programs. They only wanted relief from the immeasurable misery they had been enduring, and they welcomed the winds of change that blew over the land with Roosevelt in the White House. A group of North Dakota farmers expressed this sentiment in a resolution they adopted and sent to the president in December 1933: "Even those who now oppose you will be happier when the shadow of fear and despair has been driven into a past we all want to forget."[2]

No state was in worse economic shape in 1933 than North Dakota. Historians have noted that the state was "on the verge of economic collapse,"[3] and that "conditions in North Dakota were about as bad as any in the United States."[4] Drought in the western part of the state increased the severity of hard times, and the impact was felt in urban areas as well. In Grand Forks County, the Depression caused tax receipts to dip drastically, making it difficult for officials to meet the county's payroll and pay its operating expenses. A solution for human suffering was needed.

Among the programs Roosevelt would institute in his first year of office was the Civil Works Administration (CWA), a short-term and, consequently, less well-known employment program that would provide important assistance to North Dakotans beset by the hardships of the Depression. This essay will seek to enhance our understanding of the Civil Works Administration by examining the agency's activities in Grand Forks County, in eastern North Dakota.[5] Such an inspection of the impact of one modest aspect of the New Deal on one small portion of the U.S. will allow us to comprehend better how the Roosevelt plan of economic recovery worked and why those who received its benefits were so appreciative of the help and hope it offered them.

Roosevelt moved quickly to institute relief programs.[6] In May 1933 the new president, and the Congress elected along with him, created the Federal Emergency Relief Administration (FERA) to give money to the destitute and "make-work" jobs to those who were nearly as forsaken.[7] This was followed in June by the Public Works Administration (PWA), established by the National Industrial Recovery Act. The PWA gave large grants and low-interest loans to local governments to finance projects that were beneficial to the public such as street paving and the construction of schools and sewage disposal plants.[8] As the cold winter months of 1933–1934 approached, however, Roosevelt and his advisors concluded that more had to be done to put people to work. Consequently, in November 1933, the president created the Civil Works Administration by executive order.[9]

The CWA existed for less than five months, going out of business at the end of March 1934. Begun with $400,000,000 transferred from the budget of the PWA and later refinanced with an infusion of an additional $450,000,000 from Congress and approximately $89,000,000 of FERA money, the CWA eventually put over four million workers on the federal payroll.[10] The agency had a substantial short-term economic impact throughout the United States, and two fairly recent books have examined its national significance.[11] But the importance of the CWA and, perhaps the entire New Deal, was its effect on the local level—in the homes and businesses of the cities and counties of the country.[12]

Roosevelt wanted to implement the CWA as quickly as possible. Thus, he added administration of the agency to the duties of Harry Hopkins, head of the FERA. Hopkins, in turn, used the FERA administrative structure to put CWA programs into effect on the local level. In North Dakota, Hopkins appointed Supreme Court Justice A. M. Christianson, the state emergency relief administrator, to conduct the state's CWA operation. Christianson appointed a local CWA committee in Grand Forks County to suggest projects for agency funding. Those seeking employment on

CWA undertakings filed applications in the office of Grand Forks County Judge E. C. Lebacken who was already acting as the local federal re-employment director for the FERA.[13]

The CWA put two groups of people to work. Half of those employed on its projects were transferred from the FERA relief rolls. The other half did not have to be that destitute, but they did have to register for employment through their local re-employment office. This latter group was included in CWA plans because Roosevelt and Hopkins believed that many people who needed help had not applied for relief because they had too much pride to ask for handouts.[14] The *Grand Forks Herald* editorially lauded the plan, noting that the CWA's "primary purpose is to provide immediate opportunity for those who have no other employment to perform some useful work . . . and to enable those who are receiving assistance to preserve their own self-respect."[15]

Because it was to be implemented speedily and was to exist for only a short period of time, the CWA financed smaller projects than did its sibling agency, the PWA. In an informational meeting held in Bismarck on November 22, 1933, State Superintendent of Public Instruction A. E. Thompson, a member of the state CWA committee, stressed to local administrators that CWA projects should be those that could be begun with little advanced planning and that made capital improvements on public facilities. Ideas suggested by the Roosevelt administration for CWA funding included improving parks and playgrounds, paving roads and streets, and repairing public buildings and utility systems.[16]

Grand Forks County officials had no difficulty thinking of worthwhile proposals for the CWA. While the state and federal governments occasionally initiated projects, most originated at the local level. In Grand Forks, seventy-three projects were the proposals of local governmental units, five were state-created, and the federal government operated three. Of the local undertakings, approximately two-thirds originated during the first two weeks of the agency's operation.[17] This was crucial to the CWA's success since the state committee had to approve local projects before workers could be hired. By moving quickly, the Grand Forks committee assured some of the county's unemployed that they would be working soon.

One of the first actions the CWA national office took was to devise a quota of workers for each state based upon population and the number of people on relief. Under this system North Dakota could initially hire 13,000 people for CWA projects. The state CWA then apportioned this number throughout the state's fifty-three counties. Grand Forks County

DISTRIBUTION BY COUNTIES OF NORTH DAKOTA'S INITIAL CWA JOB ALLOTMENT

COUNTIES	NO. OF JOBS	COUNTIES	NO. OF JOBS
Adams	100	McLean	321
Barnes	329	Mercer	132
Benson	232	Morton	384
Billings	53	Mountrail	260
Bottineau	453	Nelson	266
Bowman	140	Oliver	64
Burke	231	Pembina	230
Burleigh	402	Pierce	134
Cass	784	Ramsey	285
Cavalier	260	Ransom	191
Dickey	278	Renville	269
Divide	248	Richland	385
Dunn	234	Rolette	204
Eddy	130	Sargent	329
Emmons	175	Sheridan	110
Foster	100	Sioux	89
Golden Valley	70	Slope	85
Grand Forks	480	Stark	266
Grant	309	Steele	124
Griggs	103	Stutsman	468
Hettinger	158	Towner	147
Kidder	152	Traill	187
LaMoure	215	Walsh	311
Logan	119	Ward	631
McHenry	325	Wells	205
McIntosh	174	Williams	445
McKenzie	224	TOTAL	13,000

Source: *Grand Forks Herald,* November 23, 1933, p. 8.

was allotted 480 workers, the third highest total in the state behind Cass County's 784 and Ward's 631. Most of these workers were categorized as unskilled but each county could hire a few semi-skilled, skilled, and supervisory personnel. Wages for most workers were set by the national office based upon the cost of living and other local economic factors. Workers in some parts of the country, consequently, were paid at the maximum level: unskilled workers received fifty cents an hour while skilled ones were paid $1.20. Semi-skilled laborers were paid an amount determined by the local committee, which had to be between the figures for unskilled and skilled workers. The few semi-skilled employees in Grand Forks County received sixty cents an hour. CWA employees were limited to thirty hours' work per week; thus Grand Forks County wages ranged upward to a weekly maximum of $15 for unskilled, $18 for semi-skilled, and

PEOPLE EMPLOYED AND WAGES PAID BY THE CWA IN NORTH DAKOTA

Week	People Employed	Wages Paid
1. Dec. 7, 1933	9,717	$106,432
2. Dec. 14, 1933	13,492	186,286
3. Dec. 21, 1933	18,099	256,190
4. Dec. 28, 1933	22,301	290,045
5. Jan. 4, 1934	25,970	354,941
6. Jan. 11, 1934	32,478	455,191
7. Jan. 18, 1934	35,077	517,208
8. Jan. 25, 1934	34,963	353,090
9. Feb. 1, 1934	34,677	329,074
10. Feb. 8, 1934	34,106	332,075
11. Feb. 15, 1934	33,148	321,877
12. Feb. 22, 1934	27,706	258,628
13. Mar. 1, 1934	24,174	234,590
14. Mar. 8, 1934	21,259	220,109
15. Mar. 15, 1934	19,356	195,474

Source: *Grand Forks Herald*, March 24, 1934, p. 10.

$36 for skilled workers. Supervisors made between $18 and $45 per week depending on the technical knowledge required for their positions.[18]

The money that the CWA pledged for its projects was usually limited to paying the wages of the workers and hiring necessary equipment. Local sponsoring agencies, such as county commissions, city councils, and school boards, had to supply the materials to be used. The CWA generally exercised some flexibility on this point, however, and it paid for some of the materials used on some Grand Forks County projects. As an additional way to help the local economy, the CWA, whenever possible, used supplies purchased from community merchants. Consequently, the program's economic impact went beyond paying local people to work; it was also a boon to local businesses and to those individuals who had equipment, such as trucks and teams of horses, to rent.[19]

Grand Forks residents signed up for the new employment opportunities in great numbers. By December 2, Judge Lebacken's office had registered 1,500 unemployed people who wanted work. Obviously, not all applicants could be employed. Under CWA guidelines, preference was to be given to veterans with dependents. Beyond that, county officials could use their discretion in deciding whom to hire. Not surprisingly, many who were not employed alleged that those in charge practiced favoritism in their personnel practices. Judge Lebacken, however, defended the agency's methods, arguing that the local committee hired people based solely upon the number of dependents they had.[20] "Selection, based on the needs of the individual," he explained, "has been hurried and in some cases, perhaps, persons most deserving of jobs may have been overlooked. But this will be straightened out later."[21]

The first workers were put on the Grand Forks County CWA payroll on November 27, 1933. Unemployed people continued to register at a rapid pace, and by mid-December over 2,300 county residents had signed up for CWA jobs. At the same time, the state CWA committee decided that economic conditions dictated that Grand Forks County's quota of workers should be increased from 480 to 532. In reality, this meant that the county could pay for 15,960 hours of labor per week; how those hours were to be distributed was up to Judge Lebacken and the local committee. Grand Forks CWA leaders tried to give employment to as many people as practicable. At first, they experimented with having two groups of workers on some projects; each group worked thirty hours one week and none the next. Soon, however, this plan was abandoned in favor of merely cutting the hours of all employees to twenty-four per week. In implementing the CWA in Grand Forks County, the primary considerations of the local officials were simply to get projects approved and to put needy people to work.[22]

Thirty of the Grand Forks County projects directly benefitted the City of Grand Forks. Several others financed municipal improvements in the towns of Larimore and Northwood and in the smaller villages of Manvel, Thompson, Reynolds, Niagara, Kempton, and Inkster.[23] Obviously, most utility systems, public buildings, and parks were in cities and towns, prompting historians David R. Goldfield and Blaine A. Brownell to declare that the CWA was a "clearly urban-oriented" agency.[24] Nevertheless, the CWA had quite an impact on rural Grand Forks County. Non-urban projects in the county were most often those repairing gravel roads and community schools. Eighteen proposals led to the graveling of approximately thirty-seven miles of county roads, and one related undertaking called for the removal of rocks which made traveling down one rural road difficult. Most of the graveling projects were not completed by the time the government discontinued the CWA in March 1934, or much more road repair would have been done in the county.[25]

Eleven projects were for repair of rural school buildings, and additional ones requested renovations to institutions in Larimore, Northwood, Inkster, Niagara, Thompson, and Manvel. Most of these repairs were minor, usually consisting only of painting walls and ceilings and varnishing desks and woodwork. Occasionally, electrical systems were improved, new furniture was made, or remodeling was done on the buildings. In Thompson, repairs to a barn belonging to the school district included installing a new roof, a sliding door, and partitions between the stalls. J. E. McLean, the inspector of CWA projects in the county, noted that wooden stalls were replacing concrete ones on which "the horses were always getting hurt." Most of the school repair projects cost only a few hundred dollars each (many were under $300) and were completed within a few days' time. Only two, those for schools in Larimore and Manvel, called for major renovations, and both were incomplete when the CWA expired.[26]

Other municipal projects in the county's smaller towns included graveling city streets in several communities, making repairs to the city halls of Northwood and Inkster, building cisterns in Northwood and Kempton, moving the Kempton city dump, converting the Northwood power plant into a storage shed for city vehicles, and constructing a dam at Thompson.[27] The *Northwood Gleaner* offered the opinion that the repairs to that community's city hall made it look "several hundred percent better."[28] The paper also explained that the two cisterns being built in the city were "considered really essential" but that two additional ones were needed.[29] In his official justification for building a cistern at Kempton, J. E. McLean wrote that "the Village did not have any water supply in case of fire and water supply for drinking purposes was also short."[30] Increasing the supply of drinking water was also a concern of the residents of Thompson; they received CWA funding to build an earthen dam, sixty-five feet long and five feet high, to help them store water. "The dam has raised the water level in the wells at Thompson," McLean noted, "higher than they [sic] have been for years."[31] The citizens of Kempton further improved their city by buying an acre of land a mile from town to use for a new city dump; they cleaned up the old dump ground on the edge of town and planted a garden in it.[32]

Like the rural areas and small towns of Grand Forks County, the City of Grand Forks used CWA funds to improve its public schools. This aspect of the agency's work caused perhaps the greatest physical change in the city as all but one of the municipal schools were painted and repaired. The community's only high school at the time, Central, underwent major renovations. Workers redecorated all classrooms and hallways, repaired the roof, installed a new heating system, made a new entrance to the gymnasium, moved classroom partitions, and repaired the plumbing. Construction work on the older of two junior high schools included converting two classrooms and a cloakroom into one large music hall with a band platform installed at one end of the new room. Similar remodeling was done at the city's five elementary schools as well. At Wilder School, for example, CWA employees reshingled half of the roof, removed twenty-five trees and did other landscaping work, painted all classrooms and hallways, installed four electric lights in each classroom, replaced 40 percent of the school's blackboards, varnished the woodwork, made a bookcase, repaired library books, built a stairway, and installed a new floor in part of the building. In all, CWA projects expended over $35,000 to repair Grand Forks city schools. Moreover, none of these construction jobs was completed under the CWA; instead, each was transferred to the FERA where additional monies were spent to upgrade the community's educational facilities.[33]

Perhaps the next most significant group of CWA projects in Grand Forks included those designed to improve the city's parks. Of the six programs in this category, the most ambitious was a recreational ski slide built in Lincoln Park at a cost of almost $3,500. The finished structure was 100 feet high, and the trip down the slide covered 175 feet from the tower to the ground. CWA workers also remodeled the bath house at the swimming pool in Riverside Park, reconstructed the club and caddy house at the golf course in Lincoln Park, and built six new holes on the Lincoln course.[34] All of these projects were typical of local CWA undertakings throughout the country.[35] Park landscaping was the primary focus of two Grand Forks projects. Along the bank of the Red River from Riverside Park to Central Park, a distance of 1.8 miles, CWA workers removed all underbrush and trimmed trees. They also removed 300 trees from a median in University Avenue where it passes through the campus of the University of North Dakota and replanted them on the school's grounds and throughout city parks.[36]

Civil Works Administration funds were also utilized to improve other Grand Forks public facilities. The agency financed remodeling of the county courthouse basement to provide club rooms for several area veterans' groups. In addition, its money paid for repairs to the city auditorium, the municipal airport, and the National Guard armory rifle range. CWA employees modernized the city's sewer and street lighting systems, and they repaired the Grand Forks public library and the books in it. They converted an old pump house into a storage building for city equipment and built a similar structure for state highway department vehicles. The CWA cleaned up the city's dump, repaired its incinerator, and installed pipes to extend water service to several area cemeteries.[37]

A few projects headquartered at the University of North Dakota (UND) gave employment to additional county residents. These programs were under the control of the state and federal CWA committees; consequently, the people working on them were not included in the county's employment quota. Several hundred workers, including students, made improvements to the university's physical plant, repaired the bindings on thousands of library books, and collected historical data on former students and other North Dakotans. The engineering department conducted a survey of township lines in ten counties of the state, including Grand Forks, and installed benchmarks at one-mile intervals throughout the region. The economic impact of these special projects is readily apparent in an examination of the CWA payrolls for the county during two weeks in January 1934. For the week ending January 4, county projects employed 665 people and paid them $13,504.71 in salary. The state and federal projects at UND utilized 586 additional workers at salaries totalling $8,227.55. Two weeks later, 1,094 employees on county projects earned $17,742.20 while 352 workers at the university received checks for $6,108.18.[38]

One of the more political, as well as more interesting, incidents concerning the CWA in Grand Forks County took place on the university campus. North Dakota's governor, William Langer, had for some time pressured state employees to subscribe to a newsletter published by his supporters. State workers paid 5 percent of their salaries for the newsletter and Langer put the money into his campaign fund. The governor decided to sell newsletter subscriptions to CWA workers at the same 5 percent rate state employees paid even though CWA employees, including those on the state programs being managed at UND, were answerable not to the Republican Langer but to the state committee appointed by the Democratic administration in Washington. Not too surprisingly, when Harold McDonald, a young Bismarck man who worked for Langer, came to UND to solicit subscriptions, a group of students grabbed him and threw him into the coulee that bisects the campus. Langer was removed from office in 1934 after being convicted of conducting the subscription scheme, and McDonald pleaded guilty to conspiracy to obstruct administration of an act of Congress. When, however, Langer and his codefendants were, upon retrial, ultimately acquitted of all charges, the state's attorney allowed McDonald to withdraw his plea, leaving him with a clean record.[39]

If one shortcoming of the CWA in Grand Forks County was that its workers were subjected to the governor's political pressure, another was that it was operated almost exclusively for men. This was also true of the national program in which women comprised slightly less than 10 percent of the agency's workers.[40] Judge Lebacken, while promising to find jobs for county women, stated flatly that his primary goal was "to get men to work."[41] This attitude, reflective of that of the CWA hierarchy, was anchored in the traditional belief that earning a family's living was the man's responsibility and ignored the fact that many women were heads of households. Local officials wanted to put women to work on projects that they considered suitable for their gender, and they apparently never entertained the idea of employing women on construction jobs. Instead, women with expertise in home economics were employed to conduct a survey of farm houses in the county and gather information on needed services that the CWA might provide. Female nurses were hired to provide in-home care to the needy ill, and women teachers conducted classes in sewing, cooking, typing, stenography, and other subjects for women on relief. Other women taught classes for the CWA in such areas as choral singing, public speaking, and English as a second language. One project employed several women for three weeks to sew clothing to be distributed to the poor. Women also worked on some of the projects conducted at the university and in clerical jobs in the local CWA office. In all, 211 women worked on CWA projects in Grand Forks County in contrast to 2,181 men, a proportion (8.8 percent) comparable to that of the figures for the agency as a whole.[42]

The Civil Works Administration was created to last only through the winter of 1933–1934. On March 4, 1934, the Roosevelt administration decided to end the program on May 1, but the termination date was later moved up to March 31 because the agency was running out of money. At the same time, officials in Washington resolved to cease operation of the program on March 15 in a few states including North Dakota. Thus, Grand Forks County officials were forced to finish the agency's work with only eleven days' notice. As a result, some projects were never completed. A few were turned over to local government entities for completion, and others were transferred to the FERA's Work Division. On March 15, all CWA employees in the county were laid off except for a few office workers who were given an additional week to wrap up the agency's business.[43]

Other and bigger "make-work" programs followed the Civil Works Administration as Roosevelt and the people of the country struggled to get out of the Depression. Yet, the CWA's brief existence proved significant in Grand Forks County. Certainly, without the CWA, no road or building repair would have been possible that winter. Other worthwhile improvements such as cleaning up parks, planting trees, and repairing books would never have been undertaken. But more important than the physical improvements of local facilities was the economic impact the agency had on the county. An analysis of all Grand Forks County CWA projects shows that between November 1933 and March 1934, the agency pumped slightly more than $230,000 into the local economy. Most of this was in the form of wages, but small portions were used to rent equipment and to purchase necessary supplies. In addition, local governmental units spent almost $17,000 on agency projects, mostly for materials bought from county merchants. Thus, the Civil Works Administration was responsible for approximately a quarter of a million dollars going into the pockets of the 2,392 people on its Grand Forks payroll and into the cash registers of countless businesses throughout the county.[44] Critics charged that the CWA did virtually nothing to get the country out of the Depression, but that was never its intent. What it did was simply to help the people of Grand Forks County (and every other county in the country) survive one of the harshest winters of the worst economic crisis in the history of the United States.

NOTES

1. The best treatment of the Roosevelt economic relief agenda is William E. Leuchtenburg, *Franklin D. Roosevelt and the New Deal, 1932–1940* (New York: Harper and Row Publishers, 1963).

2. *Northwood Gleaner*, December 22, 1933, p. 2.

3. D. Jerome Tweton and Theodore Jelliff, *North Dakota: The Heritage of a People* (Fargo: North Dakota Institute for Regional Studies, 1976), p. 157.

4. Richard Lowitt, *The New Deal and the West* (Bloomington: Indiana University Press, 1984), p. 10.

5. An earlier draft of this article was written in a seminar conducted by Stanley Murray at the University of North Dakota. UND history professors D. Jerome Tweton and Albert I. Berger were kind enough to read the original version and offer suggestions for improvement. The author chose to incorporate some of those suggestions into the final draft of the article while ignoring others. Consequently, he alone is responsible for the article's contents and conclusions.

6. The Roosevelt program of work relief is considered in Arthur W. Macmahon, John D. Millett, and Gladys Ogden, *The Administration of Federal Work Relief* (Chicago: Public Administration Service, 1941; reprinted, New York: Da Capo Press, 1971). The impact of that program on the urban areas of the country is presented in Mark I. Gelfand, *A Nation of Cities: The Federal Government and Urban America, 1933–1965* (New York: Oxford University Press, 1975), pp. 23–156; and in Zane L. Miller and Patricia M. Melvin, *The Urbanization of Modern America: A Brief History* (2nd ed.; New York: Harcourt Brace Jovanovich, 1987), pp. 158–72.

7. The FERA is discussed in Doris Carothers, *Chronology of the Federal Emergency Relief Administration: May 12, 1933, to December 31, 1935* (Washington: United States Government Printing Office, 1937; reprinted, New York: Da Capo Press, 1971); James T. Patterson, *The New Deal and the States: Federalism in Transition* (Princeton, N.J.: Princeton University Press, 1969), pp. 50–73; Douglas L. Smith, *The New Deal and the Urban South* (Baton Rouge: Louisiana State University Press, 1988), pp. 62–85; and "Employment Conditions and Unemployment Relief: Federal Emergency Relief Work Since May 1933," *Monthly Labor Review* 38 (May 1934): 1050–54.

8. *Grand Forks Herald*, November 14, 1933, p. 1; November 16, 1933, p. 10; January 5, 1934, p. 1; and February 13, 1934, p. 4.

9. Forrest A. Walker, *The Civil Works Administration: An Experiment in Federal Work Relief, 1933–1934* (New York: Garland Publishing, Inc., 1979), p. 37.

10. *Ibid.*, pp. 33, 58–59, and 67; and *Grand Forks Herald*, November 9, 1933, p. 1.

11. See Walker, *The Civil Works Administration*; and Bonnie Fox Schwartz, *The Civil Works Administration, 1933–1934: The Business of Emergency Employment in the New Deal* (Princeton, N.J.: Princeton University Press, 1984).

12. A recent excellent examination of the impact of the New Deal at the local level is D. Jerome Tweton, *The New Deal at the Grass Roots: Programs for the People in Otter Tail County, Minnesota* (St. Paul: Minnesota Historical Society Press, 1988).

13. Walker, *The Civil Works Administration*, pp. 36–37; and *Grand Forks Herald*, November 9, 1933, p. 1; November 23, 1933, p. 8; November 24, 1933, p. 10; and November 27, 1933, p. 7.

14. Macmahon, Millett, and Ogden, *The Administration of Federal Work Relief*, p. 35; Walker, *The Civil Works Administration*, p. 28; and *Grand Forks Herald*, November 23, 1933, p. 8; and November 28, 1933, p. 7.

15. *Grand Forks Herald*, November 23, 1933, p. 4.

16. *Ibid.*, November 9, 1933, p. 1; November 23, 1933, p. 8; December 15, 1933, p. 4; and December 23, 1933, p. 4; Walker, *The Civil Works Administration*, p. 38; and Schwartz, *The Civil Works Administration*, p. 38.

17. Microfilm Reel Number 35, Orin G. Libby Collection No. 807, "North Dakota: Federal Relief Programs, 1933–1943," Elwyn B. Robinson Department of Special Collections, Chester Fritz Library, University of North Dakota, Grand Forks, North Dakota (hereafter "OGL Collection"); and Walker, *The Civil Works Administration*, p. 84.

18. *Grand Forks Herald*, November 17, 1933, p. 8; November 23, 1933, p. 8; and December 1, 1933, p. 4; "Employment Conditions and Unemployment Relief: Work and Policies of Federal Civil Works Administration," *Monthly Labor Review* 38 (February 1934): 312–14; and Microfilm Reel Number 35, OGL Collection, project numbers 1232 and 1238. The state's quota was later increased to 17,000. A special additional allotment of 20,000 workers was granted the state because of drought conditions in the western part of the state; Grand Forks County received none of these agricultural positions. See *Grand Forks Herald*, February 7, 1934, p. 5.

19. *Grand Forks Herald*, November 21, 1933, p. 10; November 23, 1933, p. 8; December 6, 1933, p. 1; and January 22, 1934, p. 8; and Microfilm Reel Number 35, OGL Collection, project numbers 191 and 1237.

20. *Grand Forks Herald*, November 27, 1933, p. 1; December 3, 1933, p. 9; December 4, 1933, p. 8; and January 24, 1934, p. 4; Christy Brown to Judge A. M. Christianson, February 12, 1934, Microfilm Reel Number 52, OGL Collection; Walker, *The Civil Works Administration*, pp. 106–07; and Schwartz, *The Civil Works Administration*, p. 101.

21. *Grand Forks Herald*, December 4, 1933, p. 1.

22. *Ibid.*, November 27, 1933, p. 1; December 15, 1933, p. 9; December 16, 1933, p. 12; December 20, 1933, p. 10; December 23, 1933, p. 10; and December 27, 1933, p. 8. Eventually, over 4,100 people registered for CWA jobs in Grand Forks County. See *Grand Forks Herald*, January 28, 1934, p. 9. Later, hours for workers on rural projects were reduced further to fifteen per week. See *Grand Forks Herald*, January 21, 1934, p. 2.

23. Microfilm Reel Number 35, OGL Collection.

24. David R. Goldfield and Blaine A. Brownell, *Urban America: From Downtown to No Town* (Boston: Houghton Mifflin Co., 1979), p. 369.

25. Microfilm Reel Number 35, OGL Collection, project numbers 184, 193, 194, 195, 197, 200, 201, 202, 203, 205, 206, 207, 883, 1233, 1241, 1242, 1950, 1955, and 2497.

26. *Ibid.*, project numbers 1103, 1229, 1230, 1231, 1232, 1235, 1240, 1947, 1957, 1958, 2493, 2511, 2512, 2871, 2872, 2875, 3332, and 3402. Quote is from project number 1958.

27. *Ibid.*, project numbers 196, 888, 889, 1236, 1237, 1238, 1239, 1898, 1959, 2508, and 2516.

28. *Northwood Gleaner*, February 9, 1934, p. 2.

29. *Ibid.*, December 22, 1933, p. 3.

30. Microfilm Reel Number 35, OGL Collection, project number 2516.

31. *Ibid.*, project number 1898.

32. *Ibid.*, project number 2508.

33. *Ibid.*, project numbers 198, 208, 209, 210, 211, 212, 213, 886, and 1402; and *Grand Forks Herald*, March 25, 1934, p. 10.

34. Microfilm Reel Number 35, OGL Collection, project numbers 185, 186, 187, and 218.

35. Walter W. Pangburn, "Recreational Development in 1933," *The American City* 49 (February 1934): 55.

36. Microfilm Reel Number 35, OGL Collection, project numbers 188 and 214.

37. *Ibid.*, project numbers 189, 190, 191, 215, 216, 217, 1379, 1948, 1949, 1951, 2496, 2522, 2974, 3045, and 4228; and *Grand Forks Herald*, November 25, 1933, p. 10; December 30, 1933, p. 10; February 7, 1934, p. 5; February 15, 1934, p. 9; and March 1, 1934, p. 10.

38. *Grand Forks Herald*, November 28, 1933, p. 7; December 24, 1933, p. 14; January 11, 1934, p. 2; January 14, 1934, p. 14; January 20, 1934, p. 5; January 24, 1934, p. 8; February 4, 1934, p. 13; and March 11, 1934, p. 9; and Microfilm Reel Number 35, OGL Collection, project numbers 199 and 1401.

39. *Grand Forks Herald*, November 23, 1933, p. 8; March 3, 1934, p. 1; April 12, 1934, p. 1; April 17, 1934, p. 1; November 7, 1935, p. 1; November 9, 1935, p. 1; and December 20, 1935, p. 1; and Elwyn B. Robinson, *History of North Dakota* (Lincoln: University of Nebraska Press, 1966), p. 410.

40. Schwartz. *The Civil Works Administration*, pp. 156–80.

41. *Grand Forks Herald*, December 4, 1933, p. 8.

42. *Ibid.*, December 3, 1933, p. 9; December 5, 1933, p. 10; December 21, 1933, p. 10; December 22, 1933, p. 12; December 23, 1933, p. 10; December 24, 1933, p. 14; January 4, 1934, p. 10; January 10, 1934, p. 3; January 11, 1934, p. 2; January 27, 1934, p. 10; January 28, 1934, p. 9; and March 25, 1934, p. 10; and Gilbert Moskau to John E. Williams, February 17, 1934, Microfilm Reel Number 52, OGL Collection.

43. *Grand Forks Herald*, March 5, 1934, pp. 1 and 7; March 16, 1934, p. 12; and April 1, 1934, p. 11; Microfilm Reel Number 7, OGL Collection; and Microfilm Reel Number 35, OGL Collection, project numbers 197, 203, 215, 1241, 1898, and 2522.

44. *Grand Forks Herald*, December 31, 1933, p. 9; and March 25, 1934, p. 10; and Microfilm Reel Numbers 35, 49, and 52, OGL Collection.

The PWA in Tampa:
A Case Study

CHARLES B. LOWRY

This selection illustrates the difficulty that the New Deal often encountered in achieving cooperation between federal and local agencies. It also shows how the private sector, in this case, exacerbated this difficulty, largely through the impact of a colorful and determined local figure, Ernest Kreher, head of a Tampa shipbuilding and engineering company. In Baton Rouge, Louisiana, friction between Harold Ickes, head of the federal Public Works Administration, and the state legislature, among others, delayed the construction of a bridge across the Mississippi. Initially proposed in 1933, it was not built until 1940.

THE stock market crash of 1929 and the ensuing depression resulted in the first attempts by the federal government to stimulate the economy on a massive scale at a time of economic collapse. President Hoover moved reluctantly in this area, but Franklin D. Roosevelt, although poorly grounded in economics, avidly applied Keynesian economic theory to an extent unacceptable to his Republican predecessor. The programs of the New Deal affected vast numbers of individuals and businesses, both large and small. The Tampa Shipbuilding and Engineering Company (T. S. & E.) founded by Ernest Kreher, a German immigrant, was among the latter. In 1932, while Hoover was still in office, Kreher attempted to acquire a federal loan to construct a much-needed dry dock in Tampa. Fully five years were to

From the *Florida Historical Quarterly*, 52 (April 1974), 363–380.

elapse before he completed his venture. His successes and failures illustrate how Roosevelt's administration sought to implement programs to end
the depression. The Tampa dry dock project is, moreover, a good case
study of the adaptations in national legislation which are necessary to meet
local needs and the flexibility of the New Deal in making such adaptations.

Among the important tools used by the Republicans to allay the impact of the depression was the Reconstruction Finance Corporation (RFC),
created in January 1932 "to lend money to banks, railroads and other institutions threatened by destruction." It was claimed, however, that "because of Hoover's misgivings about federal intervention, the agency made
so little use of its powers that it frustrated the intent of Congress."[1] Though
the policies of the RFC during the latter part of the Hoover years did
much to reduce the impact of the depression on larger business organizations, thus slowing the downward economic spiral, they ultimately failed
to give relief to those most in need. This was the result of the fundamen-
tal philosophy "that prosperity would somehow trickle down from the
banks and industries to workingmen at the base of the economic pyra-
mid."[2] Ernest Kreher had used this philosophy as his justification in applying for an RFC loan.

Born January 10, 1874, in Limbach, Germany, Kreher followed his
brother Paul to Philadelphia in 1890, and two years later he moved to
Tampa. Like his father, he was a mechanical engineer, and he helped
build ships, dredges, and machine works.[3] After the Spanish-American War
he worked for a while for Krause and Wagner, a small machine works, but
by 1900, with the aid of Captain S. L. Varnedoux, he had bought out his
employers and established the Tampa Foundry and Machine Works. In
1917 he acquired Varnedoux's holdings, and changed the name of the company to Tampa Shipbuilding and Engineering Company. The business
prospered during the post-war years.[4]

Kreher saw in the dry dock enterprise a partial solution to a number of
economic problems—including the burgeoning demands of Gulf shipping, the financial wants of his company, the strengthening of Tampa's
role within the shipping industry, and the relief of the hard-pressed, unemployed mechanics and common laborers of the Tampa Bay area—by
creation of both temporary and permanent jobs. He was quick to grasp the
opportunities offered by the RFC, particularly when Harvey Couch, RFC
director, began urging businesses in 1932 to make application for "small
self-liquidating loans."[5] By September 17 Kreher had a loan application
pending before the RFC in Washington.[6] Processing moved slowly, how-

ever, and before it was completed Roosevelt had taken office, and the precise role of the RFC was in doubt. Kreher was informed in early June 1933 that his request should be resubmitted with increased collateral.[7]

Enlisting the assistance of the port development committee of the Tampa Chamber of Commerce, the loan was pursued with increasing urgency.[8] A report prepared by construction engineer Francis L. Judd of the Chamber was submitted to the RFC, January 24, 1933. It met the two major RFC objections that had delayed granting the loan. First, the RFC was reluctant to aid the "construction of a facility which may be competitive with other institutions of like nature located in other sections of the country."[9] Against this objection the Judd Report argued that a dry dock of 10,000 tons' lifting capacity located in Tampa would not compete for existing business, but would rather fill a very pressing demand for repairs in the form of "new business." The report provided a comprehensive account of shipping conditions from New York to Galveston, thereby presenting a cogent argument to back the Tampa company's contention.[10] The RFC's second objection concerned the "nature of the security, that is, what disposition the corporation [RFC] could make of the dock should the Company [T. S. & E.] default in their obligations."[11] In the initial loan application, waterfront properties had been offered as collateral. Kreher, though irritated by the request for further securities, agreed to submit "whatever else is required within the Company's ability and within reasonable limits."[12] At this juncture the RFC proposed a loan of $600,000, if the company would invest $100,000 of its own or borrowed funds. This remained the RFC's answer to the question of collateral.

Kreher pursued three alternatives to the RFC objection and solution. First, he attempted to borrow an additional $100,000 from banks in Tampa, but this was virtually impossible since T. S. & E. was encumbered by predepression debts.[13] State property taxes were also in arrears for $57,000.[14] Besides, banks in Tampa and elsewhere would have had difficulty floating such a loan.[15] With little prospect for a bank loan, Kreher next sought to convince the RFC that his company had already "invested over $100,000 in the dry dock enterprise by partly dredging the basin, by building the railroad tracks leading from the main line to the [site of the] dry dock, [and] by furnishing the necessary cranes."[16] When the RFC rejected a real estate appraisal submitted by Kreher, he asked Elbert L. Smith, assistant to the RFC's director, to suggest an acceptable appraiser.[17] Kreher's hopes for the success of this second alternative increased after Washington asked that he revise his loan proposal, appending to it three appraisals of work already done. Official reaction thus seemed increasingly favorable toward granting the loan.[18] Kreher's third solution was to increase the amount of his collateral. The original appraisal of his collateral had been devalued, but it still totaled $298,812.50, besides the $750,000 value of the completed dry dock which would be added.[19] Kreher now offered securities worth $1,922,250, the bulk of his wealth, which included most of his company assets.[20] He was offering to commit his entire financial holdings to the venture. Ultimately the latter two approaches were combined but only after a new obstacle, governmental reorganization, had been surmounted.

The question of what the new Roosevelt administration would do with the RFC had figured increasingly in the negotiations for the loan. By March of 1933 Kreher concluded "that the reorganization of the RFC must be over first before really anything can be done but we are very glad to be able to prepare our case in the meantime."[21] He and other company officials were thus aware of the RFC's reorganization; they did not realize how complete that activity would be. By June the RFC had withdrawn "from virtually all activities except those of banking and supplying money for other federal offices," and many of its operations had been transferred to other government agencies.[22] As a result the Federal Emergency Administration of Public Works, the PWA, inherited the question of the Tampa loan, and some of its new regulations were to have marked effect on both acquisition of the loan and the construction of the dry dock. Important in this regard was the requirement that "non-Federal public works had to be 'self-liquidating' in character. They had to . . . earn income."[23] From the time of the initial application to the RFC, Kreher had envisioned the prospective dry dock project as extremely lucrative, and in all the documentation he stressed the profitable future of the venture.[24] Thus, the loan application satisfied the requirement of self-liquidation. Significant also for the job of constructing the dry dock were certain requirements concerning labor on PWA-financed projects. The agency stipulated that all contracts contain provisions that "no individual shall work more than 30 hours in any 1 week." It also established a Southern wage scale of $1.00 per hour for skilled labor and forty cents for unskilled labor.[25] The PWA insisted that its officials had to come to Tampa for on-site inspection.[26] In the case of the Tampa company, these regulations contained cause for conflict, and in time they would impede the progress of the project.

Although Kreher had attended *Realschule*, secondary school, only to third grade, he had displayed an engineering ability equal to university study.[27] He was acquainted with many influential Hillsborough politicians and businessmen and was held in high regard by professional and academic engineers in the state.[28] He had built a considerable fortune by his

own talents and was justly proud of his achievements. Such a man was unlikely to adapt well to supervision by government-appointed engineers. In
the ensuing events a subordinate role proved to be intolerable to Kreher,
who was long accustomed to wielding authority. Circumstances thus required of PWA officials an ability to handle not only challenging engineering problems, but also more important and complex problems of
interpersonal relations. The first appointees had difficulties with both.

Two other provisions of the National Industrial Recovery Act (NIRA)
were to be of major importance in the imbroglio surrounding the construction of the Tampa facility. First, the original act of 1933 allowed the
federal government to make an outright grant of thirty percent of the face
value of the loan. Under the Relief Appropriation Act of 1935 the grant was
increased by executive order to forty-five percent.[29] Kreher later buttressed
his arguments against on-site supervision with the fact that his firm never
received a grant of either thirty or forty-five percent.[30] Secondly, because
of the potential for graft, open competitive bidding was required on PWA
work. This requirement was designed to protect contractors and officials,
and in the long run millions of federal and local dollars were saved by ruling out favoritism in the award of contracts.[31] Although necessary for NIRA
projects, the use of competitive bids in the case of the dry dock had pe-
culiar and unfortunate results.

With the creation of the PWA in June 1933, and the final disposition
of the role of the RFC, the dry dock loan application neared completion.
Kreher now had documentation for the loan transferred from the RFC to
the PWA.[32] He included the final supplement (June 30, 1933) to the Judd
Report, embodying both increased collateral and the investment already
made in the dry dock project. After appraiser's devaluations the total came
to $1,754,812.50.[33]

At first Kreher had pursued the loan with little outside assistance.[34]
Judd had compiled the statistics for the revised RFC loan application of
January 24, 1933, but Kreher had done all the other paper work.[35] George
F. Corrigan, a Tampa businessman and president of the Franklin D.
Roosevelt-for-President Club of Hillsborough County, had solicited the assistance of Congressman J. H. Peterson of Hillsborough, as did former
mayor and publisher D. B. McKay.[36] Some moral support came from two
members of T. S. & E.'s board of directors: W. H. Jackson of the law firm
Jackson, Dupree, and Cone, and George B. Howell, president of the Exchange National Bank of Tampa. Their assistance was significant during
the problem-filled period of construction.

In the final stages of negotiation Kreher found more support both at the state level and in Tampa. On July 6, Tampa businessmen, meeting at the Chamber of Commerce, pledged $10,000 in order to present four major programs to the PWA for consideration, including funds for a study headed by R. V. Brown "to prepare & present a program for a floating dry dock for Tampa, which will have long term benefits for employment."[37] This belated financial support was of no help to Kreher. Five days later a state board was organized to coordinate as "intermediary between public, semi-public and private interests" on the one hand and the federal government on the other.[38] Although this plan did not become effective soon enough to influence the pending loan, it meant Florida was one of ten states that acted to assist the federal government and to accelerate "the creaking machinery which seemed inadequate to meet the emergency of the situation."[39] Finally, Hillsborough County and the City of Tampa organized the Tampa Industrial Recovery Committee, which at its July 25 meeting pledged active support of five proposals, including a dry dock project for which the PWA was asked to supply $180,000 and the participating company the balance of $420,000.[40] This was obviously an unrealistic proposal considering the nationwide collapse of local credit.[41] R. V. Brown, by this time conversant with Kreher's activity, informed the Tampa Committee that the dry dock project was "fairly safe" already.[42] While none of these efforts affected the status of the loan, they did demonstrate that there was a strong commitment in Florida to the PWA concept and a desire to expedite its implementation. These efforts could only help Kreher's activities.[43]

Kreher traveled to Washington in late June 1933 to be present at the last loan negotiations. He was assisted by G. B. Howell, who made several trips during succeeding months.[44] Their activities were expedited by the support of United States Senators Park Trammel and Duncan Fletcher and Congressman Peterson, all of Florida.[45] In addition many Tampans were in Washington during the height of Kreher's negotiations lobbying for aid for various city programs.[46] In particular, Angel L. Cuesta, Jr., son of the cigar magnate, as president of the Tampa Industrial Recovery Committee sought to assist in securing the dry dock loan.[47] Perry G. Wall, former mayor of Tampa, solicited the aid of Postmaster General James Farley, Roosevelt's patronage chief, but to no avail.[48] When the PWA Cabinet Board first refused the loan, all Kreher's efforts seemed in vain, but subsequent deliberations quickly reversed this decision.

Kreher's optimism continued until he returned to Tampa in January 1934, and he wrote thanking those who had supported efforts to secure the loan.[49] At the same time he advised the newspapers that details had yet to be worked out and that no workmen should apply for jobs, even though approximately 300 men would ultimately be employed on the project. Tampa businessmen congratulated themselves because the facility promised considerable employment, even after construction, and a marked increase in port activity.[50] The need for the dry dock had been clearly demonstrated, and it was hoped that Kreher's experience and ideas would "make the structure superior to any dock in the country as far as methods of operation are concerned."[51]

Kreher remained in Washington for several weeks arranging details of the loan contract.[52] Formalities were not completed until January 22, 1934, when the mortgage papers were filed in the circuit court in Jacksonville. This was something of an event, with Kreher's brother Max, G. B. Howell, W. H. Jackson, and Jacksonville banker George S. Vardaman, Jr., on hand for the proceedings. Kreher then returned to Tampa to begin work on the dry dock, which he hoped could be completed quickly.[53] By this time the first deposit of $156,000 had been made in the Exchange National Bank of Tampa, enhancing prospects for an early completion.[54] However, just as the acquisition of the loan had been delayed by numerous unforeseen difficulties, so too was construction. After his return to Tampa, Kreher learned that he could not utilize the money on deposit to begin the construction until he had submitted detailed plans. He was disturbed that the PWA had not requested them three months earlier when the loan had been approved. The company was now obliged to pay interest on the money it could not use.

This PWA requirement caused no great delays or financial losses since certain construction materials had not yet arrived and work could not begin anyway.[55] But, by early March 1934 there were problems. James E. Cotton, state engineer for the PWA, was demanding that the company advertise for competitive bids on equipment. The question of competitive bids was a matter of contention for many months, although Cotton had realized that the application of this requirement to the Tampa company was anomalous. Kreher wanted to use second-hand equipment, and he considered the PWA requirement impractical. He also believed that his company could build much of the equipment more cheaply than it could be contracted. Cotton's refusal to approve either equipment acquired earlier or the purchase of rejected railroad ties, which were serviceable for dry dock construction and which could be purchased at a considerable savings, aggravated Kreher.

These difficulties were exacerbated by the fact that Cotton and his representatives were frequently absent from Tampa. Kreher complained that this caused delay and forced him to pay unnecessary interest on funds tied up in the bank.[56] This problem should have been resolved by the appointment of L. P. Slattery, March 13, 1934, as supervising engineer for the dry dock work, but it was not.[57]

The question of wages was a major impediment to construction.[58] Kreher's original loan application to the RFC had budgeted labor costs, and final negotiations had been based on a scale of thirty to sixty cents an hour for common laborers and sixty-five to seventy-five cents an hour for mechanics, i.e., skilled labor. However, based on PWA requirements, Cotton ordered Kreher to pay laborers forty cents and mechanics $1.00 an hour.[59] Kreher pressed for a lower wage based on the Civil Works Administration (CWA) scale, arguing that this was necessary if workers in his shipyard, not on the dry dock project, were to be fairly treated. He noted that the original contract had stipulated such a scale, and claimed that he would be hard pressed to pay the higher scale. He pointed out that on the Clearwater Bridge job, an RFC project, laborers were receiving twenty-five cents per hour and mechanics a similar amount. Government policy was obviously inconsistent. Kreher also argued that since the PWA called for $1.00 an hour for mechanics with a maximum of thirty hours per week the incentive of his foremen would be destroyed if they could not receive a higher rate. His arguments contained flaws. For example, PWA policies allowed foremen not a maximum, but a minimum of $30.00 per week. The contention that the scale would destroy incentive was true only if Kreher himself refused to pay foremen more than the minimum scale for skilled labor. Kreher, aware of the inconsistencies in his arguments, proposed alternative solutions to resolve the problem:

> All this can be avoided by our paying the code rates throughout our establishment. Or if you will raise the Shipbuilders' and Ship Repairers Code Scale [thus raising the minimum his competitors would have to pay] to a minimum of $1 for mechanics and 40¢ for laborers, the same as you ask us to pay, we would readily agree to such an arrangement as long as we are placed on an equal footing with our competitors.[60]

In early April Cotton instructed Kreher to engage only men sent by the local office of the National Re-Employment Service. The loan contract provided that employees should be selected from lists submitted to the company.[61]

In the main, these conflicts arose because the loan contract originally submitted to the RFC had not been modified to conform to the PWA code, and because the state PWA officials were making no exceptions in applying the code. The wage-scale debate could not be resolved until it was decided who had authority to make a final disposition. On April 5 Cotton called for temporary suspension of construction on the dry dock until Washington reached a decision concerning the wage dispute. By this time all concerned were growing testy. Kreher was mailing numerous complaints to Washington, and Cotton, supported by Major Crawford, an assistant to the deputy administrator of the PWA, was demanding that Kreher stop going over his head.[62]

On the issue of bids, Cotton and Slattery now agreed that the terms of the loan required all mortgage (dry dock) construction to be done under contract rather than by force account, that is, direct construction by the borrower. This solution was wholly unacceptable to T. S. & E., and the last week of April found Howell and Jackson in Washington representing the company. Their trip was successful, for PWA officials decided that construction could be done by either force account or contract bids. They recommended that Howell and Jackson apply to Cotton to use the method most acceptable to the company. Returning to Florida, both men met with Cotton on May 8, and the request to complete the construction in five sections by force account was again discussed and forwarded to Washington.[63]

At the same time, the wage-scale issue moved towards resolution. At first it was thought Cotton would make the decision.[64] However, it was ultimately determined that Hunt, legal advisor of the PWA, would make the final disposition after Cotton's recommendations were received in Washington.[65] Kreher, though he was not without misgivings in the matter, assumed that Cotton had recommended not only the use of force account construction but also the application of the lower CWA scale. He expected a decision from Washington no later than May 20.[66] That decision called for wages based on the higher PWA scale. These were minimum standards.

Kreher expressed the fear that George Hills, who was a power in Democratic politics,[67] had influenced the appointment of Cotton and was now swaying the decision on the force accounts in order to get the dry dock building account for his own Jacksonville engineering firm.[68] But the second portion of the decision favored T. S. & E. on the issue of force accounts and the company immediately began the preliminary construction. The dry dock project was divided into five different force accounts. Some work had already been done on the four preliminary divisions—preparation of the site, re-conditioning the dredge, dredging operations, and construction of the mooring pier. By early October this work was completed,

and on the thirteenth of the month the company reached a milestone
when the first rivet was driven in the dry dock, the fifth and final force account, which was to be built in five sections.[69]

Although the completion of the dry dock now appeared a certainty, serious new friction arose as Ernest Kreher and his brother Max attempted
to work with Slattery, the resident engineer, and Arthur D. Newkirk, PWA
supervising engineer for Tampa. Because of their disputes the auspicious
beginning of construction in October proved by the end of the year a false
start, and the solution had to be found in Washington. As early as May, in
a complaint to Washington about Slattery, Ernest Kreher wrote:

> It seems to me that the P.W.A. when given sufficient security should let
> the borrower alone and that the Trustee Bank should be responsible for
> the correctness of the expenditures. An engineer's inspection once a month
> would be ample to check up on the job. . . .
>
> We have in our office a P.W.A. accountant, who gets $4000 per annum.
> We have also a supervising engineer [resident engineer] who evidently gets
> more than the accountant. We had to hire two typists to help the engineer.
> He now uses only one. I do not think we were obliged to do so, but gladly
> did it to keep the peace. The engineer's name is L. P. Slattery. He is the
> brother of Mr. Slattery, the undersecretary for Mr. Ickes. The accountant
> is Mr. William W. Terrell, a personal friend of Mr. Parker, Chief Ac-
> countant of the P.W.A. Both of these are plainly patronage jobs. It is an
> awful feeling when you have to watch your own money being squandered
> in political debts and useless red tape to give sham employment.[70]

Kreher's contention with Slattery served as a backdrop for his more serious struggle with Newkirk. This conflict derived from both personality
differences and divergent views about control and implementation of dry
dock construction. On November 1, Newkirk met with Kreher and William
Lamb, Slattery's successor, in hopes of correcting what he considered in-
efficiencies in organization.[71] He recommended that Kreher remove his
brother Max from contact with the construction; Newkirk regarded Max's
presence as both detrimental and obstructive. He also called for the replacement of Mr. Crowell, superintendent of construction. Although agree-
ing with Kreher that Crowell, a man with considerable experience in dry
dock construction, was competent, Newkirk felt that he hindered construction because he depended heavily on Kreher for advice concerning
the work, rather than on Lamb, the new resident engineer. Newkirk declared Crowell unsuitable because he was superannuated, had "very poor"
eyesight, and was perhaps suffering from the after-effects of a stroke. These

allegations were transparent. Newkirk actually wanted "both your president [Ernest Kreher] and your Secretary [Max Kreher] to confine their duties to those customarily performed by such officials of well organized corporations and that they refrain from attempting to personally attend to any routine duties usually performed by subordinates. We particularly feel that the efficiency of your president is greatly lowered and that the work on Docket No. 45 [the dry dock] is suffering through his tendency to give his personal attention to minor matters."[72]

Newkirk finally drove Kreher to open opposition when, on December 4, he announced that he would assume the interviewing and hiring of workers from among the men sent by the National Re-Employment Service, a job that had until then been the responsibility of Max Kreher. Ostensibly, Newkirk wished to ascertain the reason for "a considerable amount of comment which has come to the writer's ear regarding the quality of labor furnished by the National Re-employment Service."[73] Newkirk also submitted to Kreher for his consideration and signature a contract between T. S. & E. and Lamb. This contract was to go into effect on December 16, and its terms gave Lamb complete control of construction, organization of the labor force, discharge of employees, and ordering of materials. In addition, the company was to have responsibility only for the engineering design of the dry dock, subject to Newkirk's approval. Lamb was to work full-time on the dry dock, for which services the company was to pay him $375 per month, and he could not be removed without the "consent of the Administrator."[74]

Kreher balked at what seemed an arbitrary extension of Newkirk's authority. Refusing to sign the contract after consultation with the company's board of directors, he decided to resist Newkirk's attempted coup. He now called on Deputy Administrator Fleming of the PWA to arrange an investigation of the whole affair and began to organize his own case and to rally support.[75] On January 4, 1935, dry dock construction stopped altogether, and lay-offs began. [76]

From January through April Washington was inundated by mail on behalf of the Tampa company. Senators Trammel and Fletcher, Representative Peterson, and Harold Ickes, together with other PWA officials, received letters from a wide variety of people and organizations—Mayor Chancey of Tampa; U.S. District Attorney H. S. Phillips; Claude H. Stone, an IRS tax investigator and friend of Peterson; R. R. Roberts and H. M. Day, both employees of T. S. & E.; W. L. Sherrod (chairman) and W. M. Wagnon (secretary) of the newly formed employees organization at the company; and American Legion Post Number Five. Perhaps the most desperate pleas came in the form of a petition signed by 242 of the company's employees which was addressed to Ickes.[77]

On January 9 F. E. Schnepfe, PWA director of project division, arrived in Tampa to investigate the conflict and inspect the construction conducted under Newkirk and Lamb. Kreher believed Schnepfe's report would be unbiased and most probably favorable to his position.[78] By the sixteenth Kreher was in Washington to present his case to the PWA, and he was still there in July.[79] He contended that both Newkirk and Lamb had unwarrantably extended their authority. Furthermore, he asserted, the two men had caused a prolongation of the time necessary to complete the dry dock, extremely poor workmanship, high construction costs, and a serious increase in injuries to laborers. In short, Kreher charged both PWA officials with grossly inefficient if not negligent management. As usual, his arguments were well documented, and he had potent support from Schnepfe and George F. Widmyer, PWA officials who had investigated the situation in Tampa.[80] The supporting testimony, which was most telling, came from a curious source—Lykes Brothers, the insurance company that wished to cancel T. S. & E.'s accident insurance.

Lykes Brothers Insurance of Tampa held the Tampa company's account for Hartford Accident and Indemnity Company. By December the accident rate on the job had increased so sharply that Alex Findlay, a marine surveyor from the American Bureau of Shipping, was sent to investigate.[81] Findlay blamed the high incidence of injuries on the mismanagement of Lamb and Newkirk. He also criticized the quality of work under their supervision, stating that much of the work already completed would have to be redone.[82] Lykes Brothers decided that the policy could be maintained only with a fifty percent rate increase and the removal of Newkirk and Lamb from control. They agreed to continue the policy until the issue was resolved in Washington, but only so long as work on the dry dock was shut down.[83]

Kreher won on all points when the PWA, in July 1935, resolved the various disputes in his favor. Kreher and PWA officials on July 30 made arrangements to renew construction, and work resumed two days later after an eight-month hiatus. The entire project was given over to the management of the Tampa Shipbuilding and Engineering Company, thus removing the possibility of interference. The PWA also appointed Widmyer, who viewed Kreher's case sympathetically, as its chief representative to the dry dock job.[84] The two men enjoyed a cooperative relationship, and work on the dry dock progressed rapidly.[85]

The dry dock was about fifteen percent complete when the stoppage occurred in January 1935. With the resumption of work in August Kreher predicted that completion would take a year.[86] By April 1937 all but the final section of the dry dock was in operation, and Kreher took preliminary steps to secure another loan from the PWA.[87] Late in the month the yacht *Alva*, owned by Commodore W. K. Vanderbilt, put in for dry dock at Tampa to repair a broken propeller shaft.[88] Four years before, in April 1933, the *Alva* had come to Tampa for dry docking.[89] This visit had resulted from mistaken information that Tampa had sufficient facilities, and the captain and crew of the *Alva* had been chagrined by the useless voyage.[90] Kreher noted the coincidence with amusement and justifiable pride in the fact that the vessel could at last be serviced.

NOTES

1. William E. Leuchtenburg, *Franklin D. Roosevelt and the New Deal* (New York, 1963), 71n.

2. Samuel Eliot Morison and Henry Steele Commager, *The Growth of the American Republic*, 2 vols. (New York, 1962), II 648–49.

3. Karl H. Grismer, *Tampa: A History of the City of Tampa and the Tampa Bay Region of Florida* (St. Petersburg, 1950), 351–52.

4. D. B. McKay, ed., *Pioneer Florida*, 3 vols. (Tampa, 1959), III, 380–81.

5. *Tampa Tribune*, September 20, 1932.

6. Kreher to James Hardin Peterson, January 14, 1935, box 74, James Hardin Peterson Papers, P. K. Yonge Library of Florida History, University of Florida, Gainesville. Hereinafter cited as PP.

7. Peterson to Kreher, June 6, 1933, box 74, PP.

8. *Tampa Tribune*, September 14, 1933.

9. Report compiled by Francis L. Judd for Kreher arguing the loan then pending before the RFC, January 24, 1933, 1, box 74, PP.

10. *Ibid.*, 2–15.

11. *Ibid.*, 1.

12. *Ibid.*, 15–16.

13. Grismer, *Tampa*, 246, 277–78.

14. *House Reports*, 78th Cong., 1st sess., no. 938, "Investigation of Certain Transactions of the Tampa Shipbuilding Co." [successor to T.S.&E.], 13–14.

15. Kreher to Peterson, April 7, 1933, box 74, PP.

16. *Ibid.*, March 7, 1933, box 74, PP.

17. Kreher to Smith, March 18, 1933, box 74, PP.

18. Peterson to Kreher, March 15, 1933, box 74, PP.

19. Supplement to the Judd Report, June 30, 1933, *passim*, box 74, PP.

20. Kreher to Peterson, March 7, 1933; Kreher to H. M. Waite, deputy administrator, PWA, March 8, 1934, box 74, PP.

21. Kreher to Peterson, March 18, 1933, box 74, PP.

22. *Tampa Tribune*, June 27, 1933.

23. U.S. Federal Works Agency, Public Works Administration, Division of Information, *America Builds: The Record of PWA* (Washington, 1939), 6.

24. Supplement to the Judd Report, November 25, 1932, 2–5, box 74, PP.

25. U.S. Federal Works Agency, *America Builds*, 39, 84–85.

26. *Ibid.*, 79.

27. McKay, *Pioneer Florida*, 380.

28. T.S.&E.'s board of directors included Angel L. Cuesta, Sr., Peter O. Knight, and Perry G. Wall. George B. Howell played an important part in the success of the dry dock project. Kreher was associated with Howell continually from these years until his death. He remained a consulting engineer to Tampa Shipbuilding Co., the successor to T.S.&E. organized by Howell in 1940, and was on the board of directors of Marine Bank and Trust Co., which in 1944 selected Howell as its president. See also Jacksonville *Florida Times-Union*, August 2, 1933, March 10, 1934, April 7, 1935.

29. U.S. Federal Works Agency, *America Builds*, 43.

30. Kreher to Waite, March 8, 1934; Kreher to M. C. MacDonough, director of engineering, PWA, March 27, 1934; Notes: Addressing the officials of the PWA by Ernest Kreher with reference to suspension of Docket 45, February 1935, box 74, PP.

31. U.S. Federal Works Agency, *America Builds*, 88–89.

32. Kreher to Peterson, January 14, 1935, box 74, PP.

33. Supplement to the Judd Report, June 30, 1933, 1–2, box 74, PP.

34. *Tampa Tribune*, September 14, 1933.

35. Judd was well informed on issues related to rivers, harbors, and shipping, and his expertise was often used during these years by state and city officials. Jacksonville *Florida Times-Union*, January 3, 1934. March 25, 1935; Fred Carter, acting secretary, Tampa Chamber of Commerce, to Peterson, June 6, 1935; J. A. Waterman, chairman of the Tampa Chamber of Commerce Aviation Committee, to Judd, June 7, 1935; Peterson to Waterman, June 10, 1935, box 88b, PP.

36. Corrigan to Peterson, December 30, 1932; McKay to Peterson, March 28, 1933; Peterson to McKay, April 5, 1933, box 74, PP.

37. *Tampa Tribune*, July 7, 1933.

38. *Ibid.*, July 12, 1933.

39. U.S. Federal Works Agency, *America Builds*, 52.

40. *Tampa Tribune*, July 26, 1933.

41. U.S. Federal Works Agency, *America Builds*, 37, 61–63.

42. *Tampa Tribune*, July 26, 1933.

43. An indication of Florida's enthusiasm for the PWA was the alacrity with which the state overcame constitutional obstacles blocking municipal and county governments from acquiring federal funds. Jacksonville *Florida Times-Union*, October 10, 1934. In general, Florida actively pursued federal funds. For instance, during the period up to January 1934, over 100 separate applications were made to the RFC and PWA for major public work projects. Jacksonville *Florida Times-Union*, January 24, 1934. A detailed account of all federal projects for this period is to be found in "Minutes of Semi-Annual Statewide Coordination Meeting of Federal Agencies in Florida, Held Under Auspices of the National Emergency Council, December 19, 1935, Jacksonville, Florida," box 111, James B. Hodges Papers, P. K. Yonge Library of Florida History. Hereinafter cited as HP.

44. *Tampa Tribune*, September 14, 1933.

45. Kreher to C. D. Cordner, president, Propeller Club of the Port of Tampa, September 14, 1933, box 74, PP. Senator Trammel sought the aid of President Roosevelt with Secretary Ickes for the "Tampa Harbor Project." Presumably their conversation referred to the proposed dredging of the harbor, but it is likely that Trammel also solicited aid for the dry dock. Franklin D. Roosevelt to Park Trammel, May 18, 1934, box 6, Park Trammel Papers, P. K. Yonge Library of Florida History.

46. Jacksonville *Florida Times-Union*, July 17, 29, 1933.

47. *Ibid.*, July 14, 1933.

48. Wall to J. B. Hodges, chairman, State Democratic Executive Committee, telegram, September 11, 1933; Hodges to Wall, September 18, 1933, box 89, HP.

49. Kreher to Peterson, September 26, 1933, box 74, PP.

50. *Tampa Tribune*, September 14, 1933.

51. *Ibid.*, January 23, 1934.

52. Kreher to Cordner, September 14, 1933, box 74, PP.

53. *Tampa Tribune*, January 24, 1934.

54. Kreher to Peterson, January 14, 1935, box 74, PP.

55. *Ibid.*, January 31, 1934. Kreher's complaint that the PWA request for plans caused delays and cost money is somewhat at odds with his assertion in June, 1933 that "complete drawings are ready and every preparation has been made to start work immediately on this project." Supplement to the Judd Report, June 30, 1933, box 74, PP.

56. Kreher to Waite, March 8, 1934, box 74, PP.

57. This term is used interchangeably with resident engineer in the sources. Slattery's position should not be confused with that of Arthur D. Newkirk, who was supervising engineer of the PWA for all of Tampa and Hillsborough County. H. A. Gray, director, Inspection Division, PWA to Peterson, March 21, 1934, box 74, PP.

58. Kreher, as a standard business practice to help maintain low costs in his yard, budgeted for low wages in his contract bids. In the construction of the dry dock, in its later operation, and in the construction of ships for the Maritime Commission and the United States Navy this was a partial cause of the financial embarrassment of his firm when wage costs exceeded budgeted estimates. *House Reports.* 78th Cong., 1st sess., no. 938, 1–35, *passim.*

59. Kreher to Waite, March 8, 1934, box 74, PP.

60. Kreher to MacDonough, March 27, 1934, box 74, PP.

61. Kreher to Peterson, April 7, 1934, box 74, PP.

62. *Ibid.*

63. Jackson to Peterson, May 11, 1934, box 74, PP.

64. Peterson to Kreher, copy of telegram, May 8, 1934, box 74, PP.

65. Jackson to Peterson, telegram, May 8, 1934, box 74, PP.

66. Kreher to Peterson, May 9, 1934, box 74, PP.

67. William T. Cash, *History of the Democratic Party in Florida, Including Biographical Sketches of Prominent Florida Democrats* (Live Oak, Florida, 1936), 209; Hills, president of George B. Hills Company, Jacksonville, to Hodges, July 27, 1933; Hills to Charles W. Hunter of the Tallahassee *Florida State News*, July 27, 1933; Hodges to Hills, July 28, 1933, box 147, HP; Wayne Flynt, *Duncan Upshaw Fletcher, Dixie's Reluctant Progressive* (Tallahassee, 1971), 168.

68. Kreher to Peterson, May 26, 1934, box 74, PP.

69. *Tampa Tribune*, October 14, 1934.

70. Kreher to Peterson, May 26, 1934, box 74, PP.

71. The author did not discover the precise time of or reason for Slattery's replacement in those documents perused in this research. As early as 1936, Slattery was serving as PWA state engineer inspector in Columbia, South Carolina, presumably the position he left Tampa to fill. Both his salary and authority were considerably improved by this move. U.S. Civil Service Commission, *Official Register of the United States 1936, Containing a List of Persons Occupying Administrative and Supervisory Positions in the Legislative, Executive and Judicial Branches of the Government, Including the District of Columbia* (Washington, 1936), 154. Kreher's opinion of Lamb was even lower than that which he held of Slattery. He was especially critical of Lamb's engineering ability. Kreher to Peterson, January 14, 1935, box 74, PP.

72. Newkirk to T.S.&E., November 2, 1934, box 74, PP. Newkirk's perception of Kreher was obviously misconceived in view of the high opinion held for the latter's engineering work by all who had occasion to examine it. In fact it was Kreher's business acumen which was ultimately found wanting, as is evidenced by the denouement of his firm. See *House Reports*, 78th Cong., 1st sess., no 938, 1–35, *passim.* This report is somewhat confused concerning the actual stock transactions relative to the 1940 re-organization of T.S.&E. The matter is amply clarified in *Kreher et al. v. United States*, No. 47413, 87 *Federal Supplement*, 881–88, *passim*, 1950; and *Ernest Kreher, Max Kreher, Paul Kreher, Trustees of Tampa Shipbuilding and Engineering Company, a dissolved corporation, v. the United States*, No. 47413, *Cases Decided in the United States Court of Claims December 1, 1949, to February 28, 1950, with Report of Decisions of the Supreme Court in Court of Claims Cases*, 355–56.

73. Newkirk to T.S.&E., December 4, 1934, box 74, PP.

74. Contract between T.S.&E. and William B. Lamb, undated, unsigned, box 74, PP.

75. Kreher to Peterson, December 31, 1934, box 74, PP.

76. *Ibid.*, January 14, 1935, box 74, PP.

77. Various documents, January to April 1935, box 74, PP.

78. Kreher to Peterson, January 14, 1935, box 74, PP.

79. Jacksonville *Florida Times-Union*, June 28, July 27, 1935; *Tampa Tribune*, July 27, 1935.

80. Notes: Addressing the officials of the PWA, February 1935, box 74, PP.

81. Glen Evins, manager of Lykes Brothers Insurance Agency, to Kreher, December 27, 1934, box 74, PP.

82. Findlay to T.S.&E., January 11, 1935, box 74, PP.

83. Evins to Kreher, January 12, 1935, box 74, PP.

84. *Tampa Tribune*, August 1, 1935.

85. Kreher to Peterson, April 12, 1937, box 74, PP.

86. *Tampa Tribune*, August 1, 1935. Under some apparent duress Kreher signed the completion certificate for the dry dock December 28, 1936. The fifth section was not at that time complete. Kreher to Peterson, July 27, August 4, 1937; and Horatio B. Hackett, PWA assistant administrator, to Peterson, August 7, 1937, box 76, PP.

87. Kreher was not to repeat his earlier success in this second round of negotiations with the PWA. In fact, the exchanges between Washington and Tampa grew increasingly heated, and Kreher contemplated a civil suit to recover damages. His grievances were ultimately litigated in 1948–1950 to the Supreme Court. See April 1937, *passim*, box 74, PP; April 1937 to August 1937, *passim*, box 76, PP; *Kreher et al.* v. *United States*, No. 47413, 87, *Federal Supplement*, 881–88.

88. Kreher to Peterson, April 12, 1937, box 74, PP.

89. *Tampa Tribune*, June 18, 1933.

90. Kreher to Peterson, April 7, 1933, box 74, PP.

"State of Emergency": Key West in the Great Depression

GARRY BOULARD

In Key West the depression began in 1926. In 1934 the governor of Florida, David L. Sholtz, responded to a request from the city that he assume all legal powers of Key West's government. Under this unusual transfer of authority, the Federal Emergency Relief Administrator of Florida, the colorful Julius F. Stone, Jr., was assigned the responsibility of providing direct relief. A plan to jump-start work relief and to begin a limited rehabilitation of the city became a comprehensive effort to create a tourist mecca, transcending the attack on unemployment. On a small scale, this is an example of irony in history, or unintended consequences. The Key West program was also marked by a strike threat by relief workers, who were not ordinarily expected to employ labor-union tactics. After the first year of federal relief activity in Key West, Stone declared that the most important change was in people's minds: hopelessness and resignation gave way to hope and confidence. (See Durward Long, "Key West and the New Deal, 1934–1936," Florida Historical Quarterly, 46 [January 1968], 218.)

On July 1, 1934, elected representatives of the Key West City Council and the Monroe County Board of Commissioners drew up two separate resolutions that said the same thing. The island city, the ordinances declared,

From the *Florida Historical Quarterly*, 67 (October 1988), 166–183.

was more than $5,000,000 in bonded debt, with at least eighty percent of its inhabitants on the welfare rolls. City services were reduced to almost a non-existent level as employees went without pay for weeks at a time. Furthermore, the lack of a viable industry to employ local residents, coupled with a greatly decreased island tax base, foretold a dire economic future for the city.[1]

The resolutions said that nine factors led to Key West's economic misfortunes: the loss of cigar manufacturing; the reduction of the island's army base; the abandonment of Key West as a naval base; removal of the Coast Guard's district headquarters; abandonment of the city as a port-of-call for the Mallory Steamship Lines' passenger ships; the reduction of freight from Key West to Cuba; the collapse of the island's once-vibrant pineapple-canning business due to higher tariffs on pineapples; the decrease in revenues from the fishing industry as a result of the Great Depression; and the removal of the sponge industry from Key West to mainland Florida.[2]

The resolutions jointly declared Key West in a "state of emergency" and agreed to hand over local powers of the island to the state of Florida and Governor David Sholtz.[3] Key West was bankrupt, the resolutions said, and its financial plight, as one magazine reporter later observed, "was just about the most desperate in the country."[4]

Through an agreement of dubious legality, Sholtz quickly announced that the entire island of Key West was, in effect, on welfare relief, and hence under the jurisdiction of the newly formed Federal Emergency Relief Administration (FERA) and that agency's director for the southeastern United States region, Julius Stone, Jr.[5]

Upon acceptance of the resolutions, Sholtz contacted Stone, sending him copies of the city and county documents, and said that since federal relief funds were administered through FERA he thought it wise that Stone act as the government's agent in Key West, heading up rehabilitation efforts there. Stone quickly accepted the assignment from Sholtz, replying that he was committed to helping "the citizens of Key West" once again to "become self-supporting."[6]

Key West's financial troubles coincided with the nation's, which by 1934 was in its fifth year of the worst economic crisis in the country's history. But the elements of high unemployment, bulging relief rolls, and a dwindling tax base—a potent combination of fiscal trouble that severely tested the financial capabilities of dozens of municipalities throughout the United States—were only part of the island's story. Even without the ripple-effect ravages of the depression, Key West would undoubtedly have faced a troubled financial future in the mid-1930s due to its inability to diversify economically, its reliance upon several dying local industries, and the drop in property values relating to the Florida land boom and bust of the 1920s.[7]

Since its discovery in the early 1500s by the Spanish, who dubbed it "Cayo Hueso" or "Island of Bones," Key West had been subjected to an inordinate amount of financial speculation, real estate development and redevelopment—even for a Florida community.[8] By 1822, the island was sold for $2,000 by a Spaniard, Juan Salas, to a Mobile, Alabama, businessman, John Simonton, and during the next century it became an American possession, a haven for pirates and Cuban fishermen, a United States military outpost, and finally, the rainbow's end for colorful entrepreneur Henry Flagler's extension of his Florida East Coast railroad to Key West.[9]

The island's population grew to nearly 2,700 by 1855, when an influx of New Englanders and English Bahamanians were attracted to Key West's growing business of salvaging ships wrecked on the coral reefs. In the next five decades, thousands of island residents and Cuban immigrants further contributed to Key West's population boom by becoming part of a bustling cigar-manufacturing business that employed more than 11,000 people by 1910, the same year the island's population passed the 25,000 mark.[10]

Key West also became the home of a vigorous pineapple-canning enterprise, which employed more than 750 residents in 1910, and a sponging industry that hired hundreds of men harvesting millions of sponges, making the island responsible for almost ninety percent of all the sponges sold in the United States. In addition, the island remained an important strategic naval base for the United States government, prompting the flow of thousands of dollars from servicemen's pockets into the local economy.[11]

But by 1930, a series of unfortunate market upheavals threatened to undo the previous century's economic progress in Key West. A federal tariff change in the late 1920s, upping the fee for imported pineapples, caused Key West pineapple canners first to reduce and then eliminate their island operations. Greek immigrant spongers in Tarpon Springs, Florida, reduced their operating costs and produced sponges at a greater rate, thus eating into a Key West sponge market already under siege by the introduction of synthetic sponges on the Atlantic coast. Finally, the once-giant Key West cigar industry largely transferred its operations beginning in the late 1880s to Tampa, where city tax incentives and modern facilities proved an irresistible attraction. Between 1920 and 1930, Key West lost more than 14,000 payrolled jobs due to unforeseen developments in these three most vibrant industrial-based enterprises. During this same decade, the city's population dropped from 19,350 to 12,831.[12]

Where once in the mid-1880s Key West was listed as the richest city per capita in the United States, by 1934 its per capita monthly income was less than $7.00. On top of the $5,000,000 bonded debt was a bond interest of more than $270,000, past due operating expenses of $150,000, and more than $113,000 in unpaid city employee salaries.[13]

The abdication of local sovereignty to FERA in 1934 was a matter of fortuitous circumstance. The year before, President Franklin D. Roosevelt had proposed the formation of FERA as part of his New Deal package of reforms designed to reinstate morale among the 5,500,000 unemployed workers collecting local, state, and federal relief. FDR wanted, he said, such relief recipients to be "paid in cash for the work that they do on all kinds of public works."[14]

FERA, then, according to its planners, became an agency that not only strived to provide work for the idle relief recipient and served as a mechanism to funnel unspent energies into public works, it also was a program masked as "self-help" rather than charity.[15]

According to the intra-departmental FERA rules promulgated by the Roosevelt administration, all FERA funds had to be used by FERA agents to pay directly to relief recipients who "voluntarily" worked a set number of hours per week on a public project.[16] The emphasis, according to both Roosevelt and Harry Hopkins, the national FERA director, was on work and the psychological effect of giving projects to those who were idle, depressed, and despondent. "Give a man a dole and you save his body and destroy his spirit," Hopkins said. "Give him a job and pay him an assured wage, and you save both the body and the spirit."[17]

Hopkins divided the nation into several districts and appointed Julius Stone, Jr., a former New York state welfare administrator, director of the FERA southeastern region, which included Florida, Puerto Rico, and the Virgin Islands.[18]

Stone was a 1926 Harvard graduate who caught both Hopkins's and Eleanor Roosevelt's attention for his administrative talent and skill as a departmental leader in New York in 1933. When Stone arrived in Key West in July 1934, he brought with him eleven FERA staffers, including a public relations writer, several engineers, architects, and city planners, and at least one lawyer.[19]

The challenge before Stone was daunting. Not only was he charged with the economic and spiritual revitalization of the entire city, but he was also immediately placed in the center command position of a constitu-

tionally questionable governmental arrangement which saw all local powers of authority abrogated to his control. Stone was allowed carte blanche
leverage to change or amend the city charter, hire or fire any number of
relief workers, and, perhaps most importantly, to use the more than
$2,000,000 relegated to his district from FERA almost any way he saw fit.[20]

Stone gave every evidence of enjoying such unprecedented collective
powers; he told the local *Key West Citizen* several weeks later, "With a
scratch of my pen I started this work in Key West, and with a scratch of
my pen I can stop it—just like that!" He also wisely realized the inherent
publicity value of the island's "state of emergency." Within days of Stone's
arrival, the FERA press office churned out story after story on Stone's acceptance of the emergency powers and the economic lot of Key West. "I
knew it didn't mean a thing," Stone later said of the officially declared
state of emergency, "but I thought it sounded pretty dramatic. So did the
newspapers. It put us on the front page in practically every city in the
country, and a lot of editors remembered the story and kept checking up
every so often on what we were doing here. It was the first publicity lift we
got."[21]

The state of emergency did, indeed, capture press attention. Within
two days after the official city-county declaration, two of the major national
wire services reported the story, supplemented by lengthy accounts in the
*New York Times, New York Herald Tribune, Atlanta Journal, Miami Her-
ald,* and *Chicago Tribune.*

But Key West's woes would not be solved by any amount of imaginative publicity drum-beating. The island's problems were seemingly infinite,
varied, and demanding of immediate attention. Perhaps the greatest short-
range demand concerned what to do with the tons of garbage piling up
on city streets and vacant lots, long neglected by the garbage haulers who
months earlier had resigned their jobs due to a lack of pay. "If someone
had constructed small bungalows, say 42 feet x 20 feet with a 9 foot ceil-
ing, the garbage and trash would have filled 176 such bungalows," one
writer observed.[22]

With the enthusiasm of a Yankee entrepreneur, Stone began to organize the more than 10,000 relief recipients into what he called the "Key
West Volunteer Corps." He spoke in front of crowded city hall assemblies
and exhorted the downtrodden to "make Key West a spotlessly clean town."
Stone told the crowd, according to one of his assistant engineers, "your city
is bankrupt, your streets are littered and filthy; your homes are rundown
and your industry gone. We will begin by cleaning up. Then we will re-
build."[23] Within days more than 1,000 volunteers began signing up, form-

ing a line three city blocks long, to work an average of thirty free hours a week cleaning up the garbage. Within the next several weeks more than 4,000 people had volunteered.[24]

As some twenty trucks were put into action hauling off the city trash and wreckage, Stone began devising more projects to rehabilitate the community and provide yet more work for the FERA volunteers. Stone's wide range of projects exhibited both his ability to target problems that might later be turned to an economic advantage and his proclivity toward whimsical, celebratory theater.[25]

Thus, Stone's program to renovate the small residential wood-frame houses known as "conch houses" won instant popular approval as both an aesthetic improvement and potential money-making venture. At the same time his formation of a Key West Volunteer Corps marimba band and his move to honor Cuban patriots through the El Grita de Yara celebration, complete with athletic contests, a parade, and the coronation of a king and queen, was much less successful.[26]

Stone deemed the home renovations essential if Key West was to recover financially. Key West, Stone said, should exploit its greatest strengths—the natural beauty of the island, the Caribbean climate, and the distinctive, intricate detail of its structural architecture—and become a tourist mecca. But to accomplish this task, he noted, immense improvements to the island requiring hundreds of man hours would be needed.

Stone's list included, besides the renovation of more than 200 residences into guest houses, construction of a series of thatched huts on Rest Beach for visitors; painting and cleaning several restaurants, pubs, and nightclubs; remodeling the once-elegant Casa Marina Hotel; landscaping the major thoroughfares; planting dozens of coconut palms; destroying scores of dilapidated buildings; constructing a dozen playgrounds, parks, and at least one major swimming pool; creating an experimental farm where relief recipients could learn to grow their own foodstuff; and organizing classes to teach the natives how to make hats, pocketbooks, mats, and other items from coconut fiber.[27]

Almost all of these goals were reached in a remarkably industrious five-month period from early July to mid-December 1934. But FERA's most ambitious innovations came in two seemingly unrelated pursuits in both 1934 and 1935—real estate and art. When government architects discovered row after row of preserved, solid, hand-hewn, wooden residential homes, Stone and his fellow administrators approached the property owners with the idea of renting the houses to winter tourists. As with Stone's accumulated emergency powers, the legal status of the FERA/Key West rents was dubious. There were no provisions in FERA guidelines for entering into contractural arrangements with private enterprise, let alone individual homeowners. But the property owners were eager to lease their homes with the understanding that after the relief workers renovated, repaired, and painted the structures, and FERA realized a profit for such work on tourist rentals, the properties would be returned to their owners with no financial or legal obligations to FERA, save the commitment to continue renting the homes to tourists.

This was a broad interpretive use of FERA funds and manpower, and, for Stone, a harbinger of more financially suspect deals to come. But the concept worked. In the winter tourist season of 1934–35 enough visitors stayed in the homes to realize FERA's investment and also to give the homeowners a profit. Years later, Stone seemed unconcerned over the potential legal ramifications of the rental-renovations project. "I got away with it," he told writer Richard Rovere, "because we were so far off that no one knew what we were doing, and also because I chose a time when Hopkins was on a long vacation."[28]

Stone's second major innovation evolved from his penchant for publicity. Because tourist brochures in the 1930s advertised certain locations through the means of attractively created sketches and drawings, Stone decided that Key West needed more artists to pursue such creations and that FERA could pay their fees. Even before the formation of the WPA's Federal Arts Project, Key West began, in 1934, its own federally funded artists colony inspired by Stone. Painting oils and water colors of conch houses, beaches, Cuban fishermen, shady lanes, and restful street cafes, the FERA artists produced colorful, pleasant works, some in the popular Diego Rivera style of the day. Artists such as Edward Bruce, Adrian J. Dornbush, and Bill Hoffman took part in the program. Stone also enticed an island lithographer to reproduce the art on post cards and brochures which were distributed nationally in time for the winter season.[29]

Two final Stone-inspired projects garnered decidedly different results. Under the impression that snow-bound Northerners liked to visit places where the natives wore shorts and rode bicycles, Stone rode around Key West on a bike, wearing his shorts, and encouraging local residents to do the same. But this time his lead was not followed. *Key West Citizen* reporter Dorothy Raymer said the residents of the island thought such attire "laughable." Another writer remembered seeing a FERA volunteer arriving in his undershorts, announcing "If Julius Short can come to work in his underwear, so can I!"[30]

Another technique by Stone proved more lucrative. Placing ads in such newspapers as the *New York Times*, *New York Herald Tribune*, *Philadelphia Inquirer*, and *Atlanta Journal*, Stone wrote that Key West was an island of "fantastic plants, Spanish limes, sapodillas, anemones, dates, pomegranates and coco palm . . . sun-streamed, shuttered, balconied houses, the aroma of ardent tropical flowers and the salty sea air." But Stone even specified how long a visitor should stay: "To appreciate Key West with its indigenous architecture, its lands and byways, its friendly people and general picturesqueness, the visitor must spend at least a few days in the city; a cursory tour of an hour or two serves no good purpose. Unless a visitor is prepared to spend at least three full days here, the Key West Administrator would rather he did not come."[31]

If the success of Stone's program must necessarily be measured in terms of how many tourists visited the island, rather than through the traditional social welfare prism of how many residents on relief bettered their economic condition, then the FERA/Key West project was a stunning triumph. More than 30,000 tourists visited Key West during the 1934–1935 winter season. In November, December, January, and February the island's hotels had 7,909 guests, compared with 4,264 the year before, an eighty-five percent increase. Passenger travel into the city by plane, rail, boat, and automobile was up by 42.5 percent. One restaurant reported an eighty-four percent increase in business from the season before, while a laundry service said trade was at its highest level since 1926. The peak of the season was reached in February 1935, when hotels counted 3,214 registered guests compared with 1,278 during the previous season. In addition, the national press lauded the Key West project, with the *New York Times* noting that the FERA program had transferred an "old pirate city" into a "clean and shining tourist haven." *Harper's Magazine* described it as "the New Deal in miniature . . . accomplishing something much better than what had been there before." *American Magazine* claimed that Key West might become a "hot-cha roaring whoopee town. If so, all luck with them—certainly that's better than the desolation of 1934."[32]

The FERA/Key West project was also popular within the New Deal bureaucracy as witnessed by the report of a WPA engineer who wrote to Hopkins after visiting the island in March 1935: "This program has completely changed the attitude of the population of Key West from one of apathy to one of energetic hope. This program bids fair to succeed in rehabilitating a stranded population in its tracks and is one of the most imaginative approaches to the relief problem which I have seen."[33]

In a special brochure produced by the FERA writers and distributed throughout the island at the end of the 1934–1935 winter season the government publicists took note of the successful winter season and claimed: "Nineteen Hundred Thirty-Four began as the darkest year in its history, and the last year, it may be, of the old order with its woes and confusion. What the moral of the story is, the observant visitor will not need to be told. As one of Key West's citizens once pointed out, the day of the pirates is over, and perhaps all the treasure they buried among the keys has long ago been found; but there still is treasure here. It needs only to be discovered, and willing hands to bring it to light."[34]

Perhaps inevitably, though, the casual mixing of private enterprise and government design, coupled with Stone's occasionally boastful pride in his one-man rule in Key West, prompted some critics to look at the FERA/Key West project as socialism in New Deal clothing and Stone as a dictator. Leading the offensive against Stone and the FERA/Key West project was the conservative *Florida Grower* which charged in a March 1935 issue that the "Rule of FERA is the rule of fear." It claimed that Stone was the island's own "Kingfish"—a reference to Louisiana Senator Huey Long, whose Kingfish appellation symbolized both his grandiose manner as well as his strong-arm governing in his native state. "No American city is more completely ruled by one man than is this small island city," wrote the *Florida Grower*, which characterized Stone as a "terrible tyrant. . . . Mr. Stone admits he is the big boss and can do just about as he pleases down there."[35]

Many of the reporters and publications claiming that Stone was enjoying his position of power pointed to his remarks as reported in the *Key West Citizen*: "With a scratch of my pen I started this work in Key West, and with a scratch of my pen I can stop it—just like that!" Even as the FERA/Key West project was winning supportive approval in the press, increasing attention was given to Stone's emergency power status. Wire press reporter Harry Ferguson, in a series of articles, charged that Stone was "the king of a tight little empire consisting of Monroe County. . . . Call it a 'dictatorship', a 'kingdom within a republic', or anything you choose." Even *American Magazine*, in an otherwise favorable profile of Stone, felt compelled to point out that he was "in fact if not in law, the virtual dictator of Key West." In addition, author Ernest Hemingway, who made Key West his home in 1931, proclaimed his criticism and loathing of governmental activities on the island in both his 1937 book *To Have and Have Not* and an earlier *Esquire* article. To some, the implication was clear: Hemingway, through his own stated opinions, was anti-Roosevelt, anti-Hopkins, anti-New Deal, and particularly anti-Stone and FERA's projects in his hometown.[36]

The defense in favor of Stone's one-man rule was easily launched, particularly among Florida newspapers more familiar with Key West's plight. The *Palatka Daily News* editorialized that Stone had brought "new hope and life to Key West," calling him a "regular savior, a modern Santa Claus," and attacking the *Florida Grower* article for its "excessive enterprise." The *Daytona Beach News Journal* said Stone's work put a "bankrupt city back on the map." While a third Florida newspaper wrote, "innuendo cannot besmirch" Stone's record, "Stone need offer no apologies for what has been done at Key West."[37]

What was more difficult to counterattack was the assertion that Stone was irresponsible with government funds, giving loans to several Key West nightclubs and subsidizing a local airline. The *Florida Grower* charged that Stone put up $15,000 for the renovation of the Casa Marina Hotel, while reporter Ferguson said two island nightclubs were redecorated with money from the FERA treasury. "Nowhere else in the United States is the FERA encouraging wine, women, and song," Ferguson wrote. Stone responded to such criticism by noting that both the airline and the nightclubs needed money to survive, but that all such loans had been repaid. "We are happy to say there will be no loss. . . . We spent less than $75,000 a month and part of that went for ordinary relief expenses."[38]

Even though the *Florida Keys Sun* charged that Ferguson's reporting was "disgracing a profession," and that the UPI reporter came to his conclusions by keeping his "eyes rolled upward and bedimmed by the bottoms of beer and whiskey glasses," both Stone and FERA were damaged by the criticisms and in danger of losing the positive press support of the previous year. The precarious nature of such public relations was further evidenced when the *Sarasota Tribune* mockingly called for a "regular department of NCER—Night Club Emergency Relief," in reference to the revelation that Stone had made FERA money available to two Key West nightclubs. All one would need, added the *Tribune*, is a "federal grant with which to lease the building, buy the beer, and hire a floor show."[39]

Equally damaging to Stone's cause in Key West were the attacks on the New Deal in general, and FERA in particular, in the national political dialogue. As early as the summer of 1934 conservative writers were charging that Roosevelt's New Deal program represented government rule at its oppressive worst. The conservative *American Mercury* claimed Roosevelt's "Brain Trusters set about saving the capitalistic system with the New Deal. All they have achieved is to bring the United States nearer to fascism." One author, who argued against a second term for Roosevelt, said that FERA made it possible for millions to "accept these glorified soup-kitchens as something permanent. . . . We are landing back where we started, maybe further back. Federal relief and the several agencies under FERA have, therefore, been a flop." According to historian Arthur Schlesinger, Jr., private enterprise enthusiasts during this same period criticized FERA because they thought it might be the "entering wedge of socialism." Whether in response to such criticisms or as a reflection of Roosevelt's belief the government should not encroach upon private enterprise, the administration in 1935 retreated from the sort of activist, broadly interpreted, morale-building relief programs symbolized by Stone's Key West efforts. A conscious attempt to reduce FERA's funding was undertaken, perhaps to quell any business misgivings prior to the 1936 presidential campaign.[40]

Such policy shifts undercut Stone's political clout and sounded the death knell for the Key West project—even after the devastating hurricane of September 1935 which battered the Florida Keys, leaving hundreds of war veterans hired by the Civilian Conservation Corps dead and the vital highway connecting the island with the mainland in collapse.[41]

Although the city of Key West and the Monroe County Board of Commissioners would petition FERA and Governor Scholtz to end the state of emergency and return their powers of government, FERA's Key West project undoubtedly ended sooner than planned. The conflict over its activities and the stated intentions of the New Deal interfered. While all of Roosevelt's reform programs supported the values of a capitalistic tradition and assumed that after a period of recovery private enterprise would absorb the employee load taken on by relief programs, Stone emphasized the merits of collective planning and the advantages of long-range governmental work relief programs. The use of FERA funds, for example, to buttress such private enterprises as an airline service, hotels, and nightclubs went beyond the confines of New Deal methods, and probably ran contrary to the New Deal philosophy. FERA, as with other New Deal relief programs, was designed to limit governmental interference, to give people work only until the economy rebounded. FERA, said its planners, was never intended to become a vast governing agency employing people in work that they may have enjoyed. On the contrary, FERA was designed to provide low-paying jobs for workers whose every move was monitored by a social service agent. Such work, such pay, and such supervisory methods would eventually prompt all but the most reluctant relief recipients to take work when the private sector offered. With Stone's FERA/Key West project, however, work was often interesting, challenging, and even creative. It was far from a typical FERA program.[42]

Yet Stone's task was not limited to creating work for those on the dole, but to rebuilding a city's economy in hopes of developing the type of city-wide market that would employ hundreds of Key West residents and render such relief programs useless. Stone's concept targeted a long-range goal in Key West, in contrast to the typical New Deal method of attending to immediate problems and assuming better times and a stronger private market in the near future. Viewed as an effort to reconstruct Key West's economic vitality, Stone's program was both innovative and correct. Without the strength of a regular tourist trade, for example, the island had little chance for recovery. Stone, and other community leaders, believed that such industries as cigar-making and pineapple-canning could not be returned to their former preeminence as Key West employers. "It would be a mistake to make it anything but a resort city," Stone told members of the Florida legislature in April 1935. "If you brought in one or two industries, they would drive away the tourists. The industries would not support it [the demand for paying jobs among the residents] and then it would be neither fish nor fowl." Stone admitted to the legislators that his expenditures included such items as paying for home renovations and providing loans to private ventures, but, he explained, "We spent less than $75,000 a month, and part of that went for ordinary relief expenditures. We have cut the relief rolls about twenty-five percent and saved that much." However, Stone exhibited his lack of enthusiasm for administrative accounting by adding, "It is impossible to say just where ordinary relief expenses end and the rehabilitation costs begin."[43]

Even though Stone predicted the need for continued federal and state funds to keep the FERA/Key West project alive for at least an additional five years, the WPA office in Washington declared in the spring of 1936 that the Key West state of emergency would conclude July 1, 1936, marking the return of normal governmental functions as assumed by Mayor William H. Malone, the city council, and the Monroe County Board of Commissioners.[44]

By the fall of 1936, Stone had left Key West to serve as a "trouble-shooter" for a variety of WPA community programs in the southeastern region, while Key West continued its long climb toward recovery, a recovery that by 1941 and 1942 was greatly aided by the influx of servicemen stationed at the naval air base as World War II began.[45]

What writer Elmer Davis called a "history in miniature," and "hope for the future," was over—two years to the date after it began. FERA continued relief efforts on the island, but its rule was now as a submissive branch of the state and city government. Mayor Malone and the city council resumed their elective responsibilities: governing the island, appropriating local funds, hiring and firing city employees, and amending the city charter. Stone's years after the state of emergency were somewhat less distinguished. He returned to Key West in 1940 as a lawyer and investor, but eventually became involved in so many legally suspect financial transactions that he fled the island "practically as a fugitive" for Cuba in 1960. He died in Australia in 1967.[46]

But the FERA/Key West project remained a case study in a municipality's comprehensive rehabilitation. Through an unprecedented cooperative effort between a federally funded agency—however far astray from bureaucratic rules that agency went—and established private enterprise, Key West was able to discover the merits of a new island-wide commerce, greatly reduce local relief rolls, and substantially increase its self-sufficiency. The Key West that went from a sponging, cigar-manufacturing, and pineapple-canning center in the 1920s to one of Florida's most consistently popular tourist havens in the decades following World War II could trace the origins of its transformation to one man—Julius Stone, Jr.—and the unusual, controversial, rehabilitative efforts of FERA during the two years of the island's state of emergency, from 1934 to 1936.[47]

NOTES

1. Marathon *Florida Keys Sun*, July 6, 1934; *New York Times*, July 5, 1934; *Key West Citizen*, July 4, 1934; Harriet T. Kane, *The Golden Coast* (New York, 1969), 76; Joan and Wright Langley, *Key West: Images of the Past* (Key West, 1982), 99; Joy Williams, *The Florida Keys: A History and Guide* (New York, 1987), 125.

2. Durwood Long, "Key West and the New Deal," *Florida Historical Quarterly* 46 (January 1968), 211.

3. *New York Times*, July 5, 1934; Elmer Davis, "New World Symphony: With a Few Sour Notes," *Harper's* 170 (May 1935), 641–42; Marathon *Florida Keys Sun*, July 6, 1934; *Atlanta Journal*, September 6, 1934.

4. Richard Rovere, "Our Far-Flung Correspondent: End of the Line," *The New Yorker* 27 (December 15, 1951), 84.

5. Davis, "New World Symphony," 644; Rovere, "Our Far-Flung Correspondent," 83; Dorothy Raymer, "Notes & antic-dotes," Key West *Solares Hill* 9 (December 1979), 16; Williams, *Florida Keys*, 125–26; WPA/FERA Scrapbook, I, 8–12, Monroe County Public Library, Key West Archives, Key West, Florida.

6. Long, "Key West and the New Deal," 212.

7. Davis, "New World Symphony," 643–44; *New York Times*, August 12, 1934; *Miami Herald*, July 5, 1935; WPA/FERA Scrapbook, IV, 20.

8. Williams, *Florida Keys*, 121.

9. *Ibid.*, 121–23; David Leon Chandler, *Henry Flagler: The Astonishing Life and Times of the Visionary Robber Baron Who Founded Florida* (New York, 1986), 212–25. Edward N. Akin, *Flagler: Rockefeller Partner and Florida Baron* (Kent, OH, 1988), 210–24.

10. Williams, *Florida Keys*, 123; *Atlanta Journal*, September 4, 1934; Rovere, "Our Far-Flung Correspondent," 85–86; Federal Writers' Project, *Florida: A Guide to the Southernmost State* (New York, 1939; reprinted ed., New York, 1984), 198–99.

11. Williams, *Florida Keys*, 130–31; *Atlanta Journal*, September 4, 1934; Nels Anderson, "Key West: Bottled in Bonds," *Survey Magazine* 70 (October 1934), 312–13; Rovere, "Our Far-Flung Correspondent," 84–86.

12. Langley and Langley, *Key West: Images of the Past*, 99; *Atlanta Journal*, September 4, 1934; Davis, "New World Symphony," 643–44; Anderson, "Key West: Bottled in Bonds," 312–13.

13. Williams, *Florida Keys*, contends that Key West in the 1880s was "the richest city per capita in America," largely because of a bustling wrecking industry: "The men wore silk top hats, the ladies served suppers on fine china, on occasion, gold plates. All the wealth was wrecking wealth. Indeed, much of the exotic furnishings that filled the houses, and the formal clothes the people wore, came directly from the foundered ships." 123–25; WPA/FERA Scrapbook, I, 9–14; *Literary Digest*, July 28, 1934; Anderson, "Key West: Bottled in Bonds," 312–13.

14. Press conference 66, November 3, 1933, *The Complete Presidential Press Conferences of Franklin D. Roosevelt*, 25 vols. (New York, 1972), 1–11, 414–15.

15. William W. Bremer, "Along the 'American Way': The New Deal's Work Relief Program for the Unemployed," *Journal of American History* 62 (December 1975), 640–41; Arthur Schlesinger, Jr., *The Coming of the New Deal* (Boston, 1959), 279; Edward Ainsworth Williams, *Federal Aid for Relief* (New York, 1939), 91–95.

16. Williams, *Federal Aid for Relief*, 99; Doris Carothers, *Chronology of the Federal Relief Administration, May 12, 1933 to December 21, 1935*, Research Monograph No. VI (Washington, DC, 1937), 84–89.

17. Bremer, "Along the 'American Way,'" 637; Davis, "New World Symphony," 646; Henry H. Adams, *Harry Hopkins: A Biography* (New York, 1977), 51–55; Schlesinger, Jr., *Coming of the New Deal*, 279–80.

18. Adams, *Harry Hopkins*, 52; Rovere, "Our Far-Flung Correspondent," 83.

19. Davis, "New World Symphony," 645; Raymer, "Notes & antic-dotes," 16; Rovere, "Our Far-Flung Correspondent," 85–86.

20. Davis, "New World Symphony," 645; Williams, *Federal Aid for Relief*, 50; *Miami Herald*, July 5, 1935; Marathon *Florida Keys Sun*, July 6, 1934.

21. Rovere, "Our Far-Flung Correspondent," 86; Raymer, "Notes & antic-dotes," 17; Marvin H. Walker, "Key West Has Its Kingfish," *Florida Grower* 44 (March 1935), 7.

22. Williams, *Florida Keys*, 126.

23. *New York Times*, July 22, 1934; Anderson, "Key West," 313; *Atlanta Journal*, September 7, 1934.

24. *New York Times*, July 22, 1934; *Atlanta Journal*, September 7, 1934.

25. *Atlanta Journal*, September 7, 1934.

26. Rovere, "Our Far-Flung Correspondent," 90; Langley and Langley, *Key West: Images of the Past*, 104–05.

27. *Miami Herald*, July 5, 1935; Williams, *Florida Keys*, 126–28; Federal Writers' Project, *Florida: A Guide to the Southernmost State*, 199; Langley and Langley, *Key West: Images of the Past*, 99–107.

28. Rovere, "Our Far-Flung Correspondent," 88; *Miami Herald*, July 5, 1935; Davis, "New World Symphony," 647–48; WPA/FERA Scrapbook, I, 5–25.

29. *New York Times*, March 30, 1935; Davis, "New World Symphony," 646; Raymer, "Notes & antic-dotes," 16; Langley and Langley, *Key West: Images of the Past*, 106; WPA/FERA Scrapbook, I, 89.

30. Raymer, "Notes & antic-dotes," 16.

31. *New York Times*, December 23, 1934; Williams, *Florida Keys*, 127.

32. *Miami Herald*, April 1, 1935; WPA/FERA Scrapbook, VII, 9; Walker, "Key West Has Its Kingfish," 7; Langley and Langley, *Key West: Images of the Past*, 100; *New York Times*, March 30, 1935; Davis, "New World Symphony," 642; John Janney, "Recovery Key," *American Magazine* 119 (May 1935), 148.

33. Weekly report of Joseph Hyde Pratt, regional engineer for the WPA southeastern region of the United States. February 28 to March 6, 1935, Harry Hopkins Collection, Box 56, Florida Field Reports, National Archives and Records Administration, Franklin D. Roosevelt Library, Hyde Park, New York.

34. Galleys to *Key West Guide Book* (Key West, 1935), 6–7; Key West/FERA collection file, Key West Art and Historical Society Archives, Key West, Florida.

35. Walker, "Key West Has Its Kingfish," 7.

36. *Ibid.*, *Washington Post*, April 24, 1935; Janney, "Recovery Key," 41; Ernest Hemingway, *To Have and Have Not* (New York, 1937), 81, 137; Anne E. Rowe, *The Idea of Florida in the American Literary Imagination* (Baton Rouge, 1986), 92–95. Hemingway expresses his anti-FERA sentiments in *To Have and Have Not* through Captain Willie who complains that people cannot eat "working here in Key West for the government for six and a half a week," and through Freddy who observes an unattractive woman and notes, "Anyone would have to be a writer or a FERA man to have a wife look like that; God isn't she awful?" Rowe, *The Idea of Florida in the American Literary Imagination*, claims Hemingway did not like FERA because it represented change in his beloved Key West, 93–94. *The New Yorker's* Richard Rovere said that *To Have and Have Not* was a novel "in which Ernest Hemingway, an outsider who deeply resented the presence here of other outsiders, celebrated the local character and missed no opportunity to pour contempt on the government men." Rovere, "Our Far-Flung Correspondent," 87.

37. *Palatka Daily News*, April 9, 1935; *Daytona Beach News Journal*, May 17, 1935; WPA/FERA Scrapbook, II, 83.

38. Walker, "Key West Has Its Kingfish," 7; *Ocala Morning Banner*, April 24, 1934; *Tampa Morning Tribune*, April 4, 1935.

39. Marathon *Florida Keys Sun*, May 5, 1934; *Sarasota Tribune*, April 25, 1935.

40. George E. Sokolsky, "America Drifts Toward Fascism," *American Mercury* 32 (July 1934), 258; Clayton Rand, *Abracadabra or One Democrat to Another* (Newark, 1936), 19–20; Schlesinger, Jr., *Coming of the New Deal*, 279; Bremer, "Along the 'American Way,'" 643–44.

41. Transcript of telephone conversation between Harry Hopkins and a FERA agent, September 5, 1935, Harry Hopkins Collection, Box 56. The hurricane promoted another Hemingway anti-New Deal outburst. In a letter to his editor, Maxwell Perkins, September 7, 1935, Hemingway wrote, "Harry Hopkins and Roosevelt, who sent those poor bonus marchers down there to get rid of them, got rid of them all right." Carlos Baker, ed., *Ernest Hemingway Selected Letters*, 1917–1961 (New York, 1981), 186; Carlos Baker, ed., "Letters from Key West," *Tropic Magazine* (*Miami Herald* Sunday supplement), August 23, 1981, 14–15.

42. Bremer, "Along the 'American Way,'" 643–44; Davis, "New World Symphony," 652; Jane Perry Clark, "Key West's Year I," *Survey Graphic* 24 (August 1935), 402.

43. *Miami Herald*, April 24, 1935.

44. *Key West Citizen*, June 23, 1936.

45. *Miami Tribune*, May 31, 1936; Canby Chambers, "America's Southernmost City," *Travel* 68 (March 1937), 34.

46. Williams, *Florida Keys*, 127–28; *Miami Herald*, July 27, 1960, July 7, 1962, and September 15, 1970; Key West/FERA collection file, Key West Art and Historical Society Archives, Key West, Florida; Raymer, "Notes & antic-dotes," 44. Stone left the WPA in 1937 to return to Harvard to receive his law degree. Upon graduation in 1940, Stone moved back to Key West, establishing his own law firm, Harris and Stone, and eventually serving as an attorney for the Monroe County Commission and the Florida Keys Aqueduct Commission. He became involved in many financial transactions with various clients who sometimes ended up as his business partners. Because he had a variety of real estate and business investments, Stone maintained a number of bank accounts reflecting his varied financial interests. Re-

porter Raymer said Stone "juggled all of his diversified financial schemes with wiley skill for more than a decade," but "ultimately, his wizardly juggling of a wide range of business interests and investments became too complicated. He began to lose control of the precarious balance system. In short, money acquired for one thing was put into something entirely different, and some investors sustained losses. In a number of cases, invested funds disappeared entirely." In 1961 the Internal Revenue Service filed a $125,251 lien against Stone for income taxes owed from 1955 to 1959. But by that time Stone had liquidated all of his Key West properties. Raymer called Stone a "clever attorney, as well as a sharp businessman," whose life in Key West in the 1940s and 1950s was a "chronicle of wheeler-dealer expansiveness." Joy Williams is more direct. Stone, she writes, "had managed to represent and bilk just about everyone in town. In 1960, the master of the shady deal fled." See Williams, *The Florida Keys*, 127.

47. Florida Writers' Project, Work Projects Administration, *A Guide to Key West* (New York, 1941), 22–23, 52–53; *Time Magazine* (April 11, 1938); Key West/FERA collection file, Key West Art and Historical Society Archives, Key West, Florida.

The Persistence of the Past: Memphis in the Great Depression

ROGER BILES

This essay considers the impact of the New Deal on a "thoroughly South-ern city" with respect to local autonomy, the political system, social struc-ture, and the acceptance of social change along with federal funds. In Memphis, President Roosevelt had to deal with Boss Crump (as he did with bosses in other cities such as Chicago, St. Louis, and Jersey City). Some his-torians have criticized him for such dealing, while others maintain that he had to balance the maintenance of his political support and protection of his policies against local power such as that of Crump, who was often co-operative but had deep misgivings about the New Deal. The author's con-clusion here agrees with much recent literature which stresses the limits of the impact of the New Deal, especially (but not only) in the South. Obsta-cles to change resulted in a prevailing continuity.

IN *Cotton Fields and Skyscrapers*, an interpretation of southern urban his-tory, David R. Goldfield questioned the traditional concept of a resurgent New South rising from the ashes of Reconstruction. Change has come to the South, he allowed, but the transformation occurred most markedly in this century; the watershed was the Great Depression. Goldfield con-cluded that "the federal government paid for the capital facilities in south-

From the *Journal of Southern History*, 52 (May 1986), 183–212.

ern cities that northern cities had paid for themselves in earlier decades
and on which they were still paying off the debt. The almost-free mod-
ernization received by southern cities would prove to be an important economic advantage in subsequent decades." During World War II the federal
government continued to influence the region by bringing additional industry and military bases to its cities. Southern cities retained much of
their pre–Civil War identities in the aftermath of World War II, Goldfield
argued, but change was well underway. The onset of the New Deal began
the process that significantly altered the personality and characteristics of
the South.[1]

Certainly the Great Depression and the New Deal left a long-lasting
imprint on American cities, North and South. As Paul V. Betters, executive director of the U.S. Conference of Mayors, stated, "the year 1932
marked the beginning of a new era in federal-city relationships." Mark I.
Gelfand noted in A Nation of Cities that while it was revolutionizing life
in the countryside, the New Deal also brought the federal government
into urban areas in a meaningful way for the first time. Franklin D. Roosevelt's policies not only made vast sums of money available to cities, thus
providing relief and temporary employment for thousands of jobless men
and women, but they also paved the way for subsequent innovations in
housing, transportation, and public welfare. Most significant, noted David
R. Goldfield and Blaine A. Brownell in their survey of American urban
history, "The New Deal also signalled the advent of new American values
that were much more appropriate to the collective, urban realities of the
modern era than to the individualistic and largely rural ethic of the past."[2]

Nowhere was this "largely rural ethic" more firmly implanted than in
southern cities—and nowhere should the impact of the New Deal have
been more shattering. By nudging city halls throughout the South into a
closer relationship with the federal government, the New Deal presumably
punctured the isolation of these communities and forcibly brought them
into the twentieth century. Historian George B. Tindall outlined the
changes resulting from this clash:

> The programs of the New Deal, designed to meet the problems of de-
> pression, almost inadvertently jeopardized the traditional power structure
> which rested on the control of property, labor, credit, and local govern-
> ment. Relief projects reduced dependency; labor standards raised wages;
> farm programs upset landlord-tenant relationships; government credit by-
> passed bankers; new federal programs skirted county commissioners and
> sometimes even state agencies. The trends became more ominous in 1935,

when the 'Second New Deal' swung from recovery to reform with such measures as WPA, social security, the Wagner Labor Relations Act, the 'soak-the-rich' tax, and later, the Farm Tenant and Housing Acts of 1937 and the Fair Labor Standards Act of 1938.[3]

This essay attempts to test Tindall's observations in one southern city, Memphis, Tennessee. It seeks to discern the modernizing impact of the New Deal on the city, to discover to what degree the surfeit of federal programs in the 1930s contributed to the conquest of the Old South. Was the price of federal funds the surrender of local autonomy? Did local leaders want or accept social change along with federal money? Did the New Deal transform Memphis's political system or its social structure? What accommodations were made by federal agencies to local conditions and mores? If Memphis, a thoroughly southern city, proved largely immune to the powerful forces unleashed in the thirties, then a victory needs to be recorded for continuity over change in the South, for the cotton field over the skyscraper.

Prior to the 1870s Memphis sported a heterogeneous population in which Germans and Irish figured prominently in the city's economic and political affairs. After the disastrous yellow fever epidemics of that decade, which resulted in financial ruin and the surrender of the city charter to a state-administered taxing district, the foreign-born avoided the location. Whereas first-generation immigrants constituted over 30 percent of the population in 1860, the figure declined to 12 percent in 1880, 8 percent in 1890, and 5 percent in 1900. By the turn of the century Memphis had become a city, roughly half white, half black, virtually devoid of the foreign-born, whose growth had been fueled largely by rural migrants. Historian Gerald M. Capers, Jr., observed that by 1900, "Memphis presented a strange paradox—a city modern in physical aspect but rural in background, rural in prejudice, and rural in habit." These recent arrivals from the countryside who were responsible for giving the city a decidedly provincial air included in their cultural baggage such items as a nostalgic devotion to the southern Lost Cause, a propensity for violence, and belief in stringent codes of honor, fundamentalist religion, and white supremacy. The influence of this steady infusion of farm folk led H. L. Mencken to comment in the 1920s that Memphis was the "most rural-minded city in the South."[4]

During the prosperous decade of the twenties, Memphis enjoyed considerable population growth. Thanks largely to the city's annexation of 20.3 miles of suburban land in 1929, its population grew from 162,351 in 1920 to

253,143 in 1930, an increase of 56 percent. The demographic trends of earlier years continued apace: the 1930 census revealed that 61.8 percent of the city's population was white, 38.1 percent black—a racial composition virtually unchanged from the preceding decennial report of 62.2 percent white and 37.6 percent black. If anything, Memphis, long a homogeneous city, was becoming even more so; only 2.1 percent of the population was foreign-born, down from 3.6 percent a decade before. The historical pattern of immigration from nearby rural areas continued with the vast majority of newcomers hailing from Tennessee, Mississippi, and Arkansas.[5]

Traditionally dependent upon the Mississippi River for its existence, Memphis continued its economic role as a commercial entrepôt. According to the U.S. Bureau of the Census, 27.7 percent of the workforce toiled in "manufacturing and mechanical" pursuits, as opposed to 40.2 percent in Philadelphia and 36.2 percent in Chicago. One-fourth worked as domestics, the majority of them black (22,860 of 27,514). Like other southern cities that had experienced some growth in the postbellum years, Memphis maintained a predominantly mercantile cast. Still the nation's largest inland cotton market, Memphis remained a one-crop town; not surprisingly, the city's bankers, merchants, and factors sustained a keen interest in the fluctuations of the commodity's price levels. And yet, underlining the degree to which industry had not taken hold in the city, almost no textile concerns had situated there. Fourteen percent of the total U.S. cotton crop passed through the Bluff City in 1929–1930, but only 104 people worked in cotton mills. The fluffy white plant was transported to the city, was hauled about by sweating, straining, black stevedores, and was classified, sold, and shipped out again—much the way it had been done for generations.[6]

The city's preoccupation with cotton prices, which fell alarmingly from 20.2 cents per pound in 1927 to 5.7 cents in 1931, explains why most Memphians evinced so little reaction to the cataclysmic events of October 1929. The stock-market crash generated considerable panic among the denizens of the city's downtown financial district but seemingly little reaction elsewhere. No epidemic of suicides punctuated the news of financial ruin. The two daily newspapers reported the events in New York City but perfunctorily so; moreover, they declined to award them the glaring headlines prevalent elsewhere. The health of the stock market was, quite simply, irrelevant to all but a few speculators. The Memphis *Commercial Appeal* called talk of a major national disaster "unbelievably silly" and generously quoted President Hoover on the nation's health. It editorialized:

That the prices of securities will find their proper level is inescapable wherever that may be. There is not a flaw in the soundness of the country. Agriculture in the last few years may not have fared as well as industry, but it is not menaced. Financially, commercially, industrially and in all other ways the nation is as rock ribbed as Gibraltar. It refuses to be shaken by flurries one way or the other among speculators in stocks.[7]

In the months following the stock-market crash, the dailies continued to downplay bad economic news. Quoting the optimistic pronouncements of local businessmen, they predicted a short duration for hard times and reassuringly referred to the "sunshine syndrome." That is, they told readers that temporary winter layoffs in 1929–1930 would melt away with the coming of warmer weather. In fact, hard times were not all that hard in Memphis for the first year of the Depression. Few businesses failed and unemployment remained low—only 2.8 percent for whites and 3.5 percent for blacks. Since Memphis had less heavy industry than many northern and midwestern cities and relied heavily upon service and trade enterprises, the ravages of the Depression appeared very slowly. Far removed from the nation's banking and manufacturing centers, many southern cities experienced a time lag between the stock-market crash and the onset of economic dislocations.[8]

By late 1930, however, the darkening clouds over Memphis gave way to genuinely stormy weather. River trade decreased as hard-hit industrial cities dispatched fewer and fewer barges down the Mississippi. The number of unemployed in the Bluff City rose rapidly, totaling about seven thousand in November and ten thousand in December. The number of families helped by the sole existing public community relief organization, the Family Welfare Agency, rose so dramatically that many supplicants had to be turned away for lack of resources. The problems of feeding and housing transients grew as well; Salvation Army records show that in December 1929 the army gave 1,700 meals to wayfarers and 8,200 one year later. In March 1931 the number had risen to 10,250. By the winter of 1930–1931 breadlines had formed outside hospital kitchens as thousands of unfortunates queued up hoping that such institutions would share their surplus food. The increasing frequency of suicides served as a grim barometer of the worsening situation. Suddenly so many people were jumping off Harahan Bridge into the Mississippi that the newspapers printed the names and telephone numbers of clergymen and urged the dispirited to seek counseling. "Soon a Memphis preacher jumped off."[9]

With each succeeding year the situation worsened. Unemployment continued to rise, reaching 17,000 in mid-1932 (about 14 percent of the workforce). Employers responded by cutting to a thirty-hour work week and pledging not to hire women. Between 1929 and 1932 employers handed over to men approximately 6,000 jobs previously held by women. The Fisher Body Company, which produced wooden parts for automobile bodies, closed its Memphis plant, throwing about 1,200 men out of work. The Ford Motor Company suspended operations in its assembly works for several months that year. In all, the number of manufacturing establishments fell 35.8 percent from 1929 to 1933, and as result the total wages paid to Memphians fell 55 percent. Public school teachers kept their jobs but had their salaries pared and finally received payment from the city in scrip.[10]

Insolvency and foreclosure threatened businesses, and many modest enterprises went bankrupt. Even some of the oldest and most respected establishments failed to meet their financial obligations. The swank Parkview Hotel, adjacent to Overton Park, closed its doors, and the city's two daily newspapers went into receivership. Between 1929 and 1933 the number of retail establishments fell by 22.3 percent; consequently, retail sales decreased 54.3 percent. The decline in bank debits (the volume of checks drawn from local banks), usually a reliable economic indicator, clearly demonstrated the city's ill health—Memphis's rate fell 55 percent from 1929 to 1933 compared to a national average of 53 percent for 140 cities excepting New York.[11]

For embattled Memphians an influx of transients further exacerbated the situation. As the transportation hub of the Middle South, Memphis had always attracted a steady stream of rootless sojourners, usually men and women of little means. The dislocations of the Depression, especially severe among landless sharecroppers and tenant farmers, accelerated this trickle of humanity into a torrent. Arriving by the thousands in railroad boxcars and beat-up jalopies, these desperate unfortunates found an atmosphere uncongenial to their arrival. Unhappy city officials tried to discourage transients from disembarking and spoke to those who did in sobering tones about moving on.

Panic enveloped the city in the spring of 1932 when word spread that thousands of veterans would be descending upon Memphis en route to Washington, D.C. These were the men of the Bonus Army, preparing to demand early payment of their World War I gratuities. Rumors circulated that the penniless veterans had stayed on in the towns along the line where the railroads booted them off the trains. In early June some two hundred members of the Texas Bonus Army arrived on a special train provided by the mayor of Little Rock, Arkansas. They pitched camp at the Mid-South

Fairgrounds and waited for the wherewithal to continue on the next leg of their eastward journey. Noting that the city could not care for the veterans, Police Commissioner Clifford Davis beseeched the railroads to provide transportation, but to no avail. When an additional 225 bonus soldiers arrived from Oklahoma, the Southern Railroad posted guards around their trains and refused to transport anyone unable to pay. The Veterans of Foreign Wars and the American Legion fed the expanding settlement as the impasse dragged on. Exasperated by the railroad's intransigence, Davis hinted that his men would not try to stop veterans from stealing a train. Finally, the city trucked the veterans to Nashville where the buck passed to another city's government.[12]

With local and state governments pleading insufficient resources, shocked and weary citizens turned hopeful eyes to Washington, D.C. The inaction of the Hoover administration left Memphians feeling bitter and disillusioned. No longer minimizing the severity of conditions, the *Commercial Appeal* criticized the president for his incessant attempts to gloss over a worrisome situation and called his administration's economic policies "disappointing." It remained vague on what the federal government legitimately could do and always cautioned limited involvement, but nonetheless the paper haltingly advocated federally funded public works projects, noting in particular the need for flood control improvements on the Mississippi River. Not surprisingly, the local Democrats took advantage of the administration's slackening popularity to gain partisan advantage. Both Boss Edward H. Crump, autocratic ruler of Memphis and the most powerful politician in Tennessee, and Senator Kenneth D. McKellar lambasted Hoover for his insensitivity to the suffering of the masses and for his chummy relations with the plutocrats of the Northeast. The haughty Hoover, who had made much of "Republican prosperity" in 1928, became an inviting target, and Memphis Democrats went after him with a vengeance.[13]

Significantly, they attacked him as much for his attempts to expand the role of the federal government in combating the Depression as they did for the failure of his earlier "do-nothing" policies. Ed Crump, who had been elected to the House of Representatives in 1930, voted for the Reconstruction Finance Corporation, but he scored Hoover for his inattention to the need for reduced spending and emphasized the importance of continuing to balance the federal budget. McKellar was even more critical, calling the RFC the "greatest pork barrel that was ever established in the history of time." While favoring some form of relief and a token veterans' bonus, McKellar became the chief spokesman in the Senate for trimming all House-approved appropriations by 10 percent. In discussing governmental strategy for combating the Depression the senator emphasized the need for fiscal orthodoxy, saying:

> The real remedy and the only remedy is to live within our income. We have no moral right to expend more money than we have collected or to expend money that we have not collected in order to carry on the ordinary operations of the Government.[14]

Indeed, this hidebound commitment to conservative economics characterized the Memphis municipal government's response as well. Like most other southern cities, it had traditionally denied its citizens substantial welfare services. The business aristocracy, infused with the interrelated ideals of physical growth and economic expansion, considered aid to the city's unfortunates a low priority. The creation of community welfare organizations lagged behind population growth, an error compounded in Memphis by the previous annexation of a large section of contiguous land. Alarmingly few avenues for philanthropy existed. In 1929 only the Memphis Community Fund, organized six years earlier through the efforts of the Chamber of Commerce and the Council of Social Agencies, functioned as a welfare agency. This privately funded charitable organization would bear the brunt of the relief burden.[15]

As its officers readily admitted, the Community Fund fell far short of being equal to the task. In its inaugural year the agency raised $477,000 in pledges; in 1929 it mustered $551,000. Thus while the city population grew by 35 percent in the intervening six years, the amount of money pledged rose only 16 percent. In depression-torn 1930 the amount amassed actually decreased by $23,000 from the previous year. Noting that the per capita gift in Memphis for 1931 was a miserly $1.83, the fund took the city's wealthy to task for their indifferent response. It concluded:

> Comparisons with cities both north and south show that the per capita giving in Memphis is low. . . . Our difficulties of financing will continue until the men and women of wealth within our city give more generously of their means to the causes of social welfare than they have been in the habit of doing in the past.[16]

In its plea for more money, the fund's spokesmen attributed the stinginess of the well-to-do to their assumption that the vast majority targeted for assistance were black. Granting that this was so, welfare workers argued for contributions on the basis of "selfishness," contending that the "economic situation and the health condition of the colored affects the entire community." Further, they chastised city government for its failure to shoulder any part of the load and cited for credibility a study by the Children's Bureau of Washington, D.C., that detailed the proportion of family relief borne by public and private sources in twenty-four cities. Ranging from 100 percent private funds in New Orleans to 98 percent public funds in Detroit, the average allotment for relief was 85 percent public and 15 percent private. (The only regular appropriation made for family relief from tax funds in Memphis was a $40,000 annual allotment by the county for mothers' aid.) The study's conclusion was that "Communities can carry their immensely greater loads only as public resources assume responsibility for a larger part of them."[17]

The city government responded to the charges of apathy, but not in a substantial way. In December 1930 Mayor Watkins Overton, Boss Crump's surrogate in city hall, met with Community Fund officials to create the Mayor's Commission on Unemployment and Relief. Not intended as a comprehensive relief program, the Mayor's Commission attempted only modest involvement on an extremely limited scale. (In its two years of operation, the commission spent only $50,000.) It underwrote the "Buy an Apple" campaign, for example, by supplying eighty men with produce for sale on downtown street corners. It also paid a handful of men each day to chop kindling at a city-owned wood yard. But mostly the commission served as an employment agency, bringing together unemployed workers and potential employers. It arranged for area cotton planters to use unemployed Memphians to pick the crop, albeit at the rock-bottom wage of forty cents per one hundred pounds. The city sold work tickets that provided the buyer ten hours of unskilled labor for each one-dollar work ticket purchased (the worker received in turn relief commodities from the commission) and served as a clearinghouse for donations of food and clothing from concerned citizens. Even this limited activity strained the community's meager resources and, refusing to extend a plea for emergency operating revenues, the Mayor's Commission closed in 1932.[18]

During these years Mayor Overton constantly complained about the unrealistic demands placed upon city government. First, Overton lashed out at the Community Fund, which, he claimed, "is refusing to help us and are spending their money paying salaries and the like." More frequently, he lamented, "The entire burden of taking care of the unemployed is being put on the cities. . . ." Why, he repeatedly asked Congressman Crump, could not the federal government assume a larger role? In one of many letters he sent to Crump regarding the worsening situation in 1931–1932, he wrote: "I wonder if it would be possible to try to get the Federal Government to try to employ some of these unemployed on river work. I know there is a lot they could do if they would."[19]

The city government could have done more but not without incurring a much greater deficit. In 1929 the city's net debt was $25,553; by 1933 it had increased only to $27,386. Municipal expenditures necessarily remained low, because tax revenues trickled in at a snail's pace. Assessed property valuations, always comfortably low for premium commercial establishments, remained so. Owners of more expensive homes and friends of the Crump machine faced lower actual levies than did less affluent homeowners who typically suffered more in the Depression. The inability or unwillingness of taxpayers to meet their obligations further diminished the resources available to city officials. Mayor Overton reported to Crump in late 1931 that $1.5 million in delinquent taxes remained unpaid; by 1933 that figure exceeded $4.6 million. Only then did the city launch a massive, though ultimately unsuccessful, drive to collect back taxes.[20]

To generate the payment of delinquent taxes the city employed several tactics: Mayor Overton asked the Real Estate Board to urge its clients to pay back levies; the city announced a special dispensation waiving costs, commissions, or penalties for any taxpayers owing unpaid levies from 1921 to 1931; and City Attorney Walter Chandler produced a brochure, "Progress Promoted By Taxes," in which he listed all of the municipally funded improvements—improvements, of course, dependent upon taxes—enjoyed by the citizens of Memphis. By imploring, cajoling, threatening, and reasoning, the administration conducted an extensive campaign to collect back taxes; they were met, however, with unified and concerted opposition. Far from a haphazard effort by scattered individuals, resistance to payment crystallized into a formal organization—the Property Owners Association. This group employed newspaper ads, radio appeals, and telephone campaigns to advance its cause. Members even staged demonstrations in the city commission chambers, totally disrupting official government functions on several occasions. As a result of such spirited opposition, tax delinquency remained a severe problem throughout the decade.[21]

The city, lacking full revenue, failed to contribute more than a token amount for relief and was forced to cut other expenditures to keep from going heavily in the red. This resulted in paltry appropriations for vital city services. Memphis, the thirty-sixth largest city in the nation, spent overall only $18.21 per capita in 1933, ranking sixty-fifth out of the sixty-eight cities with over 120,000 population and leading only Chattanooga, Birmingham, and San Antonio. For health and sanitation, Memphis ranked fortieth with a per capita expenditure of $1.84. For charities, hospitals, and corrections it ranked fifty-third, spending $1.45. And most disgraceful, for education its annual per capita outlay of $7.06 ranked sixty-sixth nationally. In 1937 a U.S. Office of Education study listed Memphis dead last in that category. The city's school system went broke for several months in 1932, and schools remained open in 1933 only because teachers, who actually went unpaid for months at a time, accepted a 17 percent salary cut.[22]

With municipal government scrupulously playing a limited role, it fell to the community's citizens to organize whatever ad hoc organizations they could to meet the crisis. Soon after the demise of the Mayor's Commission in 1932, a group of prominent residents formed the Committee of One Hundred to deal with unemployment. The committee, short-lived and lacking a clear mandate, sought only to duplicate the earlier limited efforts of the Mayor's Commission. Another voluntary organization, Community Kitchens, Incorporated, dispensed hot meals to indigents. Dependent upon gifts from merchants, it could afford to serve only one meal a day before closing abruptly in 1933 for lack of donations. A more unorthodox experiment, the Unemployed Citizens' League of Memphis, yielded only slightly better results; members of this cooperative bartered their labor for food, secondhand clothing, and furniture. Articles of payment went into the co-op's inventory where they could be purchased by other members. In February 1933 all work commissioned by the cooperative yielded wages or barter totaling $23.85; the March profit amounted to $6.50. Ultimately, this flirtation with communalism failed simply for lack of money.[23]

Fully engaged at last in the battle against the Depression, the *Commercial Appeal* joined with other civic groups to sponsor fund-raising enterprises. It also made its classified advertisement columns free to all prospective employers, and while the paper carried approximately seventy-five free "help wanted" ads daily, only a few hundred persons secured work during the several months' life of the experiment. Jobs were in such short supply that the paper's editors looked elsewhere to promote recovery. Noting that the economic health of Memphis and the entire Mid-South region depended heavily on cotton, the paper surmised that an assault on the one-crop economy would compel farmers to grow food crops and thus lead to a more enviable diversification. That the idea of reducing the amount of cotton planted interested Memphians, and not just those farmers living in the surrounding countryside, was demonstrated by the involvement of the city's chamber of commerce in the paper's scheme.

Dubbing the campaign "Plant to Prosper," *Commercial Appeal* editor
Frank Ahlgren launched it as a contest in 1934.[24]

The creators of the contest sought to encourage compliance with the
Bankhead Cotton Control Act, which provided for compulsory reduction
of cotton by limiting the amount of land in production. The goal was
the cultivation of less cotton and more food, thus creating greater self-
sufficiency. Under the rules of the contest, the winning farmers in several
categories ("best use of land removed from cotton in the reduction program, soil conservation, home improvement, and preservation of food and
seed") were awarded cash, emblems, and certificates of merit. In its first
year 1,780 farmers, cultivating 469,000 acres of land, entered the contest.
In subsequent years, participation and prize money increased. Officials in
1936 divided the entrants into two categories: landowners, and sharecroppers and tenant farmers. In 1938 they added yet another category for blacks
who owned no land. By 1940 more than 50,000 families had entered, and
its founders could boast that the overwhelmingly successful program, the
subject of several magazine articles, had been copied in other parts of the
country and abroad.[25]

The community's concern with low cotton prices led to another De-
pression-era innovation, Cotton Carnival. Based upon the Mardi Gras cel-
ebrations in New Orleans, Mobile, and Pensacola, and the Veiled Prophets'
Carnival in St. Louis, it could not claim, as the others did, to have any
particular religious significance. From the outset Cotton Carnival was a
business venture that sought to stimulate interest in the product at a time
when market prices had dramatically fallen. As a stimulus to economic recovery, it failed; as a symbolic event, however, Cotton Carnival assumed a
significant role. Conceived by wealthy businessmen, it became the best-
known and certainly the most generously endowed community response to
the Depression. Its genesis and subsequent development shed considerable
light on local priorities.[26]

Members of the Chamber of Commerce thought of resurrecting the
Reconstruction-era Memphis Mardi Gras with a cotton motif. They turned
the project over to Everett R. Cook, president of the Memphis Cotton Exchange, who sold the idea to the city's prominent businessmen. (Cook also
had the good sense to enlist the support of Crump, thus ensuring the success of the venture.) Cook served as president of the first carnival in 1931,
which chose the "Old South" as its theme. This seemed an appropriate
title since blacks as well as horses and mules pulled the floats. Almost immediately the elitism and exclusivity of participation resulted in the found-
ing of secret societies open only to the wealthy and well born.[27]

Barred from equal participation in Cotton Carnival festivities, blacks formed their own annual celebration, "The Beale Street Cotton Makers' Fiesta." Despite opposition from whites who refused to permit advertising for the gala on Main Street and from many resentful blacks who found no reason to celebrate the role of cotton in Afro-American history, the festival survived, in large part because of the generous support of the local black American Legion post. Later renamed the Cotton Makers' Jubilee, it lasted as a segregated institution into the 1980s.[28]

The Memphis Cotton Carnival, a lavish spectacle closed to all but a relatively few insiders, struck many citizens as an insensitive display of wealth at a time of widespread misery. Moreover, its goal to elevate cotton prices defined recovery in terms that advanced the city's wealthy cotton interest. While it could be argued that the carnival's "trickle-down" effect would benefit all the people, the inattention of wealthy merchants to persistent unemployment seemed to indicate a consistent self-interest and lack of altruism. Those in a position to contribute significantly to relief did so sparingly. Indeed, the philosophy behind Cotton Carnival was in harmony with the approach to Depression-induced hard times espoused by Memphis decision makers. City hall closely adhered to a policy of low taxes and limited expenditures, while striving for a balanced budget. The Chamber of Commerce averred that the road out of destitution led to "more business in government, less government in business," a view echoed by the ledger-minded *Commercial Appeal*. It intoned:

> The Commercial Appeal long ago took the position that two objectives were necessary to put business back on its feet in this country: 1. Reduce the cost of government. 2. Get the government out of business.... This government cannot exist with one-half of the people paying taxes to keep up the other half.[29]

Reacting to the prospect of increasing participation by the federal government in recovery, the paper warned that "political nostrums never solved an economic problem." As the presidential election of 1932 approached, the *Commercial Appeal* noted sadly that "nothing short of a miracle" could prevent the defeat of the incumbent. Yet it took comfort in the fact that the Democratic front-runner, Governor Roosevelt of New York, seemed to understand the importance of fiscal orthodoxy. Others were not as sanguine. The Memphis Cotton Exchange and the Memphis Merchants' Exchange sent telegrams to Senator McKellar urging the nomination of the more conservative Albert C. Ritchie of Maryland. They suspected that Roosevelt might be too "socialistic" in his outlook toward

business. Clearly, in the last days of the Hoover presidency, Memphis
community leaders continued to cling to a most conservative economic
and political view—one opposed to any sort of "new deal."[30]

During the "Hundred Days" of feverish legislative activity stimulated
by the new president, the uncertainty with which his vague campaign
promises had been greeted gave way to genuine enthusiasm. By moving
first to safeguard the country's banks and credit system, Roosevelt assured
conservatives that the major thrust of his "new deal" would be preserva-
tive, not destructive. His continued obeisance to the sacrosanct balanced
budget, as demonstrated in the Economy Act, further assuaged the fears of
the business community. Admittedly, some of the administration's bolder
initiatives gave the *Commercial Appeal*'s editors pause, but they continued
to support the president. Maintaining that "natural laws" must ultimately
decide the fate of farmers, the editors conceded that the Agricultural Adjustment Act (AAA) would not do any harm. Ignoring one of the pillars of
fiscal orthodoxy, they endorsed the abandonment of the gold standard and
embraced the revolutionary National Industrial Recovery Act (NIRA) as
the "most comprehensive plan for . . . rehabilitation anyone has yet offered." When the "Hundred Days" ended, the paper called the Seventy-
third Congress's achievements "momentous" and the president's leadership
"courageous."[31]

The Chamber of Commerce also expressed faith in the president's initiatives in the spring of 1933, and Memphis representatives in the U.S.
Congress did likewise. Congressman Crump voted for each and every administration bill, in two cases at least drawing the ire of many of his constituents. Remembering that the liquor issue had been used to oust him
from the mayoralty seventeen years before, Crump gleefully endorsed the
repeal of prohibition, arousing temperance advocates in western Tennessee. And his support of the AAA elicited protest from many of the city's
powerful cotton interests who rued the entry of government into their domain. Crump explained his vote to Memphis Cotton Exchange president
Henry Haizlip:

> The Farm Bill may or may not afford the remedy. If it does, well and
> good—if it fails, I have no doubt the President will very quickly chart a
> new course and tackle the problem from some other angle. . . . I voted for
> the Farm Bill, hoping and believing that the President would exercise the
> practically unlimited power which it vests in him, cautiously and wisely.[32]

Because of the indispensability of cotton to the Memphis economy, no
New Deal measure commanded more attention than the AAA. Despite

initial misgivings on the part of local factors and merchants, the early success of the cotton acreage reduction program allayed many doubts. Certainly the situation had reached desperate straits by 1933; thirteen million bales, three years' supply, had accumulated and, as a result, prices fell to five cents per pound, approximately half of parity. In the initial year of AAA operation, the government plowed under 10,487,991 acres of cotton, prices rose to an average of 9.7 cents per pound, and Department of Agriculture economists estimated that a quarter of a billion dollars in income went to cotton growers. Crop receipts plus benefit payments gave planters more than double the income of the previous year. In 1934 the AAA retired nearly 40 percent of the cotton land normally under cultivation, and prices rose again.[33]

Threats by the U.S. Supreme Court to abrogate the AAA led the *Commercial Appeal* to argue that its dissolution would be "disastrous." When the Court fulfilled its threat in the 1936 Butler decision, the paper called for a speedy replacement, "some sort of regulation, some method of control, some aid to fair price returns." Subsequent bumper crops in cotton, with attendant price drops, renewed demands for federal intervention. The Soil Conservation and Domestic Allotment Act of 1936, the replacement for AAA, was initially seen as a "fairly good makeshift," but ultimately it proved unsatisfactory because of its voluntary nature. The Second AAA, passed in 1938 as a compulsory measure, received a warm welcome from the newspaper.[34]

Planters and cautious newspaper editors came to embrace the federally sponsored cotton reduction program not only because prices rose, but also because agency officials administered it in a conservative manner. New Deal incursions into cotton plantations could have disrupted traditional work patterns and, more importantly, economic and class distinctions. The AAA did not. As one agricultural specialist observed in 1935, "the whole action of the AAA to the present time appears to have the effect of not only maintaining the status quo in landlord-tenant relations, but of actually strengthening the foundations upon which they are built." Planters continued to prosper, and tenants eked out a marginal existence—a condition assured by the act's provisions. The government awarded all subsidy payments to landlords who in turn distributed an unspecified portion to their tenants. The landless workers had no voice in the contract between the AAA and landowners and relied totally on the planters to pass along to them a just portion of the government subsidy. AAA representatives even advised planters how to circumvent the few provisions safeguarding the rights of tenants. In a December 1933 visit to Memphis, AAA administra-

tor Oscar G. Johnston counseled landlords that if they signed an AAA contract before reaching an agreement with their tenants, they would not have
to share profits. If, however, they already had agreements with tenants,
profits would have to be shared. In short, Johnston advised landlords to
sign the 1934–1935 contracts before negotiating with their tenants.[35]

The withdrawal of thousands of acres from use made sharecroppers ex-
pendable, and the AAA's reluctance to invade the landlord's domain freed
them suddenly to release idle workers. Ironically, the federal government's
policies laid the foundation for wholesale evictions. Secretary of Agriculture Henry A. Wallace sent a telegram to the Memphis Chamber of Commerce in which he acknowledged that AAA contracts did not bind
landowners to employ the same tenants. As a result some dispossessed
sharecroppers were forced to accept "day labor" and remained in the
countryside in an increasingly destitute state. Many others picked up and
moved into the nearest sizable city; their exodus from the bootheel of Missouri, eastern Arkansas, western Tennessee, and the delta of Mississippi
ended in the ramshackle slums of Memphis. New York Times reporter Raymond F. Daniell found scores of rural migrants on the city's relief roles, a
situation that proved most unsavory to Memphis officials.[36]

Lorena A. Hickok, a roving observer for New Deal administrator Harry
L. Hopkins, reported the resentment among Memphis businessmen toward these new arrivals. Among the malcontents were "the conservative
editor of the conservative Memphis Commercial Appeal, who thinks we've
got a big rural relief load that will stay on our hands forever, if we don't
drop 'em pretty soon" and a wealthy cotton magnate who suggested that
"all tenants are lazy beggars and should be treated as serfs and would
rather see the price of cotton stay down at five cents a pound forever than
be boosted with Government control and Government insistence on any
sort of fair play for sharecroppers and laborers." Local leaders encouraged
newcomers to return to the countryside, even providing free transportation
for those willing to resettle. But for most Memphians involved with cotton, a few unwanted sharecroppers descending on the city constituted a
small price to pay for rebounding prices, especially since the care of these
indigents fell to the federal government. As Memphis Press-Scimitar editor
and staunch New Dealer Edward J. Meeman summarized to Hickok:
"Take our cotton planters and our merchants here in Memphis. They are
a lot better off than they were a year ago. So, aside from kicking a little
about Government expense, they're perfectly contented as long as they
aren't interfered with."[37]

The business community's accommodation to the New Deal agricultural program after initial misgivings contrasted with its growing disenchantment with the NIRA. At first Memphis greeted the NRA with enthusiasm. The *Commercial Appeal* cited the marching of hundreds behind the blue-eagle banner in an NRA parade as "visible evidence of a community solidly behind the president and committed to the program of the administration." Within a few weeks of the program's launching, 75 percent of the city's manufacturers and retailers displayed blue-eagle emblems as evidence of their participation. The Chamber of Commerce took the lead in urging all businessmen to comply with NRA codes; its president called loyalty to the program "a very definite responsibility." A local businessman, cotton oil magnate Hugh Humphreys, became the NRA's code-compliance director for Tennessee with the state office located in Memphis. For the first few months, at least, all signs indicated a hale and hospitable welcome for the NRA in the Bluff City.[38]

By late 1933, however, problems began to surface. In September the NRA's Memphis district office reported wavering loyalty "pending the effective work of the compliance boards." It chronicled the growing disenchantment among those who adhered to the codes while violators, largely ignored by the compliance boards, grew increasingly brazen in their peculations. In February 1934 the Chamber of Commerce sponsored a public meeting to air grievances. Merchants complained about the faulty enforcement provisions, the seemingly endless red tape, and the recurring bureaucratic snafus. Many of their problems, they felt, had to do with over-centralization and an insensitivity to the concerns of southern cities. Specifically they referred to the need for different wage scales for the North and the South, the absence of sufficient representation on the national code authorities by southern industry, and the need for more local code authorities for purely local industries. By mid-1934 the dissatisfaction boiled over into virtual noncompliance, so that when the Supreme Court struck down the NIRA in the 1935 Schechter decision, it merely confirmed existing views in Memphis.[39]

Of most immediate concern to the city, of course, was unemployment and the relief crisis. Given the Overton administration's miserly bent, the provision of millions of federal dollars for local use must have seemed fortuitous. In July 1932 President Hoover authorized the Reconstruction Finance Corporation (RFC) to provide relief loans to cities, but a political war between Congressman Crump and Tennessee governor Henry Horton delayed the arrival of federal funds until January 1933. In the early months of that year the RFC employed several thousand men to work a maximum of four days per week for $1.25 to $2.40 a day on highway construction sites and on creek beds within the city. The RFC-sponsored projects employed fewer than one-third of the idle men registered for work relief; the rest looked to the new, vastly more extensive New Deal programs created in the spring of 1933.[40]

In May 1933 Congress created the Federal Emergency Relief Administration (FERA) and authorized it to distribute 500 million dollars through state and local agencies. Immediately Governor Hill McAlister named the Tennessee State Relief Administration (later renamed the Tennessee Emergency Relief Administration [TERA]) to preside over the dispensing of both direct and work relief. For the former, it distributed salt pork, eggs, clothing, shoes, and coal to the needy of Memphis; for the latter, it employed jobless men to clean streets and drain ditches. Despite these efforts great numbers of Memphians remained outside of the federal government's relief net. By late 1933, with winter approaching, it became evident that FERA's resources would be inadequate and additional federal assistance necessary.[41]

The Civil Works Administration (CWA) assumed control of work relief in November 1933. Unlike the FERA, the CWA did not operate through state and local intermediaries but paid wages directly to workers. Created as a stopgap measure to help the unemployed through the winter, it disbanded promptly in the spring of 1934. During its brief existence, the CWA funneled over $2 million into Memphis and at its height employed some 8,000 men. Even so, fewer than one-third of the city's idle received jobs from the CWA which, like the FERA before it, lacked the funds commensurate with the gravity of the conditions. As late as April 1934 the FERA remained the only federal agency dispensing relief to cities and in quantities far below that of the previous months.[42]

In May 1934 the Public Works Administration (PWA) office opened in Memphis. Unlike other New Deal agencies that concentrated on short-term, low-cost projects for the unemployed, the PWA made grants to cities for large-scale construction projects. (The cities had to augment these grants with sizable contributions of their own.) In PWA projects, about 70 percent of funds went for materials and the remaining 30 percent for wages. Since "make work" was never a goal, the agency directly employed relatively few men; moreover, the PWA hired indiscriminately, not just from the relief roles, so that it had only an incidental impact on gross unemployment figures. Nevertheless, the amount of money spent and the construction projects completed constitute a formidable list; all told, the PWA lavished $8,494,048 on Memphis. (The city spent over $14 million, mostly obtained from loans.) Buildings erected included John Gaston Hospital, a new grain elevator, the juvenile court, dormitories at the University of Tennessee Medical School, and several public schools. Improvements for streets, parks, bridges, sewers, and drainage ditches accompanied construction. In conjunction with the Army Corps of Engineers, PWA workers built Riverside Drive along the Mississippi River, providing the city a safe thoroughfare at the base of the bluffs.[43]

PWA largess also made possible the construction of the first public housing projects in Memphis. Mayor Overton in 1934 created a municipal housing commission to investigate the need for slum clearance and to select sites for construction. On the basis of its recommendation, the PWA authorized the building of two projects on cleared bayou slum areas adjacent to downtown at a cost of $6.5 million: Lauderdale Courts with 449 units for whites and Dixie Homes containing 663 units for blacks. Both complexes, which limited tenant selection to families whose income totaled less than $1,000 a year and charged rent of $15–$16 per month, opened in 1938. By that time the U.S. Housing Authority had assumed the functions of the PWA's Housing Division and promised aid for three additional public housing projects: Lamar Terrace (478 units for whites) opened on May 1, 1940, William H. Foote Homes (900 units for blacks) on August 10, 1940, and LeMoyne Gardens (500 units for blacks) on December 4, 1941.[44]

President Roosevelt created the Works Progress Administration (WPA) in 1935 to employ men at higher wages than the relief rate. Recognizing that "make work" had little intrinsic value, he nonetheless favored it over the dole. Organized in July, the Tennessee WPA absorbed the work-relief program of the TERA. By late summer the WPA was employing 7,000 Memphians, most of whom performed manual labor. WPA administrators set them to work repairing streets, digging ditches, painting buildings, and resurfacing sidewalks—all low-cost maintenance assignments. A few major construction projects were undertaken, most notably the erection of Crump Stadium and additions to the municipal airport.[45]

By 1938, when Congress mandated draconian cuts in relief appropriations, the WPA had spent $5.2 million on work relief in Memphis, a substantial contribution but considerably less than the PWA spent in Memphis over a comparable period. The disparity can be accounted for, at least in part, by the incompetence of the local WPA office. In 1936, for instance, a greater number of certified persons awaited placement than actually held make-work jobs. Local director Tate Pease went about his work so slowly and haphazardly that the city's job quota went unfilled for months at a time. Mayor Overton, recognizing Pease's shortcomings, spoke of him as

likeable but "a little old to keep up with details." City engineer Will
Fowler was less charitable, calling Pease "a senile old man." Despite these
criticisms, Pease, a loyal Crump supporter of long standing, kept his patronage job.[46]

This seemingly cavalier attitude toward relief surfaced in several other
ways. Memphis had the distinction, for example, of being the last major
southern city to establish a permanent welfare department. In 1935 the
city's board of commissioners created the Memphis Welfare Commission,
composed of volunteers serving without pay to "study, investigate, and cooperate with all agencies now operating in the city." As the language of its
charter made clear, the commission existed to coordinate efforts among existing federal, state, and philanthropic agencies and not to spend municipal money. Mayor Overton assured his constituents that it "is not an
organization for using tax money to buy groceries." Concerned about the
number of recipients receiving aid to which they might not be entitled and
skeptical of the thoroughness of the WPA's screening process, the Welfare
Commission devoted much of its time to investigating all relief applications for WPA certification. Those families fortunate enough to be found
needy received the "princely" sum of $18.51 per month.[47]

Similarly, members of the Chamber of Commerce registered their in-
dignation when WPA employees refused to relinquish their "make work"
to pick cotton in the surrounding fields. The chairman of the chamber's
agriculture committee, owner of an Arkansas cotton plantation, called
upon the local WPA office to suspend all work until the cotton harvest
ended. The federal government intervened to keep the WPA in operation,
but the city forced many relief recipients off the welfare rolls because they
were able to pick cotton. Such a policy had the dual benefits of aiding the
planters and paring down the relief rolls. In the end it was federal agencies that picked up most of the relief tab, costing the city very little, but
Memphis still took pride in the fact that 56 percent of its families had
never received any assistance.[48]

The advent of New Deal relief and employment agencies simply reinforced the city government's aversion to spending its own money. From
January 1933 until September 1934 Shelby County depended entirely on
federal and state funds for its $2 million expenditure for emergency relief.
In 1937 the county allocated one-tenth of one percent of its budget for welfare payments, while authorizing more money for maintenance of public
golf courses. WPA chief Harry Hopkins found Memphis guilty of shirking
its duty, a charge that Mayor Overton denied by arguing that Memphis
had done more than its share in 1931–1932 before the federal government

had become involved. Since that time, the mayor asserted, "it was definitely understood that the city of Memphis needed its funds to care for increased burdens on its institutions which provide for this entire section."
That Hopkins did not share this view apparently bothered Overton not at
all. As one historian noted, Crump and Overton "applauded the involvement of Washington in welfare while organizing a local relief apparatus
only marginally sympathetic to the jobless and indigent." Elmer Scott, a
WPA administrator, observed, "Memphis gave the distinct feeling that a
warm welcome was extended to government concerning itself in the plight
of the unemployed, and paying the bills—as long as it is the *Federal* government. The local city and county government thus also welcomes abso-
lution from responsibility—moral or financial."[49]

Referring to the feelings of the community as a whole, not just to the
leadership, the same observer concluded: "Thus the local conscience is at-
rophical and that is in itself the greatest tragedy." Another WPA visitor,
Lorena Hickok, also commented on the apathy of the populace. She wrote
to Hopkins:

> One thing I've noticed particularly. That is that people outside the relief
> business aren't thinking much about it. They are more like they used to
> be last summer, when things were booming and, if they were conscious of
> relief at all, they were bored by it—not critical, just bored. . . . The com-
> ment you usually hear is, 'You've got a lot of people on relief who are
> there to stay as long as you'll let them.' And that's all they have to say. No
> criticism. No condemnation. They're just indifferent.[50]

Memphis gave only cursory attention to the relief crisis during the Depression, a response in keeping with its traditional refusal to allocate funds
for indigent care. These unfortunates, always a small minority, multiplied
during the Great Depression and assumed greater visibility, but they still
fell far short of a majority of the population. Moreover, many were considered "undesirable" groups—blacks, recent rural migrants, and members
of the lower classes. Any New Deal enterprise serving such a constituency
naturally met with ambivalence, if not with outright hostility. Despite
some reservations about specific federal initiatives, the Democratic leadership of Memphis remained firmly in the Roosevelt fold. As a Democrat in
a solidly one-party region, Boss Crump could be expected to hew the party
line, but his loyalty was such that he could rightfully claim to be a consistent New Dealer.

First as a congressman and later as a private citizen, the Memphis boss
fell in line behind all New Deal measures. While serving in the House,

Crump voted for every Roosevelt-endorsed law, remained unstinting in his praise of the New Deal, and argued that "Roosevelt . . . has done more for the South than any President—aid to the farmers, public works, TVA. . . ." Noting in 1940 that "there is tremendous sentiment against Roosevelt," Crump rejoined: "There wouldn't be any, however, if every one was fair enough to compare conditions when he went in and now." Crump's cohort, Senator McKellar, evinced the same loyalty, not only voting "right" but also championing some of the more controversial administration measures in the South. When speculation surfaced that the Crump machine would desert Roosevelt in his 1944 reelection bid, McKellar wrote reassuringly to the president: "Enclosed please find an interview given out by Mr. Edward H. Crump to the *Commercial Appeal*. . . . He is one of your tried and true friends from 1931–32 to date, who has always upheld and supported you. You have never had to bother about Tennessee and you will not have to do so this time." Roosevelt responded, "Ed's interview was typical and I got quite a chuckle out of it. He is in a class by himself."[51]

The president's reply seems to indicate that he, like many other distant observers of the Memphis political landscape, found Crump to be a colorful character. According to his biographer, Boss Crump "liked the President's energy, flair, and forcefulness; he was especially impressed with the way in which Roosevelt had risen above his physical handicap." Also, "both were of the aristocracy of their particular regions, yet both came to be thought of as the benefactor of the 'little' man." Although there may have existed a mutual admiration between the two politicians, the strongest bond between them was one of self-interest. As the most powerful figure in Tennessee politics in the thirties, Crump, along with his ally McKellar, held the balance of power in the state. But as head of the Democratic party and godfather of patronage, Roosevelt had much to offer local politicians.[52]

Liberal backers of Roosevelt and the New Deal had some difficulty accepting support for the president from big-city bosses. Liberals failed to recognize that the president, a cold-blooded realist, saw in these urban chiefs a source of votes that he could not spurn for reasons of ideological purity. As several recent studies have shown, Roosevelt dealt with these uneasy allies on an ad hoc basis; as long as they delivered the votes and kept their defalcations to an acceptable limit, they were tolerated. If they asserted too much independence or greed, as in the cases of Kansas City's Thomas J. Pendergast or Jersey City's Frank Hague, the administration moved against them. Ed Crump, fortunate enough to maintain his power and sufficiently loyal to the New Deal, remained in the president's good graces.[53]

Even though the Memphis Democratic machine never strayed from the New Deal line, Crump did not always feel at ease with decisions made in Washington. Nor did the boss approve of his fellow New Dealers. Asked what he and other Memphians thought about Roosevelt's "Brains Trust" advisors, Crump responded, "Oh, just a necessary evil, I guess." Particularly galling to the thoroughly southern boss was the New Deal's concern over the issue of race. Admittedly, Roosevelt initiated few efforts designed specifically to aid blacks; his administration's reputation as pro–civil rights can best be attributed to the unofficial efforts of a few liberals such as Harold L. Ickes, Aubrey Williams, and Eleanor Roosevelt. Nevertheless, these meager efforts, symbolic though they might have been, aroused Crump's ire. By 1944 he found the situation serious enough to write McKellar:

> The negro question is looming big in this part of the country—in fact, all over the South. . . . The Roosevelts dug up the negro question. . . . There was a big dinner, social equality—negroes and whites—at the Roosevelt Hotel in New York last Thursday, honoring Walter White, a negro leader. Mrs. Roosevelt and Wendell Willkie spoke, as well as two or three negroes. If they load down the Chicago platform with repeal of Poll Tax, Anti-Lynching and endeavoring to erase the Jim Crowe [*sic*]—that will certainly be something for us to think about. . . . We may have to be for Roosevelt whether we like it or not, but I would hate to think it wise to be placed in that position.[54]

Crump need not have worried, for the New Deal made no attempt to interfere with local race relations. The federal government exercised no control over the administration of the city's relief program and its effect on blacks. Long before the U.S. Supreme Court struck down the NIRA, many Memphis employers simply disregarded the codes mandating color-blind wage scales. Local CWA personnel assigned black women to the homes of personal friends for domestic work as a prerequisite for their receiving aid. The National Youth Administration office limited its job training programs for blacks to domestic work in response to the cry that "good help" was becoming increasingly hard to find. The agency's regional director established a policy of not recommending blacks for positions if whites needed work. Segregation proved to be unassailable even in New Deal agencies; Civilian Conservations Corps (CCC) camps that opened throughout the South relied upon strict separation of the races. Boss Crump refused to countenance a mixed CCC facility for Memphis and then raged when the War Department opened only a small camp for blacks in nearby Collierville. Despite the protestations of area whites, the black camp remained in operation. CCC officials, however, did not challenge the local proscription of integration.[55]

Publicly Crump never criticized Roosevelt or the New Deal; privately he occasionally exhibited an independent streak. Crump's hard line against the Congress of Industrial Organizations proved embarrassing to the Democratic party outside the South, and in 1940 Roosevelt attempted in vain to moderate Crump's position. Later the president decided to oppose Senator McKellar's 1946 reelection due to the aged solon's increasing conservatism and implacability. Roosevelt wanted Crump to abandon his longtime ally and throw in with the insurgency, a request that the Memphian refused to honor. Whether Crump demurred out of loyalty to an old crony or out of an informed conviction that McKellar had the power in his native state to withstand the coup, he had the resolve to say no to the president.[56]

Crump clashed with Roosevelt on occasion and balked at the more liberal New Deal experiments, but he remained loyal because of the largess afforded the machine and the autonomy the boss enjoyed in presiding over its distribution. City government appropriated very little money, but Crump was empowered to name local relief agents who took charge of dispensing federal funds. As Douglas L. Smith has noted, "Washington never federalized the TERA." Indeed, no one in the Roosevelt administration protested when Senator McKellar fired TERA director Walter L. Simpson for ordering agency officials to stay out of politics. Moreover, New Dealers in Washington awarded Memphis a number of plums eagerly sought by competing localities, among them the Collierville CCC camp and the regional offices for the NYA and the Home Owners Loan Corporation.[57]

The bulk of federal money came to Memphis under the auspices of federal relief, and with it came patronage. Shelby County, with roughly one-ninth of the state's population, received one-seventh of the WPA jobs. As Tennessee's senior senator, McKellar monopolized almost all of it, much to the chagrin of junior Senator George L. Berry, who protested the inequity. Harry Hopkins backed McKellar as did Postmaster General James A. Farley, who said, "McKellar was my friend, and I certainly tried to prove that I was his." Over the years the combined enrollments of the FERA, CWA, PWA, and WPA brought thousands of jobs to Memphis—jobs which, though created and funded through the federal government, passed into the hands of needy Memphians through the good offices of the Crump organization.[58]

Crump undoubtedly used the WPA for political purposes. Memphis Democrats probably coerced the recently unemployed into repaying their benefactors because laborers not only voted for the machine candidates but also contributed to their campaign chest. The WPA, which had been taken over by the Crump machine, was turned into a veritable army for the purpose of administering collections. Crump opponents complained about such practices with a steady stream of lamentations that turned into a torrent during the 1938 elections. And a few members of the WPA workforce responded to the machine's heavy-handedness with angry letters charging electoral irregularities. A U.S. Senate investigating committee corroborated these allegations but took no action. Even Hopkins tried to foil the Memphis machine. But Crump had become so accustomed to using the WPA as an arm of his political machine that he resented any interference by public works administrators in the local organization. In the heat of the 1938 campaign the miffed boss wrote McKellar: "Harry Hopkins is certainly putting it on thick—these letters for the WPA workers to read (accompanying their paychecks)—telling them they must vote their own choice—no politics—no interference. Is this being done all over the United States or has Senator Berry been getting in some work in Tennessee?"[59]

The New Deal proved to be a boon not just to the Crump machine but to the community as well. By 1938 the various work-relief agencies had spent $15.6 million on relief and $6.4 million on housing construction in Memphis. Evidence of the federal government's presence was everywhere—in street and bridge improvements, landscaping in parks, new viaducts and drainage culverts, and countless other improvements to the physical appearance of Memphis. The city could also boast a new and modern airport, hospital, grain elevator, juvenile court facility, and football stadium. The Tennessee Valley Authority (TVA) brought electricity to thousands of homes at a much cheaper rate, and the money spent on improved sanitary facilities, especially in low-lying areas on the periphery of the city, all but eradicated the traditional scourge of the city, malaria.[60]

Despite these highly visible improvements, the Roosevelt administration's popularity had dwindled by the late 1930s in the Bluff City. The president's 1936 reelection bid received the endorsement of the progressive *Press-Scimitar*, but from the *Commercial Appeal*, always more reflective of the community's attitudes, came only ambivalence. The editors raised no objections to Roosevelt, but hoped that he would become less liberal and would give business a "breathing spell." Ambivalence gave way to outright opposition when in 1940 the conservative organ called for the selection of Tennessean Cordell Hull as the Democratic party's presidential candidate. After Roosevelt's nomination, both papers deserted him, and only the strenuous efforts of a worried Boss Crump kept Memphis safely in the president's corner that autumn.[61]

Why had Memphis grown disenchanted with the New Deal? In large part because the New Deal had taken on a decidedly liberal cast over the years. Measures like the Wagner Act and the Social Security Act, linch-pins of the Second New Deal, aroused considerable opposition. The fed-eral wage and hour provisions of the Fair Labor Standards Act cut deeply into the low-cost incentives Memphis offered northern businessmen who were considering relocation (local businessmen argued that low wages compensated for their higher freight rates.) Southerners were further dis-pleased by the administration's mild endorsement, if not sponsorship, of a federal antilynching law. According to the *Commercial Appeal*, the New Deal had fallen prey to "professional agitators and adventurers" who were taking aim at "southern customs, southern traditions, southern institu-tions." By 1940 the paper sadly alluded to the "pinkish rind of sociology which surrounds the core of administrative policy" and the "steady and heavy pressure toward the centralization of government."[62]

Although fearful of an expanding federal government dominated by northern liberals, Memphians actually had little cause for concern. While the New Deal had altered the face of the city, in fact, the addition of new buildings, roads, sewers, and parks was essentially a cosmetic change. No clash of titanic forces, one demanding change and the other girded to pre-serve an older way of life, occurred. Ed Crump and his minions had no intention of altering their city's character, and the federal government made no effort to dislodge the conservative defender of local customs. Roosevelt stopped short of demanding the surrender of local autonomy as the price of federal aid; instead, he worked hand-in-glove with the local Democratic organization—an organization that had an unsavory reputa-tion but produced a rich bounty of Democratic votes. New Deal agencies, controlled by local politicians, dispensed aid to indigents and the unem-ployed but exerted little impact on the majority of the residents. Mem-phians continued to look to city hall, not to Washington, D.C., for leadership. Inadvertently, federal policy reinforced the essentially rural character of the city, as New Deal farm programs drove thousands of Mid-South sharecroppers and tenant farmers off the land and into the region's major city. Once in Memphis, they continued to infuse the city with rural mores, ideas, and values. Spared encroachments by the federal government, the social structure survived unchanged. Memphis remained a magnet for rural transplants, a haven for conservative cotton interests, the domain of an omnipotent political machine, and the guardian of a rigid racial caste system.

NOTES

1. Goldfield, *Cotton Fields and Skyscrapers: Southern City and Region, 1607–1980* (Baton Rouge and London, 1982), 181–82 (quotation). See also David R. Goldfield, "The Urban South: A Regional Framework," *American Historical Review*, LXXXVI (December 1981), 1009–34.

2. Betters quoted in Blake McKelvey, *The Emergence of Metropolitan America, 1915–1966* (New Brunswick, N.J., 1968), 85; Gelfand, *A Nation of Cities: The Federal Government and Urban America, 1933–1965* (New York, 1975), 384; David R. Goldfield and Blaine A. Brownell, *Urban America: From Downtown to No Town* (Boston and other cities, 1979), 371. For a sampling of urban historians commenting on the Depression and New Deal see Howard P. Chudacoff, *The Evolution of American Urban Society* (Englewood Cliffs, N.J., 1975); and Charles N. Glaab and A. Theodore Brown, *A History of Urban America* (New York, Toronto, and London, 1967).

3. Tindall, *The Persistent Tradition in New South Politics* (Baton Rouge, 1975), 71. See also Douglas Lloyd Smith, "The New Deal and the Urban South: The Advancement of a Southern Urban Consciousness During the Depression Decade" (unpublished Ph.D. dissertation, University of Southern Mississippi, 1978).

4. Capers, *The Biography of a River Town. Memphis: Its Heroic Age* (Chapel Hill, 1939), 206 (first quotation); Memphis *Commercial Appeal*, August 10, 1901; Gerald M. Capers, "The Rural Lag on Southern Cities," *Mississippi Quarterly*, XXI (Fall 1968), 260 (second quotation).

5. U.S. Bureau of the Census, *Fifteenth Census of the United States: 1930, Population*, Vol. II (Washington, 1939), 69, 213–15; Smith, "The New Deal and the Urban South," 3; Richard K. Thomas, "The Residential Distribution of Immigrants in Memphis, Tennessee" (unpublished M.A. thesis, Memphis State University, 1970), 7, 36–37.

6. U.S. Department of Commerce, *Statistical Abstract of the United States, 1932* (Washington, 1932), 758, 790, 796; U.S. Bureau of the Census, *Fifteenth Census of the United States: 1930. Population*, Vol. IV: *Occupations by States* (Washington, 1933), 423, 1384, 1516, 1536–38.

7. U.S. Department of Agriculture, "Some Facts About the Cotton Outlook For 1932," Miscellaneous Publication No. 139, January 1932 (Washington, D.C.), 1–5; Memphis *Commercial Appeal*, October 26, 1929.

8. Smith, "The New Deal and the Urban South," 27–28; Robert A. Sigafoos, *Cotton Row to Beale Street: A Business History of Memphis* (Memphis, 1979), 166–67.

9. Thomas H. Baker, *The Memphis Commercial Appeal: The History of a Southern Newspaper* (Baton Rouge, 1971), 282; Memphis Community Fund, "Annual Report, 1931" (Memphis Public Library, Memphis, Tenn., hereinafter cited as MPL); Memphis *Commercial Appeal*, February 9, 1931; Shields McIlwaine, *Memphis Down in Dixie* (New York, 1948), 178 (quotation).

10. Sigafoos, *Cotton Row to Beale Street*, 167; Stanley J. Folmsbee, Robert E. Corlew, and Enoch L. Mitchell, *History of Tennessee* (4 vols., New York, 1960), II, 300; Smith, "The New Deal and the Urban South," 36–44.

11. Ralph C. Hon, *Memphis, Its Economic Position* (Memphis, 1935), 19–22; Videotape interview, "Conversations with Prominence: Null Adams of the *Press-Scimitar*," 1979 (MPL).

12. Memphis *Commercial Appeal*, June 4–8, 1932.

13. *Ibid.*, March 2, August 19, 1930; Robert D. Pope, "Senatorial Baron: The Long Political Career of Kenneth D. McKellar" (unpublished Ph.D. dissertation, Yale University, 1976), 205–12; *New York Times*, October 7, 1932; William D. Miller, *Mr. Crump of Memphis* (Baton Rouge, 1964), 171–73.

14. Miller, *Mr. Crump of Memphis*, 171, 173; Pope, "Senatorial Baron," 205–206 (first quotation); *Congressional Record*, 72 Cong., 2 Sess., 2592–93 (January 26, 1933) (second quotation).

15. Memphis Community Fund, "Annual Report, 1940" (MPL). See also Charles L. Meyers, "Evolution of the Jewish Service Agency in Memphis, Tennessee: 1847 to 1963" (unpublished M.A. thesis, Memphis State University, 1965). On the pattern of a few social welfare organizations in southern cities see Goldfield, *Cotton Fields and Skyscrapers*, 39–44.

16. Memphis Community Fund, "Annual Report, 1931," 2–5.

17. *Ibid.*, 8, 12.

18. "Public Works Program, Memphis, Tennessee," September 1938 (MPL); Memphis *Commercial Appeal*, April 2, 1933.

19. Watkins Overton to E. H. Crump, December 21, 1931, Folder 33, Box 3, Watkins Overton Papers, Mississippi Valley Collection (Memphis State University Library, Memphis, Tenn.). See also Overton to Kenneth D. McKellar, telegram, January 28, 1932, Folder 34, Box 3, *ibid.*

20. U.S. Department of Commerce, *Statistical Abstract of the United States*, 1932, 217; U.S. Department of Commerce, *Statistical Abstract of the United States*, 1934 (Washington, 1934), 213; Overton to Crump, December 7, 1931, Folder 33, Box 3, Overton Papers; Walter Chandler, "Progress Promoted By Taxes," December 1933, Folder 7, Box 12, *ibid.*

21. Sigafoos, *Cotton Row to Beale Street*, 199; Chandler, "Progress Promoted By Taxes," Overton Papers; Overton to Crump, April 27, 1932, Folder 37, Box 3, Overton Papers; Memphis *Commercial Appeal*, May 5, 1944.

22. U.S. Department of Commerce, *Statistical Abstract of the United States*, 1935 (Washington, 1935), 220–21; Sigafoos, *Cotton Row to Beale Street*, 170; Overton to Crump, February 19, 1932, Folder 35, Box 3, Overton Papers. On the plight of the schools see David M. Hilliard, "The Development of Public Education in Memphis, 1848–1945" (unpublished Ph.D. dissertation, University of Chicago, 1946).

23. Memphis *Commercial Appeal*, March 25, 26, 1932, July 27, 1933; "The Barter Movement in Memphis," *Monthly Labor Review*, XXXVI (April 1933), 769.

24. Memphis *Commercial Appeal*, November–December 1930; Everett R. Cook, *Memphis, Cotton's Market Place* (Memphis, 1942), 13; interview with Frank Ahlgren, Memphis State University Oral History Project, Mississippi Valley Collection.

25. Cook, *Memphis, Cotton's Market Place*, 13; Memphis *Commercial Appeal*, July 1, 1934, February 10, 11, 12, 1935, April 10, 1938, January 1, 1940.

26. Memphis *Commercial Appeal*, March 2, 1931.

27. Ed Weathers, "Carnival Knowledge," *City of Memphis*, II (April 1977), 34–35; Miller, *Mr. Crump of Memphis*, 164.

28. Weathers, "Carnival Knowledge," 34.

29. Memphis Chamber of Commerce, "Annual Report, 1931," p. 32 (MPL); Memphis *Commercial Appeal*, March 12, 1933.

30. Memphis *Commercial Appeal*, September 6, 1931 (first quotation), October 29, 1932 (second quotation), June 29, 1932.

31. Memphis *Commercial Appeal*, March 24, 1933 (first and second quoted phrases), April 30, 1933, May 1, 1933 (third quotation), June 17, 1933 (fourth and fifth quoted words).

32. Miller, *Mr. Crump of Memphis*, 179; Crump to Henry H. Haizlip, March 23, 1933, Folder 44, Box 3, Overton Papers (quotation). See also Thomas H. Coode, "Tennessee Congressmen and the New Deal, 1933–1938," *West Tennessee Historical Society Papers*, XXXI (1977), 132–58.

33. David Eugene Conrad, *The Forgotten Farmers: The Story of Sharecroppers in the New

Deal (Urbana, 1965), 43–49; Charles S. Johnson, Edwin R. Embree, and W. W. Alexander, *The Collapse of Cotton Tenancy* (Chapel Hill, 1935), 47–49; Howard Kester, *Revolt Among the Sharecroppers* (New York, 1936), 29.

34. Memphis *Commercial Appeal*, July 21, 1935 (first quotation), January 7, 1936 (second quotation), August 8, 1937 (third quotation), July 14, 1938.

35. Harold Hoffsommer, "The AAA and the Cropper," *Social Forces*, XIII (May 1935), 501 (quotation); Conrad, *The Forgotten Farmers*, 52; Memphis *Commercial Appeal*, December 12, 1933.

36. Donald H. Grubbs, *Cry From The Cotton: The Southern Tenant Farmer's Union and the New Deal* (Chapel Hill, 1971), 58; Kester, *Revolt Among the Sharecroppers*, 30–31; Wilson Gee, "Acreage Reduction and the Displacement of Farm Labor," *Journal of Farm Economics*, XVII (August 1935), 522; Clayton R. Robinson, "The Impact of the City on Rural Immigrants to Memphis, 1880–1940" (unpublished Ph.D. dissertation, University of Minnesota, 1967), 80–94; Gunnar Myrdal, *An American Dilemma: The Negro Problem and Modern Democracy* (New York and London, 1944), 253–58. Throughout the South farm tenancy declined, so that there were 150,000 fewer blacks so employed in 1940 than in 1930. Myrdal, *An American Dilemma*, 253.

37. Lorena A. Hickok to Harry L. Hopkins, June 11, 1934, Folder "Reports, May Through August 1934," Box 11, Lorena A. Hickok Papers (Franklin D. Roosevelt Library, Hyde Park, N.Y., hereinafter cited as FDR Library). See also Robinson, "The Impact of the City on Rural Immigrants," 92–93.

38. Memphis *Commercial Appeal*, November 25, 1933 (first quotation), January 13, 1934; Memphis *Press-Scimitar*, September 1, 1933 (second quotation); John Dean Minton, *The New Deal in Tennessee, 1932–1938* (New York and London, 1979), 91–92.

39. "Report from Memphis District Office to Leighton H. Peebles," September 23, 1933, Compliance Records, Records of the NRA, Record Group 9 (National Archives, Washington, D.C.) (quotation); "Report from Hugh Humphreys to John Swope," March 2, 1934, Public Attitude Reports, Records of the NRA, Record Group 9; Memphis *Press-Scimitar*, May 11, 1935.

40. Memphis *Commercial Appeal*, January 23, 1933; Memphis *Press-Scimitar*, July 6, October 5, 1933; Sigafoos, *Cotton Row to Beale Street*, 178.

41. Minton, *The New Deal in Tennessee*, 64–65; Virginia Ashcraft, "History of Public Welfare Legislation in Tennessee" (unpublished M.A. thesis, University of Tennessee, 1947), 160–62.

42. Smith, "The New Deal and the Urban South," 151–54. For a comprehensive list of CWA projects in Memphis, see Memphis Municipal Reference Library, "Public Works Program," n.p., 1938 (MPL).

43. Arthur M. Schlesinger, Jr., *The Age of Roosevelt: The Politics of Upheaval* (Boston and Cambridge, Mass., 1960), 266–67; City of Memphis, "Public Works Program, January 1, 1928–August 31, 1938," n.p., n.d., Folder 12, Box 8, Overton Papers; Memphis *Press-Scimitar*, May 6, 1937; Department of Streets, Bridges, and Sewers, "Annual Report, 1935," Drawer 1, Mayors' Office Files (Memphis-Shelby County Archives, Memphis, Tenn., hereinafter cited as MSCA); Memphis Municipal Reference Library, "Public Works Program."

44. "Memphis in the Heart of the Mid-South: A Story of Progress Made Possible By Taxes," n.p., 1936, Drawer 1, Mayors' Office Files; Minton, *The New Deal in Tennessee*, 112–13; William F. Larsen, *New Homes for Old: Publicly Owned Housing in Tennessee* (Knoxville, 1948), 21–22; Memphis Housing Authority, "More Than Housing," Annual Report of the MHA, 1939 (MPL).

45. Minton, *The New Deal in Tennessee*, 70–72; City of Memphis, "Public Works Program, January 1, 1928–August 31, 1938," Overton Papers.

46. City of Memphis, "Public Works Program, January 1, 1928–August 31, 1938," Overton Papers; Overton to Crump, July 19, 1937, Drawer 7, Mayors' Office Files (first quotation); Will Fowler to Harry S. Berry, n.d., Drawer 7, *ibid.* (second quotation).

47. Smith, "The New Deal and the Urban South," 265–66; Memphis Board of Com-

missioners, "Resolution," December 3, 1935, Folder 9, Box 10, Overton Papers (first quotation); Memphis *Commercial Appeal*, July 9, December 14, 1935 (second quotation); Memphis Welfare Commission, "Annual Report, 1936," Drawer 1, Mayors' Office Files.

48. Memphis *Press-Scimitar*, September 9, 1936, March 22, 1937.

49. Memphis *Press-Scimitar*, February 18, 1935; U.S. Bureau of the Census, *Financial Statistics of Cities Over 100,000 Population*, 1937 (Washington, 1940), 186–87; Overton to Hill McAlister, August 30, 1933, Folder 7, Box 47, Hill McAlister Papers (State Library and Archives, Nashville, Tenn.) (first quotation); Smith, "The New Deal and the Urban South," 264–65 (second quotation); Elmer Scott to Harry Hopkins, April 15, 1934, Folder "Tennessee Field Reports, 1933–1936," Container 60, Group 24, Harry L. Hopkins Papers (FDR Library).

50. Scott to Hopkins, April 15, 1934, Folder "Tennessee Field Reports, 1933–1936," Container 60, Group 24, Hopkins Papers; Lorena Hickok to Hopkins, June 11, 1934, Folder "Reports, May Through August 1934," Box 11, Hickok Papers.

51. McIlwaine, *Memphis Down in Dixie*, 379–80 (first quotation); Crump to McKellar, September 15, 1940, Folder 1940 Sept.–Dec., Box 4, McKellar-Crump Correspondence, Kenneth D. McKellar Papers (MSCA), (second quotation); Jeanne Graham, "Kenneth McKellar's 1934 Campaign: Issues and Events," *West Tennessee Historical Society Papers*, XVIII (1964), 118; Pope, "Senatorial Baron," 240–41; McKellar to Roosevelt, August 30, 1943, President's Personal File 3715, Franklin D. Roosevelt Papers (FDR Library) (third quotation); Roosevelt to McKellar, September 14, 1943, *ibid.* (fourth quotation).

52. Miller, *Mr. Crump of Memphis*, 179–80.

53. On Roosevelt and the city bosses see Lyle W. Dorsett, *Franklin D. Roosevelt and the City Bosses* (Port Washington, N.Y., and London, 1977); Charles H. Trout, *Boston, the Great Depression, and the New Deal* (New York, 1977); Bruce M. Stave, *The New Deal and the Last Hurrah: Pittsburgh Machine Politics* (Pittsburgh, 1970); and Roger Biles, *Big City Boss in Depression and War: Mayor Edward J. Kelly of Chicago* (DeKalb, Ill., 1984).

54. Lorena Hickok to Harry Hopkins, June 11, 1934, Folder "Reports, May Through August 1934," Box 11, Hickok Papers (first quotation); Crump to McKellar, May 29, 1944, Folder May 1944, Box 5, McKellar-Crump Correspondence, McKellar Papers (second quotation).

55. Gloria Brown Melton, "Blacks in Memphis, Tennessee, 1920–1955: A Historical Study" (unpublished Ph.D. dissertation, Washington State University, 1982), 148–49; Memphis *Press-Scimitar*, March 22, 1937; Memphis *Commercial Appeal*, July 7, 1935; Minton, *The New Deal in Tennessee*, 60.

56. Dorsett, *Franklin D. Roosevelt and the City Bosses*, 40; Miller, *Mr. Crump of Memphis*, 305–306.

57. Smith, "The New Deal and the Urban South," 145 (quotation); Crump to Hill McAlister, November 6, 1933, Folder 4, Box 20, McAlister Papers; McAlister to Crump, October 10, 1933, *ibid.*; Memphis *Commercial Appeal*, November 20, 1934, November 26, 1940.

58. Dorsett, *Franklin D. Roosevelt and the City Bosses*, 46; Pope, "Senatorial Baron," 238 (quotation).

59. *New York Times*, July 26, 1938; Dorsett, *Franklin D. Roosevelt and the City Bosses*, 46–47; Crump to McKellar, May 10, 1938, Folder May 1938, Box 3, McKellar-Crump Correspondence, McKellar Papers.

60. City of Memphis, "Public Works Program, January 1, 1928–August 31, 1938," Overton Papers.

61. Memphis *Press-Scimitar*, November 1, 1936; Baker, *The Memphis Commercial Appeal*, 301–302, 312–13; Crump to McKellar, September 15, 1940, Folder 1940 Sept.–Dec., Box 4, McKellar-Crump Correspondence, McKellar Papers.

62. Memphis *Commercial Appeal*, April 15, 1937, May 3, 1937 (first and second quoted phrases), May 20, 1938; Baker, *The Memphis Commercial Appeal*, 312 (third and fourth quoted phrases).

Politics and Relief in Minneapolis During the 1930s

RAYMOND L. KOCH

The allegation that New Dealers played politics—"vote buying"—with work relief sometimes proved true. Some federal officials engaged in active or passive participation in this political game, while conflicts between state and local officials over control of relief programs were especially severe in Minneapolis, called by some anti–New Dealers "The Moscow of America." These clashes were exacerbated by a third, leftist Farmer-Labor party led by the ostensibly radical Floyd B. Olson, governor from 1930 until his death in 1935. Statewide this party incurred substantial losses in 1934 but remained a potent force in Minneapolis.

THE Great Depression that overshadowed the 1930s brought New Deal reforms which in turn had widespread impact on local government. In particular there was a rapid expansion of public relief departments, with attendant unrest, in larger cities. A study of the turbulent situation in Minneapolis offers insight into the serious difficulties encountered in the almost overnight development of public welfare services. The one overriding factor behind the troubles was the intense pressure for immediate action due to the severity of the economic collapse and the ensuing unemployment. The fact that people had to be kept from starving influenced many

From *Minnesota History*, 41 (Winter 1968), 153–170.

of the actions of various organizations and individuals, especially politicians and social workers, throughout a harrowing decade.

At the outset of the 1929 crash, Minneapolis did not experience the immediate rise in unemployment that the Eastern cities did and consequently weathered the winter of 1929–30 remarkably well. The traditional philosophy of relief-giving—that private charitable agencies should care for the temporarily unemployed—prevailed then in Minneapolis as elsewhere.

By the fall of 1930, however, the number of unemployed requesting aid from the Family Welfare Association, the largest cash assistance private agency in Minneapolis, rose at an alarming pace. The Union City Mission, after the onset of an early October cold wave, bedded more than a thousand homeless and jobless men nightly. A similar development occurred at the Salvation Army's Industrial Home where scores of men were forced to sleep under newspapers because of a scarcity of blankets. As a result, by the end of 1930 private agencies were swamped with the first victims of the depression despite the fact that such agencies had long borne only a small proportion of the total cost for cash assistance. The public relief department still shouldered the greatest cost for needy cases, including resident unemployed and aid to dependent children (or mothers' allowances as the program was then called). Estimates of the total number of unemployed in Minneapolis ran as high as 35,000 in January, 1931.[1]

After the fall elections of 1930, which saw the Farmer-Labor party gain prominence at the state level of politics with the election of Floyd B. Olson as governor, pressure for action on relief needs rapidly increased from organizations of unemployed persons which had sprouted immediately after the great crash.[2] The day after Olson's first inaugural speech, a group of Twin Cities Communists arranged a march to the capitol and staged a demonstration for unemployment relief. They were led by Karl Reeve, district organizer of the Communist party in Minneapolis and leader of a local chapter of the Trade Union Unity League, a Communist-front organization. The group distributed a circular that blasted the American Federation of Labor and the Farmer-Labor party and even accused Olson himself of being a "henchman of the Steel Trust." Several weeks later the Trade Union Unity League scheduled William Z. Foster, a leading national Communist figure, to speak on March 2, 1931, in the Minneapolis Gateway district, a haven for transients and local homeless and jobless individuals. Mayor William F. Kunze banned the speech, but the league tried to hold a meeting anyway. The result was the "Gateway riot," as it was called the next day after police broke up the assembled group.[3]

As the depression intensified with every passing week during its second year, private agency social workers and administrators realized they could no longer assume responsibility for cases ignored by the public relief department. The government—the common social instrument of all the people—was the only effective means of alleviating the situation. So, as pressure mounted on local politicians, tension developed in Minneapolis between the city council, the board of public welfare, and the division of public relief. Although the relief division dated back to the 1890s, the welfare board dictated city relief policies. The board included the mayor, three councilmen, and three lay members. The mayor appointed the latter six for four-year overlapping terms, subject to city council approval. While the board was the official policy-maker, the council voted the relief appropriations to be distributed by the board, a function that in many instances proved to be an effective control device.[4]

Mounting demands for relief gave Farmer-Labor candidates their best issue in the 1931 city elections. Farmer-Labor–endorsed William A. Anderson replaced conservative William F. Kunze as mayor, and the party's representation increased on the Minneapolis city council. Following the Farmer-Labor victories, the welfare board was deluged with complaints about lengthening relief lines, delays in processing applications, and inadequate food orders. Richard S. Tattersfield, long-time superintendent of the division of public relief, came under heavy attack for showing more interest in conserving public funds than in supplying the needy. He resigned effective September 15, 1931, and was succeeded by his chief critic, Alderman Melchior U. S. Kjorlaug, who, unlike Tattersfield, was trained in social work.[5]

The shift of superintendents marked the beginning of a decade-long effort to achieve greater efficiency and effectiveness in processing relief applications. Kjorlaug undertook department reorganization and promoted the adoption of professional casework techniques. Several trained social workers were added to the staff. Also, the intake department took steps to insure at least a measure of privacy during its interviews.[6]

The combined efforts of public and private welfare agencies helped Minneapolis to emerge from the winter of 1931–32 in better condition than many other cities. However, local resources were nearing depletion. Social workers warned that larger expenditures would be needed for the coming year. The arrival of spring failed to decrease unemployment. Families who had already skimped along at a minimum level of subsistence were, in increasing numbers, forced to make their first application for relief. While most private relief-giving agencies had nearly doubled their

budgets over the previous year, they could not begin to keep up with demands. In the face of mounting tax delinquencies and persistent agitation
by taxpayers' associations for reduced government spending, municipalities
had to spend more and more for relief. In 1932 Minneapolis issued over
two million dollars in bonds for direct relief alone. The year 1932 also
proved to be the last in which private agencies shared any important part
of the cost of unemployment relief. The Family Welfare Association of
Minneapolis in that year was allocated over $600,000 from the Commu-
nity Chest, most of which went to aiding jobless families. In 1933 this sum
dropped below $500,000 and kept on dropping thereafter to a low of
$200,000 in 1938.[7]

Left-wing dissidents intensified their activities in 1932, further com-
pounding the tense relief situation. By summer large numbers of the unemployed were appearing at City Hall, invading council meetings and
heckling aldermen whose proposals dissatisfied them, particularly those
who suggested a work relief program. Objecting vigorously to any work
arrangement, they favored direct relief only, and that preferably in cash.
Late in June, when the relief division was faced with an imminent shut-
down owing to the inability of the board of estimate and taxation to sell
relief bonds at less than the prevailing interest rate, the *Minneapolis Journal* ran an editorial condemning relief division policies which, it said, had
led to its current plight. "Beneficiaries now boo and jeer backers of the
groceries-for-work system because they were encouraged for many months
to believe that the groceries were rightly theirs without any adequate return in labor." Inevitably, the editorial went on to cite instances of "sponging" in which several heads of families were found to have some means of
support other than direct relief. The *Journal* misplaced the blame, however, since the relief policies were established by the board of public welfare, not the division of relief. Ultimately, the policies of the board were
controlled by the city council, which determined the amount of money to
be spent and in what manner it should be granted.[8]

The summer relief crisis reached a peak on July 8, 1932, when approximately seven hundred "hunger marchers" demonstrated again in
front of City Hall. They demanded a five-million-dollar appropriation for
city relief, an eight-dollar-a-week grant to unemployed workers, and a slum
clearance program. Invading the city council chambers, the demonstrators
listened to two Farmer-Labor aldermen protest Mayor Anderson's reap-
pointment of one of the conservative members of the board of public welfare—Mrs. H. S. Godfrey—to another four-year term. One of the

aldermen, Albert G. Bastis, was a vitriolic politician who contributed considerably to the relief turmoil for the next few years. Bastis declared that the mayor's appointee did not understand the relief problem and that the welfare board was obsolete. He also accused private agencies of making money on the transients, since these agencies charged the city for the price of meals given to homeless men seeking aid. Bastis created a sensational disturbance several weeks later at another council meeting when he brought in a sack of stale bread and other food in various stages of decomposition, saying it had been given to a woman by the relief department. When Alderman Frank H. Brown ventured to challenge Bastis, his remarks were "met by catcalls and imprecations from the rear of the room. . . . 'That is exactly what we get,' 'eat it yourself and see,' and other such cries were heard above the din." Such skirmishes turned out to be the preliminary events of a battle that would continue for a number of years as the Farmer-Labor party increased its membership, both on the council and on the board of public welfare.[9]

In retrospect, 1932 was no doubt the year of discontent. The state and national governments had refused to act. Left-wing agitators were active everywhere. Social workers had long since abandoned the belief that local relief agencies could handle the crisis. Consequently, relief operations in Minneapolis throughout the winter of 1932–33 continued on the precarious pay-as-you-go system. When the situation grew drastic, the relief department threatened to close down, forcing the city council to issue bonds to provide relief for one more month. Relief rolls increased sharply in November with the arrival of bitterly cold weather. Union City Mission reported that it was serving 1,800 homeless men daily. The Community Fund drive fell short of its goal, and a resoliciting campaign had to be initiated to meet its budget. Meanwhile, several studies of city relief operations were being conducted. One report presented to the council recommended the division of the city into four relief districts and a complete reorganization of the relief department. Another study prepared by a committee which included University of Minneapolis sociologist F. Stuart Chapin indicated that the relief department was inadequately staffed and placed the blame on the lack of leadership exerted by the board of public welfare. This report pointed out that in September the fifteen investigators each averaged 311 visits, and then they reached only 4,662 cases out of a total of 8,611 families on the relief roll. Professional social workers insisted that 150 visits per month should be the maximum for adequate service.

While this recommendation was heeded and the staff increased, the proportionate rise in family cases (to over 13,000 by March, 1933) cancelled out any decrease in the number of visits assigned to each investigator.[10]

The Minneapolis mayoralty campaign in May, 1933, centered almost entirely on the relief issue. Incumbent Mayor Anderson lost the support of his own local Farmer-Labor Association, which contended that he had failed to improve relief standards. The Farmer-Laborites backed Thomas E. Latimer, who had served as an attorney for one of the local organizations of unemployed. Conservatives backed Alexander G. ("Buzz") Bainbridge, a local theater manager and director of a stock company known as the Bainbridge Players. Anderson and Bainbridge survived the primary, while the Communist candidate, Morris ("Red") Karson, for all his popularity among the unemployed groups, polled only 978 votes. Following the primaries, Bainbridge stridently attacked the failure of the board of public welfare to carry out a large work relief program. He advocated a compulsory work program and a complete reorganization of the relief department. Anderson, who tried to steer a middle course between Bainbridge's position and the radical demands of the Farmer-Laborites, was defeated easily by 10,000 votes in June. Thus, while the remainder of the country had swung to the political left in the 1932 elections, seven months later Minneapolis elected a conservative mayor.[11]

Bainbridge erased all doubts about his intentions when, a month after his election, he presented his reorganization plan. Under the guise of economy, he proposed that the relief department's entire investigative staff of fifty-seven social workers be abolished. Bainbridge argued that the police department could better handle investigations. Trained social workers, he declared, were not required in public welfare administration. Bainbridge also contended that Minneapolis had become a haven for "floaters from all over the country" and that the relief department's paternalistic policies toward unemployed transients cost the city an unwarranted thirty cents a day for each case. The new mayor proposed that all aid to nonresident transients be stopped by October 1. A majority of both the board of public welfare and the relief department resolutely objected to Bainbridge's scheme, and the investigative procedure remained intact. The squabble, however, opened up a split between Superintendent Kjorlaug and the mayor, who presided over the board. The feud flared publicly in September when Kjorlaug charged that the relief department had become a "political football" because of Bainbridge's irresponsible charges. Kjorlaug called for a public investigation of his department to clear its name. The mayor responded by demanding Kjorlaug's resignation on the grounds that the superintendent was "temperamentally unfitted for the position."[12]

The dispute was augmented when several workers in the department informed the mayor of procedures they considered unsatisfactory. One social worker, Mrs. Blanche B. van Poll, even congratulated Bainbridge on his election victory. This proved too much for Kjorlaug, who suspended her for ninety days. Throughout the controversy, Kjorlaug could count on support from a large majority of his staff, the board of public welfare, and several prominent civic organizations and church leaders. Eventually Bainbridge retreated from his adamant demands. By winter, 1933, the development of the National Recovery Administration and the creation of the Civil Works Administration had diverted newspaper headlines away from the mayor's scrimmage with the relief department.[13]

The burst of publicity over the relief situation (it made front-page news throughout most of July, August, and September) had both good and bad effects. On the positive side it made many private citizens and most public officials aware of the difficult problems faced by the relief department. For all of Bainbridge's fulminations against relief policies, his battle with Kjorlaug served to educate the mayor on matters he knew little about. By 1934 the fuss simmered down, and Bainbridge took a more moderate position on relief policy. The dispute also produced careful and more reliable checks on outside income of clients, a classification of transients, and an improved rent policy. The rent issue provided one of the major causes of the periodic "invasions" of the relief offices by client organizations which protested the eviction notices renters all too often received.[14] With the advent of the federal relief programs (Minneapolis received its first shipment of surplus commodities in October, 1933), unemployment demonstrations decreased. Left-wing agitators could not stir up as much sympathy for their marches when stomachs were filled. In addition, a number of civic associations and religious groups became more interested in relief conditions. Such "awareness" served to form at least a measure of public support for the relief department.

The unfortunate aspect of the debate was the continued exploitation of the relief question by city politicians—both liberal and conservative. Ultimately, it was the relief client who suffered. There was little doubt even in the most "liberal" of minds that a small percentage of the clients constituted a "professional relief class" that schemed and contrived to get a living out of relief without any effort to seek work. These usually formed the nucleus of groups which demonstrated at City Hall, where left-wing agitators could count on them for support. By far the largest number of cases, however, were heads of families who would have preferred work could they have found it and who applied for relief only as a last resort against starvation. This group seldom made newspaper headlines.

The rapid expansion of the relief load from 1931 to 1935 was reflected in the size of the department itself. Its 1930 staff of seven had grown to more than 350 by the close of 1935. The average monthly case load was around two thousand during the winter of 1930–31; by December, 1934, it was over 21,000. In the meantime a detailed system of investigative procedures and a comprehensive set of written personnel qualifications had been established. This process of reorganization was accomplished by Kjorlaug, who labored long and hard to bring order and efficiency into his administration.[15]

The year 1935 saw the program involved in another political crisis. Certain politicians—especially those with a large number of needy constituents—had long exerted pressure on relief officials to place their "boys" on the relief rolls. This pressure increased in 1934 after the outbreak of the sensational and violent truck strike, with many of the pickets demanding and getting public relief.[16]

The mayoralty campaign in the spring of 1935, like the one in 1933, was fought primarily on the relief issue. Farmer-Laborites again backed Thomas E. Latimer. While calling for substantial increases in relief allowances, they also demanded the dismissal of Kjorlaug. Incumbent Mayor Bainbridge campaigned mainly for economy—an unpopular issue—and he was ousted in the primary. Enough relief clients and jobless voters turned out at the polls early in June to elect Latimer over Charles F. Keyes. The election also gave liberals and Farmer-Laborites a majority on the city council, leading to a change in the composition of the board of public welfare. Two Farmer-Labor councilmen, Edwin I. Hudson and I. G. Scott, replaced board members who had lost their council seats. The third councilman on the board was its vice-chairman, William J. McGaughren, chairman of the Hennepin County Farmer-Labor Association, who, paradoxically, was considered a conservative in matters of relief. The lay members included local businessman I. S. Joseph, the only other conservative on the board, and two labor-backed members, Dr. Albert G. Herbolsheimer and Selma Seestrom, a member of the executive board of the Hennepin County Farmer-Labor Women's Federation. Mrs. Seestrom replaced Mrs. H. S. Godfrey, a long-time board member who resigned in August because (so she said) she was threatened with violence by relief clients for her opposition to increases in allowances.[17]

After the election the organizations of unemployed redoubled their efforts to insure that Farmer-Labor campaign promises would be carried out. One factor that undoubtedly contributed to the increased agitation for more relief was the sharp cutbacks in funds made by the Federal Emergency Relief Administration (FERA) during the spring and summer of 1935. Often clients eligible for work relief experienced a considerable delay in receiving assistance. They were not always put on direct relief immediately, and the Works Progress Administration (WPA) did not get under way as quickly as anticipated. The liquidation of the FERA took place by successive steps from month to month. The largest cut in the work program came in August. Many former work relief clients were thrust on the direct relief rolls, placing an unexpected burden on the city.

The Farmer-Labor–controlled board of public welfare assumed power on July 1, 1935. Two weeks later it publicized its program, calling for an increase of up to 130 percent in family relief grants and a doubling of annual relief expenditures by the city council. Board member Joseph predicted that the plan would bankrupt the city in four months.[18] Early in August, however, the majority voted for increases in relief allowances averaging approximately 35 percent.

Meanwhile, Mayor Latimer frantically held meetings with state relief officials. Along with representatives from St. Paul and Duluth, he asked the state executive council for more funds. The request was denied. Then Latimer asked the State Emergency Relief Administration (SERA) to allocate more money to Minneapolis. Again, help was denied. Moreover, federal and state relief officials threatened immediate withdrawal of financial support unless the board of public welfare rescinded its increased relief schedule. During this time city relief officials saw their funds rapidly dwindling away. The situation finally reached a crisis late in August when the city comptroller stopped honoring all relief orders because the allocated funds were gone. This placed Farmer-Labor officials in an exceedingly awkward position. They had, at the insistence of their constituents, increased relief allowances; yet because of that very policy their followers faced the possibility of receiving nothing. The board had no choice, so it rescinded the higher allowances on August 28. By this time several new WPA projects had taken some of the clients off the direct relief rolls.[19]

The August events were only preliminary skirmishes for the major battle yet to come. For some time city officials had been criticizing the SERA policy of allocating proportionately more funds to the rural counties than to the urban areas. During the summer of 1935 the SERA made a vigorous attempt to force the rural counties to furnish more money—an effort that resulted in the withdrawal of eighteen southern counties from the SERA. With funds from the FERA rapidly decreasing, the SERA found it more and more difficult to keep pace with the increasing demands from city relief officials for assistance.

The majority on the board of public welfare, spurred by Hudson and Scott, now tried a new tactic. In a concerted effort to gain control over the distribution of all relief funds, including state and federal, the board in October denied desk space in the central relief office to SERA's official representative, Edna Dumaresq. Miss Dumaresq's responsibility was to see that city officials did not misappropriate federal and state funds. Hudson and Scott charged that the SERA social service director, Benjamin E. Youngdahl, was trying to run the board. Youngdahl responded by intimating that the SERA would hold up its monthly allocation to Minneapolis if Miss Dumaresq were not immediately reinstated. The dispute brought out into the open the long-simmering conflict between the right and left wings of the Farmer-Labor party. Latimer publicly favored Youngdahl's position—as did the two conservatives on the board, McGaughren and Joseph. Paradoxically, Youngdahl believed in strong central control—the very thing that the conservatives had always objected to in federal programs. To the conservatives, however, the greater evil at the moment was the blatant attempt of local politicians to gain control of city relief funds.[20]

This direct confrontation of federal versus local authority was further complicated by an announcement from Washington that all federal relief aid to the states would cease on November 15. Since the WPA could not employ all of those eligible for work relief, the city council now had to appropriate even larger sums for direct relief. While the welfare board stumped hard for the sale of additional relief bonds, the city council remained obstinate. Council conservatives, weary of the antics of the board and of Hudson and Scott in particular, now saw their chance for revenge. During the 1930s the city council numbered twenty-six aldermen, two from each ward. Only eleven were conservative in 1935, but they could block a bond issue as it required eighteen votes to pass. Consequently, the conservatives declared they would not vote for the sale of any more relief bonds until the council majority (a coalition of Farmer-Laborites and liberals) removed Hudson and Scott from the board of public welfare. There the matter stood—deadlocked—with the conservatives holding the trump card, since relief bonds would have to be issued eventually.[21]

Meanwhile, Youngdahl engaged in a power play of his own. In the spring of 1935 the SERA, following federal instructions to get more local financial participation, had made an agreement with the welfare board. The substance of it was that the state agency would pay direct relief costs for 1935 above the sum of $1,719,000, which the city board agreed to appropriate. When the dispute erupted in October, Youngdahl, after a preliminary investigation, decided that Minneapolis had not lived up to its contract. When the board increased its individual relief grants in August, it spent more than the original agreement had called for. Beyond that, the board had spent over $75,000 for items the SERA did not consider direct relief, such as mothers' pensions, burials, and housing for homeless men. Youngdahl thus refused to release any more funds to the welfare board. This prompted Hudson to retort: "If Youngdahl is running this board and the relief department, we ought to know it right now." On Monday morning, November 18, the Minneapolis relief department did not open its doors. Hudson and Scott were now trapped; their ward constituents could receive no relief funds. After a hasty conference between the antagonists, the board agreed to reinstate Miss Dumaresq, after which the SERA released $250,000 to the board.[22]

City funds, however, were still being held up by the council conservatives. On November 20 the majority liberal bloc attempted to transfer appropriations from the council's permanent revolving fund to the relief department, but City Attorney Richard S. Wiggin (a Farmer-Laborite) overruled this action. He said it was contrary to the city charter. The next day Kjorlaug cut direct relief to food and fuel items only, giving nothing for rent, clothes, or electricity. The board was now confronted with the effects of its own folly. While claiming to represent the interests of relief clients, Hudson and Scott had succeeded in reducing the already inadequate grants to the barest minimum, leading to even more suffering for the recipients. The financial crisis eased somewhat when state Attorney General Harry H. Peterson (Farmer-Laborite) overruled Wiggin and allowed the council to "borrow" money from its revolving fund. This action automatically released additional SERA funds which were still being withheld pending the issuance of relief bonds by the city council. Although Peterson admitted his ruling was contrary to the city charter, he said that provision for the poor was paramount and overrode all other legal considerations. In December the bond question finally was resolved when five liberal aldermen joined the conservatives and ousted Scott and Hudson from the welfare board. The conservatives then quickly voted the necessary relief funds.[23]

The turmoil, however, did not cease. One of the Farmer-Labor campaign slogans during the 1935 mayoralty race had been, "Kjorlaug must

go." The basic reason for this demand lay beneath the surface of custom-
ary political oratory; it struck at the very nature of social work itself. Although a competent and not unsympathetic administrator, Kjorlaug was a
dedicated practitioner of the case-work method developed by Mary E.
Richmond, whose emphasis on "adjusting the individual to his environment" had prevailed in social work during the 1920s.[24] After 1929 it became
ludicrous to ask a relief client to adjust to an environment that had collapsed about him. Clients objected to the case-work approach. They
wanted neither to be "adjusted" nor to be psychoanalyzed; all they wanted
was their relief order. They got support from relief investigators, also called
"visitors," who by 1935 numbered over a hundred. Most of them belonged
to the Minneapolis Social Workers' Council, local branch of the national
rank-and-file movement and essentially a trade union for bettering the lot
of relief workers who labored long hours with large case loads for low
salaries.[25]

Many Minneapolis rank-and-file visitors publicly opposed Kjorlaug's
case-work policies. In response to their objections, the welfare board in August, 1935, appointed five special investigators (themselves members of the
staff) to examine relief department activities. Apparently the Social Workers' Council was experiencing its own internal power struggle as left-wing
relief visitors tried to gain control of the leadership. According to one report, when the "complaint committee" initiated its investigations, "panic
and fear began creeping among the staff. In investigating the investigators
it was meeting in semi-secret sessions with a few of the least responsible
members of the S.W.C. Rumors, veiled threats, promises of better jobs,
spying, intimidation served to disrupt morale." The complaint committee
made its first report to the welfare board on November 16 at the height of
the SERA controversy. Most of the 1,500 client complaints studied, the
committee said, were caused by lack of prompt service, but many clients
took strong exception to the case-work method of investigation. This report
was one reason why the welfare board suspended Kjorlaug on December
4 for ninety days to "discipline" him for policies it said were creating turmoil within the relief staff. The board also recommended immediate reorganization of the relief department. Board conservatives Joseph and
McGaughren opposed the suspension, as did practically all of the city's private social agencies. Kjorlaug himself refused to resign. At first the board
tried unsuccessfully to return Richard Tattersfield to his old post and then
appointed Norma Fodness, a former president of the Social Workers' Council, as acting relief superintendent. She, however, was not acceptable to
the council.[26]

Beset by pressure from all sides, Mayor Latimer organized a citizens' committee of fifty prominent civic and labor leaders to investigate all city relief operations. Labor representatives soon split off to form their own investigating committee in conjunction with organizations of unemployed. Among other things, the labor committee recommended the "new system," recently installed by the welfare board in the north and northeast districts, which operated on the premise that granting of relief was primarily a financial transaction. It did not humiliate the client by prying into his personal life.[27]

Meanwhile, increasingly irritated over the state of affairs, SERA Administrator L. P. Zimmerman issued an ultimatum that Minneapolis would receive no additional funds unless all personnel changes in the relief department were submitted to the SERA for approval. Zimmerman also insisted that relief costs be reduced and that the administration of relief be purged of politics. But Mrs. Fodness, unmoved by SERA threats, said she would continue to make personnel changes. She proposed elimination of fifty-five investigators and twenty-one clerks and recommended salary increases of $70 a month for some of the remaining workers. This ignited a violent demonstration by rank-and-file workers whose spokesman declared that the situation had become intolerable with such "snooping and sniping all the time." The board responded by halting staff reductions, removing Mrs. Fodness, and appointing a moderate Farmer-Laborite, Alderman Ole Pearson, relief superintendent. Although Joseph held out for Kjorlaug's reinstatement, most of the board felt the internal conflict within the relief department had become so vicious that he must leave. Kjorlaug finally gave up his battle and resigned late in February, 1936.[28]

After Pearson's appointment the staff hoped for a breathing spell in the ferment over relief that had been making headlines since the summer before. But in April, 1936, the administration of relief again appeared in news stories that revealed what many citizens had long suspected.

Throughout the battle between relief workers, politicians, and the welfare board, the city attorney's office had been conducting its own investigation into relief operations. By April, Joseph A. Hadley, assistant city attorney, had uncovered enough evidence to bring charges against several relief department employees and clients for defrauding the city. Five investigators had posed as "clients," filling out orders to themselves and presenting the orders to merchants. Some transient clients were found to have sold books of meal tickets (given to them by the relief department) for "de-horn" liquor. In addition, nearly two dozen cases of irregularities were uncovered among merchants who handled relief orders.[29]

Pearson, determined that all cases of fraud be disclosed, backed the investigations. He himself ordered the relief department onto a five-day week after it became apparent that some clients who had obtained work still remained on the rolls and were coming to the department on Saturday to obtain relief orders. Pearson subsequently reorganized the payroll investigation division in order to examine as many city payrolls as possible to ferret out those relief clients who had acquired jobs. The investigations resulted in the sentencing of two clients, two merchants, and one relief employee to a year in the workhouse. Furthermore, a number of merchants had their licenses revoked, and several investigators resigned. The episode served to increase public criticism of the entire relief program.[30]

Pearson intensified his drive for administrative efficiency throughout the summer of 1936. In July the welfare board ordered a reregistration of all clients on the rolls. This became necessary for two reasons: it was found that clients on WPA jobs had represented themselves as "artisans" (thus making them eligible for higher wages) when they were actually unskilled workers; and the old age assistance program (OAA) recently had been launched, providing help to many former direct relief clients. The procedure for reregistration, which applied a strict means test to close relatives, also required that the applicant take an oath and sign an affidavit that his resources, if any, were correctly represented. This precipitated a great outcry from clients—so much so that Attorney General Harry H. Peterson intervened to rule that the oath was not a part of the relief law and could not be enforced legally. During 1936 the Workers Alliance had emerged as the major organization representing the unemployed. Its leaders appeared at meeting after meeting of the welfare board during the fall of that year to insist upon a higher food allowance to counter fluctuations in food prices. Their persistence eventually brought a small victory; in December the board voted a 10 percent increase in the amount allotted for groceries.[31]

By 1937 internal relief department conflicts ebbed as Pearson worked hard to bring order and stability to his administration. Outside forces, however, were again at work. Community control over the left-wing elements in the Hennepin County Farmer-Labor Association was evidenced when Mayor Latimer failed to gain his party's endorsement for the 1937 election. The previous year Latimer had charged publicly that Communists were infiltrating Farmer-Labor ranks, particularly in Hennepin County. Left-wingers responded to Latimer's charge with the demand that he be "thrown out of the Farmer-Labor party." The quarrel intensified during the summer of 1936 when the mayor tried unsuccessfully to remove Selma Seestrom, a left-wing favorite, from the board of public welfare. He thus identified himself with the right-wing Farmer-Laborites and in doing so lost considerable support from the unemployed groups. As a result of this turmoil the Farmer-Laborites gave their endorsement to Kenneth C. Haycraft, state director of old age assistance. Conservatives supported George E. Leach, who had been mayor of Minneapolis four times during the 1920s. The squabbling within the ranks of labor and the Farmer-Labor party took its toll on election day; Haycraft was soundly beaten by Leach. Farmer-Laborites did gain some satisfaction from the aldermanic races; the progressive bloc managed to retain control of the city council.[32]

By the spring of 1937 the national economy had shown enough improvement so that President Franklin D. Roosevelt ordered a sharp cut in WPA rolls. The slash had hardly been made when an acute recession sent the economy downward during the late summer and fall. The recession, coupled with the WPA cuts, thrust a host of families and individuals back onto the direct relief rolls. These events coincided with the return of Leach to the mayor's office. City officials, civic groups, and even moderate Farmer-Laborites such as McGaughren of the welfare board voiced fears about the eventual effects of the high cost of relief. Since Minneapolis's recent laws covering old age assistance and aid to dependent children required considerable financial participation from local political units, city relief costs were rising to new heights in 1937.[33]

Efforts were made to lower the city's direct relief load, which continued to average between 12,000 and 15,000 monthly throughout 1937 despite the advent of the old age assistance program. Mayor Leach, pressured by civic groups that had supported him during the election, decided to inaugurate his own drive to reduce the relief rolls. He was supported by McGaughren, who suggested that clients should not own automobiles, telephones, and other such luxuries. Area farmers complained bitterly that the WPA had drastically reduced the available number of harvest workers, and McGaughren felt that all able-bodied single men on relief in Minneapolis should be forced to take jobs in harvest fields or be automatically cut off the direct relief rolls. Leach opened his drive by urging all civic organizations to find jobs for employable relief clients. He requested that at least one be hired in each of the thousand or more manufacturing establishments in Minneapolis. While it was a commendable idea and highly praised by the Civic and Commerce Association, only a handful of businesses hired relief clients. Leach also requested all the case records so that he could go through them and personally investigate any doubtful ones. As far as economy-minded citizens were concerned, this was another praiseworthy idea. The mayor learned, however, that case records were confidential; even he did not have access to them.[34]

The welfare board itself initiated economy steps. Since November, 1936, the board had allowed a monthly supplement of nine dollars to WPA workers. Originally, this supplement covered only fuel, but it was continued through the summer of 1937 as a food supplement, since WPA employees received equal pay (within each of its classifications) regardless of the number of dependents in each family. Early in August, however, the welfare board discontinued giving supplementary assistance to WPA workers. This action brought immediate protests from the Workers Alliance and the Federal Workers Section of General Drivers Union 544, which threatened to lead a general march of WPA workers off their projects and onto the direct relief rolls unless the supplement was restored. The board not only stood firm on its decision but went even further. In September I. S. Joseph, board finance chairman, warned that relief spending must be cut immediately or Minneapolis would suffer a possible taxpayers' strike and almost certain financial ruin. Joseph's report prompted the board to enact a series of policy changes, the most stringent being the removal of all healthy single men under forty-five and all healthy single women under thirty-five from the relief rolls until December when they would then have to reapply for aid. Other new regulations included: the adoption of a clothing-according-to-need policy, replacing the old set clothing budget allowance; insistence on contributions from all employed unmarried children in relief households; removal of automobile owners from the rolls except in emergency cases; and refusal of relief to any client who was able to obtain credit.[35]

These policy changes were brought about by a number of factors. The turmoil within the relief department itself, the lenient attitude toward clients by many relief investigators, the complex of programs which led to considerable case duplication, client reluctance to take jobs (often in fear that wages would be garnished to pay debts)—all these produced a ground swell of public resentment against certain aspects of the mass relief programs. Many still harbored traditional beliefs about relief, feeling that it should be made as difficult as possible to get and that any allowance should cover only the barest of need. Hard-pressed taxpayers resented the use of relief funds to support such "luxuries" as radios, automobiles, telephones, or even a good suit of clothes. In addition, the influence of left-wingers among the organizations of unemployed (which exacted as much as twenty-five cents per month from relief client members) became increasingly distasteful to even those who were moderately liberal. Mc-Gaughren charged that "direct relief in Minneapolis has become a racket," that the leaders of relief organizations were attempting to build direct relief into a permanent activity, and that these groups actually tried to prevent clients from performing any work. No doubt most of the criticisms against relief clients were justified to some degree, but they applied only to a small percentage of the total case load. There were still thousands of individuals and families suffering great deprivation not of their own choosing. The simple fact remained that those desperately in need of economic assistance could not get jobs of any kind.[36]

The new regulations served only to increase agitation by organizations of unemployed. Five days after the restrictions became effective, representatives of the Workers Alliance and the Federal Workers Section of Local 544 held a stormy session with the welfare board in which they vigorously protested the new policies. The meeting ended with a promise by Leach that no needy person would be denied relief. Leach also agreed to ask state WPA Director Victor A. Christgau to increase WPA employment, although he knew very well that Christgau could do nothing because all state monthly quotas were determined solely in Washington. Relief Administrator Zimmerman, however, partially sided with the relief clients and threatened to withhold state funds unless the board of public welfare dropped its harsh policy against single men and women.[37]

In the face of the deepening recession and the WPA's refusal to increase its monthly quotas, organizations of unemployed increased their agitation. They were backed by the tacit approval of Governor Elmer A. Benson and his aides. In October, 1937, WPA workers on Minneapolis projects threatened to strike unless the welfare board revoked its new regulations. Late in October the board did rescind the order barring single men under forty-five and single women under thirty-five from direct relief and the order prohibiting clients from owning automobiles. The problem of supplementary aid to WPA workers with large families still remained, however. WPA employees continued to protest by threatening strikes and insisting upon additional support. In December the welfare board voted to supplement WPA wages for needy families up to 25 percent if necessary. Thus, if a WPA worker with a large number of dependents received a "security wage" of $55 (the maximum wage for an unskilled worker at the time), he could receive an additional sum of nearly $14 from the city relief department.[38]

Through the winter of 1937–38 the recession continued, causing the highest direct relief load in Minneapolis history. There was a peak of 17,654 relief cases in March. By this time President Roosevelt had requested and received increased appropriations for the WPA. Throughout 1938, as WPA quotas for each state rose, the direct relief load declined. How to finance direct relief remained a vexing problem. Aid from the state relief administration was limited to the appropriations passed by the 1937 legislature. The president of the Minneapolis board of estimate and taxation proposed that the Minnesota income tax be increased so that the state could allocate additional sums to the urban areas. The Hennepin County grand jury, conducting its own study of relief costs, suggested a halt to the issuing of bonds and proposed that relief be financed instead by a city sales tax, thus backing Leach's demand. Farmer-Labor Alderman Harold Kauth proposed that relief funds be raised by a public lottery. This brought an avalanche of criticism from churches, civic leaders, and conservative politicians. In the end, the city council reverted to form. It continued selling relief bonds.[39]

Under the leadership of Pearson, who remained superintendent throughout the 1940s, the relief department gradually worked its way toward a stabilized and effective administration. It was aided immeasurably by the development of a permanent federal program. Also of assistance was a department survey requested early in 1938 by the welfare board and conducted by the American Public Welfare Association (APWA). Among other things, the APWA study concluded that the relief granted was adequate but that the staff lacked knowledge of modern case-work techniques. "Many cases showed an inability to evaluate the situation from any viewpoint other than relief eligibility," the report said. It contended that visitors ought to aid clients in "problem-solving." The study also criticized a lack of cooperation with other agencies as well as the excessive paper work necessitated by the setup of four district intake offices. The welfare board welcomed most of the association's suggestions and gave Pearson authority to pursue reorganization as he deemed necessary. One result was a trend toward employing professional social workers and developing higher minimum qualifications for visitors.[40]

The history of the Minneapolis relief department through the 1930s reveals the consequences of political intrigue in the development of a public relief program. The constant turmoil over the giving of assistance was enhanced by several factors present in the city's relief environment. Obviously, one factor was the general economic condition. Another was the influence of the Farmer-Labor party on the board of public welfare and in the city council. Organizations comprised of discontented relief clients and led by left-wing agitators exerted considerable pressure on the local Farmer-Labor party, and extreme left-wing members of the Hennepin County Farmer-Labor Women's Federation also became active in relief politics. A third factor contributing to the turmoil in relief administration was the "pay-as-you-go" system of financing. Relief bonds were issued irregularly by the city council on the basis of how much was needed for the next few months. Other unsettling ingredients were the uncertainty about the extent and duration of federal relief programs and the continual debate within the relief division between rank-and-file workers on one side and the more conservative supervisors on the other.

No one could have divined beforehand the extensive changes that developed during the 1930s. Most significant was the federal government's acceptance of responsibility for meeting the economic needs of distressed Americans. One historian has correctly noted that "the New Deal solved a few problems, ameliorated a few more, obscured many, and created new ones. This is about all our political system can generate, even in crisis."[41] Despite this pessimistic observation, relief programs did bring a measure of sustenance and order into the lives of thousands of Minneapolis residents. By keeping people alive, the New Deal and the Minneapolis relief department unquestionably achieved their most important and immediate goal.

NOTES

1. *Minneapolis Journal,* October 19, sec. 2, p. 2, 15, October 20, p. 15, 1930; Alvin H. Hansen, Nelle M. Petrowski, and Richard A. Graves, *An Analysis of Three Unemployment Surveys in Minneapolis, St. Paul, and Duluth,* 5–7 (University of Minneapolis, Employment Stabilization Research Institute, *Bulletins,* vol. 1, No. 6—August, 1932).

2. Several such groups were active in Minneapolis. The major ones were the United Relief Workers Association, the Unemployed Council, the Workers Alliance (which subsequently absorbed the first two), and the Federal Workers Section of Minneapolis Teamsters Local 574 (in the later 1930s, 544), which after 1935 expanded to include not only the unemployed but also direct relief clients and WPA workers. An excellent brief statement on organizations of unemployed in general is Helen Seymour, *When Clients Organize* (American Public Welfare Association, Chicago, 1937).

3. A copy of the circular is in the unemployment file, Olson Papers, 1931, Governors' Archives, in the Minnesota State Archives. For a description of the Trade Union Unity League, see Irving Howe and Lewis Coser, *The American Communist Party: A Critical History,* 255 (New York, 1962). For background on the Minnesota political scene during the 1930s, see Arthur Naftalin, "A History of the Farmer-Labor Party in Minnesota," unpublished doctoral dissertation, University of Minnesota, 1948 (copy in the Minnesota Historical Society), and George H. Mayer, *The Political Career of Floyd B. Olson* (Minneapolis, 1951). *Min-*

neapolis Journal, March 3, 1931, p. 1 describes the Gateway riot. Unless otherwise noted, all newspaper citations in this article occur on front pages.

4. For information about the administrative structure of the relief department, see Florence W. Hutsinpillar and Clara Paul Paige, *Report of the Division of Relief of the Department of Public Welfare, Minneapolis,* June, 1931, issued in mimeographed form by the United States Department of Labor, Children's Bureau; and Division of Public Relief, *Historical Review: Four Years of Depression 1931–1934,* a mimeographed report prepared for the Minneapolis board of public welfare.

5. *Minneapolis Journal,* July 23, p. 17, September 4, 1931.

6. Under Tattersfield, applications for assistance were taken over the counter in full view and hearing of others in the cramped quarters. Tattersfield would scribble "Same old bum," "Chronic indigents," and other comments on case records. See Hutsinpillar and Paige, *Report,* 56.

7. Division of Public Relief, *Historical Review,* 7; Family Welfare Association, *Agency Report,* vol. 18 of *Community Survey of Social and Health Work in Minneapolis,* appendix 1, table 1 (Minneapolis Council of Social Agencies, 1938).

8. *Minneapolis Journal,* June 27, 1932, p. 18. By 1932 many professional social workers, public and private, favored some type of work relief program.

9. *Minneapolis Journal,* July 8, p. 1, 8, July 22 (quotations), 1932.

10. *Minneapolis Journal,* November 25, December 7, p. 1, 26, 1932; Division of Public Relief, *Historical Review,* 6.

11. *Minneapolis Journal,* May 9, June 13, June 14, p. 1, 6, 1933. Another factor in Bainbridge's election was that he was a "wet," while Anderson had earlier vetoed a beer ordinance for Minneapolis.

12. *Minneapolis Journal,* July 18, September 9, 1933.

13. *Minneapolis Journal,* September 12, 1933. For background on the NRA and the CWA, see William E. Leuchtenburg, *Franklin D. Roosevelt and the New Deal, 1932–1940,* 64–66, 121 (New York, 1963).

14. Division of Public Relief, *Historical Review,* 22–25.

15. Harry Fiterman, "Relief Shown City's Greatest Problem," in *Minneapolis Journal,* April 20, 1936; Division of Public Relief, *Historical Review,* 6.

16. The strike is dealt with at length in Charles R. Walker, *An American City: A Rank-and-File History* (New York, 1937).

17. *Minneapolis Journal,* June 11, August 7, 1935.

18. *Minneapolis Journal,* July 16, 1935.

19. *Minneapolis Journal,* August 13, 16, p. 1, 28, August 28, 1935. The state executive council was composed of the governor, attorney general, auditor, treasurer, and secretary of state.

20. *Minneapolis Journal,* October 23, 1935, p. 16.

21. *Minneapolis Journal,* November 1, 8, p. 1, 28, 1935.

22. *Minneapolis Journal,* November 14, 17, p. 1, 2 (quotation), November 18, 1935.

23. *Minneapolis Journal,* November 20, 21, 25, December 20, 1935.

24. See Clarke A. Chambers, *Seedtime of Reform: American Social Service and Social Action, 1918–1933,* 97–99 (Minneapolis, 1963).

25. For general interpretations, see Jacob Fisher, *The Rank and File Movement in Social Work, 1931–1936* (New York School of Social Work, New York, 1936).

26. The quotation is from "Shake-up in Minneapolis," in *Social Work Today,* 3:19 (March, 1936). The editors of this decidedly left-wing national organ of the rank-and-file movement attributed the article to "a committee of four members of the Social Workers Council." *Minneapolis Journal,* November 16, December 4, 7, 1935.

27. *Minneapolis Journal,* December 19, 1935; January 7, p. 1, 6, 1936.

28. *Minneapolis Journal,* December 19, 1935; January 14, p. 1, 2 (quotation), February 13, p. 15, February 25, March 10, 13, p. 21, 1936. The welfare board obligingly gave Kjorlaug a clean bill of health on his administration record and praised him for his honesty. For a brief resumé of the battle leading to Kjorlaug's departure, see "Storm Over Minneapolis," in *Sur-*

vey, 72:44 (February, 1936). This was reprinted, with a few changes, in *Minneapolis Journal*, February 14, p. 6, 1936.

29. For major accounts, see *Minneapolis Journal*, April 2, 3, 4, 5, 6, 7, 10, 11, 14, 15, 1936. About four hundred merchants were licensed to do business with relief clients on the basis that they give only those articles that were specified in the order. Some were found to have given items other than those specified.

30. *Minneapolis Journal*, May 5, 1936.

31. *Minneapolis Journal*, July 28, September 14, December 1, p. 1, 6, 1936.

32. *Minneapolis Journal*, March 9, p. 6 (quotation), 13, June 28, July 31, p. 15, 1936; June 15, 1937.

33. Leuchtenburg, *Franklin D. Roosevelt*, 243; Minneapolis Council of Social Agencies, *Community Survey of Social and Health Work in Minneapolis*, vol. 1, sec. 5, p. 3 (Summary Report, 1938).

34. *Minneapolis Journal*, July 21, 28, 29, 1937. Leach also advocated a city sales tax to finance relief costs. See *Minneapolis Journal*, August 6, 1937.

35. *Minneapolis Journal*, August 6, p. 9, August 16, September 2, p. 1, 21, September 3, 1937.

36. *Minneapolis Star*, October 5, 1937.

37. *Minneapolis Journal*, September 8, 14, 1937.

38. *Minneapolis Journal*, October 28, p. 1, 28, December 7, 1937. The December meeting, attended by representatives of WPA workers, labor unions, and unemployed groups, was so stormy that a dozen policemen were called into the room to keep order.

39. *Minneapolis Journal*, April 7, p. 1, 23, June 29, 1938.

40. American Public Welfare Association, *Public Welfare Survey of Minneapolis, Minnesota* (June, 1938), a mimeographed report on the Minneapolis division of public relief. The quotation is on p. 23.

41. Paul Conkin, *The New Deal*, 106 (New York, 1967).

"Heavenly Houston" or "Hellish Houston"? Black Unemployment and Relief Efforts, 1929–1936

RANDY J. SPARKS

Historians have written a great deal about how those African Americans who could vote shifted their allegiance from the party of Abraham Lincoln to the party of Franklin D. Roosevelt. This shift was only tenuously related to the kinds of reforms sought by the civil rights movement after World War II. It was essentially the result of the New Deal relief, even though discrimination or segregation, with some exceptions, marked the administration of New Deal programs. Still, the roots of the later civil rights movement can be traced to the 1930s (see my anthology, The Negro in Depression and War: Prelude to Revolution *[1969]).*

IN 1919 the Houston Chamber of Commerce placed an advertisement in the Houston *Informer*, a leading black newspaper, boasting of the opportunities awaiting blacks in "Heavenly Houston." As a leading cotton port, railroad hub, and center of Texas's nascent oil industry, the city needed large numbers of menial laborers. Thousands of blacks moved to Houston after 1920, but in 1930 the *Informer* warned its readers that "Heavenly

From *Southern Studies*, Winter 1986, 353–366.

Houston" had become "Hellish Houston." The Great Depression devastated the black community; blacks had higher rates of unemployment than whites and desperately needed city, state, and federal relief, but discrimination prevented them from getting the assistance to which they were entitled.

This grim picture of the Depression in Houston conflicts with that painted by the city's leaders during the era and with the traditional historical view of Houston as the city the Depression forgot. David G. McComb, the author of a history of the city, observed that this traditional view "seems correct," but he did not consult sources from the black community.[1] If Houston was better off than other cities, that was true only for the white community. Houston's prosperity was only a facade, a shoddy structure which obscured reality. For black Houstonians the Depression, whether before or after the New Deal, was a devastating experience.

Houston's black population grew rapidly after 1900 as refugees from the boll weevil and agricultural depression arrived in search of city jobs. By 1929 black industrial workers were mainly employed as menial laborers in oil companies, shipping, railroads, and cotton-related firms. Other black workers found jobs as domestics or seasonal laborers on Harris County farms. When the Depression hit, the condition of black workers, never enviable, rapidly deteriorated. The ranks of menial laborers thinned; the number of domestics swelled. Black workers suffered not only because they were workers but also because they were black.[2]

Blacks suffered from intensifying job discrimination even before the Depression affected Houston, possibly because rapid black population growth in the 1920s provoked a white backlash. Jesse O. Thomas, the southern field director of the National Urban League, conducted a survey of black social welfare in Houston during May 1929 and found that because of "rapid replacement" blacks were "losing out in jobs they formerly held." Even menial occupations traditionally regarded as "Negro-jobs" went to members of other races, and such discrimination was not limited to the private sector. In January 1930 the *Informer* observed that "some dictator" in City Hall prohibited blacks from serving as clerks in the fish and oyster stalls in the City Market. The excuse for the rule was that black clerks had been "too flip" with white girls, though no black had ever been reported for this offense. The black newspaper noted that black clerks usually served only black customers while white clerks served white customers. Charging blacks with "uppitiness" or laziness, firing them, and replacing them with white workers quickly became a pattern. In February 1930 black women working in a cleaning plant were replaced by whites.

In April an ice cream factory fired all its black employees except one and hired whites. Understandably, blacks were angered and frightened by this practice. In March the *Informer* observed "reports are afloat that a movement is gaining momentum here to have most . . . concerns discharge all their colored help and replace them with whites." This pattern of discrimination also affected seasonal agricultural jobs; as agricultural prices plummeted, Harris County farmers replaced many black laborers with Hispanics who would work for even lower wages.[3]

Unemployment affected thousands of blacks from 1929 to 1936; their unemployment rate was consistently higher than the rate for the total population. A 1942 study conducted by the University of Texas with the assistance of the Works Project Administration provided the most detailed study of Houston for the 1920s and 1930s. This work divided the city into census tracts and provided employment figures for each tract. Blacks predominated in nine of the fifty-eight tracts. A summary of the study reveals that in 1928 32 percent of the total population did not report employment; the average rate for the nine black tracts was 45.8 percent. In 1934 the ratio was 37 percent of the total population and 55.5 percent of the black tracts; and in 1937–38 the ratio stood at 31 percent of the total population and 44.7 percent of the black tracts. These figures are imprecise, but they suggest that unemployment was far more serious among blacks than among the population as a whole. In February 1931, twenty-nine thousand Houstonians were unemployed. Of this number a staggering twenty thousand were black.[4]

Unemployed blacks desperately needed relief, but Houston was slow in providing even minimal aid for needy blacks. In 1930 a black man arrested for burglary in the city told policemen that he had committed the crime "because he was 'jes so hongry.'" No doubt hunger drove other blacks to such extremes. By 1930 the number of needy people applying for aid overwhelmed the city's charitable organizations.[5]

Many private organizations came under the umbrella of the Houston Community Chest. Of the thirty-three member agencies perhaps the most important for relief was the Social Service Bureau, but its 1929 budget of $37,000 was inadequate. In the first six months of 1929 blacks made up only 17 percent of the cases in the bureau's Family Department, and only 22 percent of the relief went to blacks. The bureau had one case worker to serve a black population of over sixty thousand. The Ex-Slave Home was a Community Chest organization for blacks only. This home for the elderly was located in a poorly drained, undesirable area and consisted of two one-story shacks, one for men and one for women. When Jesse

Thomas visited the home in 1929 he found "some aged men, most of whom had some kind of affliction and very poorly clad in a filthy condition and unhappy." Several of the men were ill or blind. Since there were no screens on the doors or windows, the men battled flies and other insects during the hot Houston summer. The women's quarters were much the same, though perhaps slightly cleaner. Many of the Community Chest agencies made no provisions for blacks, and others provided only second-rate service to blacks. Every year the black community joined in the annual fund-raising drive for the Community Chest and strained their meager resources to contribute. They were poorly repaid for their efforts.[6]

As relief agencies became overburdened, they chose to aid whites first. In December 1930 the *Informer* notified its readers that blacks "must take the rear in such soup lines as have been established. And it is reported that in one of the lines recently, a policeman stands on guard to prevent them from taking any place in the line. The giver of food in that place had decided that only white persons and Mexicans are to be served."[7] As the existence of soup lines indicated, unemployment was a serious problem in Houston by 1930, especially among blacks, but the city's leaders refused to recognize the grim situation. In March 1930 *Houston* magazine, published by the influential Chamber of Commerce, wrote, "There never was a time when the people of Houston had greater cause to think prosperity and talk prosperity than now." While admitting that "There has been some talk of unemployment in Houston," the magazine reported that many people did not have jobs but there was "little unemployment." They resolved this apparent contradiction by saying that transients made up most of the unemployed in the city. The business leaders found "little or no reduction of employee forces and practically no unemployment on the part of our resident population."[8]

While the chamber could deny the existence of unemployment, the city government could not continue to do so; in 1930 the city government took its first halting steps toward organizing a system of public relief. Mayor Walter E. Montieth's Houston Unemployment Aid Committee, which had one black member, set up a commissary in the city auditorium to dispense food. While the mayor organized the committee, it received no city funds. Private agencies carried the "whole burden" of relief, and Montieth opposed issuing bonds to raise funds or accepting federal appropriations to assist local governments in relief. Unlike many cities around the nation, Houston could have afforded to issue bonds or appropriate money for relief. Because of the mayor's tight-fisted monetary policies the city had a balanced budget in 1934—its first in over twenty-five years. Mon-

tieth believed that further government involvement in relief was unnecessary since "the unemployment and relief situation is not only being adequately taken care of at this time, but will be taken care of as long as the
emergency exists."[9]

Actually, as early as 1930 the city's relief program was in serious trouble. In February 1931 W. T. Carter, Jr., chairman of the mayor's committee, announced that his organization was "flat broke" and that the groceries
in the commissary were almost gone. Though funds came in to keep the
commissary in operation, the service was clearly inadequate. Considering
the appointment of a subcommittee to study the plight of the twenty thousand black unemployed, the Unemployment Aid Committee remarked:

> It is a matter of common knowledge that our Negroes have for the most
> part refused to go to the cotton patch this summer. The subcommittee to
> be appointed might well consider the wisdom of immediate registration of
> unemployed Negroes and the committee might decide to promptly inform
> all Negroes who refuse to work either in the cotton patch or elsewhere,
> when work is offered, that they will not be entitled to any aid this winter.

The committee made no reference to just wages. Backed by relief agencies, employers could easily exploit unemployed laborers. In November
1931 the unemployment committee gave groceries to over three thousand
white families and thirteen black families. The Social Service Bureau had
given aid to eight hundred black families by the same date.[10]

The city government's plan to appoint a special subcommittee on black
unemployment had been abandoned, and no one knew how many blacks
were jobless since no surveys were conducted, but Walter W. Whitson, the
head of the Social Service Bureau, thought the situation had changed
since February when twenty thousand blacks and nine thousand whites
were reported to be unemployed. He estimated that four whites were out
of work for every black, though he offered no statistics to support this
claim. The cotton-picking season did provide employment for many blacks,
and cotton-related industries like compresses and oil mills provided jobs in
the fall as cotton came into Houston,[11] but these occupations could not
have absorbed the twenty thousand blacks who had been out of work a few
months earlier.

Whitson, stung by criticism from the *Informer* and from Jesse Thomas,
wrote Eugene K. Jones at the National Urban League's New York City
headquarters. He reiterated his view that the unemployment situation had
improved for blacks by March 1931 and that by April and May most of
those who had been out of work were white. He wrote that September cot-

ton picking, cotton-related industries, and yard work employed almost all blacks who wanted to work. Whitson, who also served on the mayor's unemployment committee, reported that since black unemployment was not a problem the commissary had been closed to them. Blacks were not cut off from relief, but received aid in the "regular way," through orders placed with grocery stores. He defended the committee's record, noting that when unemployment had been high among blacks during the previous winter, between 70 and 75 percent of the families aided through the commissary were black. As the cotton season ended he acknowledged that black unemployment seemed to be increasing. The committee opened the commissary to blacks on November 30. He assured Jones that white and black cases were handled in the same way, except that blacks were asked to collect clothing for their race because the bureau's supply was insufficient for blacks and whites.[12]

Whitson could not hide his anger against Jesse Thomas. In a clever attempt to discover the presence of discrimination at the city commissary, Thomas had telephoned the agency's office pretending to be a white man opposed to giving relief to blacks. Whitson dryly observed that, "He got just about the type of information that I should think he would expect to get under the circumstances." The information Thomas got probably confirmed his fears that blacks were not getting relief in proportion to their need. In a 1932 United States Senate hearing, reports from Houston supported Thomas's charges: "Applications are not taken from unemployed . . . colored families," the report read. "They are being asked to shift for themselves."[13]

Police brutality against blacks at relief agencies occurred throughout the period from 1929 to 1936 and kept some blacks away from relief agencies. As noted earlier, some agencies had policemen on hand to turn blacks away. In May 1932 twelve blacks standing in a bread line with whites and Hispanics were arrested for vagrancy, but the whites and Hispanics in line were not molested. The *Informer* recognized this as "a scheme to intimidate Negroes joining the line." In another incident, a crowd gathered as an ambulance arrived to pick up a white woman who became ill while waiting in line to apply for relief. A policeman at the scene ordered the crowd to disperse, and just then a white man drove up, stopped his car, borrowed the policeman's blackjack, and struck an elderly black man also waiting in line. "Results—no arrests, no charges filed. The white man calmly returned the borrowed club to a policeman on duty and walked away."[14]

In March 1936 Robert Lucas, a forty-seven-year-old black man, was severely beaten by two guards at the city relief headquarters. The incident began when several white women approached a staircase landing where Lucas was standing. An officer ordered Lucas to stand back and made a motion to strike him with his club. Lucas raised his hands to ward off the blow and pleaded, "Don't hit me, Mister." Guards took Lucas into an adjoining room and left the door open while they beat him with their clubs. When Lucas asked the officer to stop twisting his arm on the way to a police car, the guards began beating him again. When Lucas resisted, one of the guards drew his gun. Hundreds of women, black and white, lined the sidewalks. Several of the women fainted, and cries for help could be heard blocks away. A white man in the crowd interceded on Lucas's behalf and convinced the officer not to shoot him. Pools of blood on the sidewalk testified to the severity of the beating, but Lucas was not given medical attention. Instead, he was jailed on charges of disorderly conduct. The following month, a jury deliberated six minutes before finding him guilty of disturbing the peace and fining him $28. He was called a "mean, impudent Negro with a chip on his shoulder" who "wouldn't stay in his place." Though a number of witnesses testified on Lucas's behalf, including a reporter from the *Informer* who was present at the scene, the all-white jury accepted the officer's story.[15]

Violence against blacks at relief agencies probably resulted from various motives. It intimidated blacks and kept many of those in need away from relief agencies. This may explain the small number of applicants that Whitson used to support his contention that no unemployment problem existed in the black community. George T. Nelson, a young barber in Houston in the 1930s, recalled that police brutality against blacks at relief agencies was "known to be true." He believed that the authorities were "tryin' to keep blacks and whites apart. A poor black and a poor white could get together and turn the town over and they figured that." As unlikely as the proposition sounds, it should not be dismissed too quickly. The 1930s were desperate times, and desperation had previously drawn poor blacks and whites together to work against a common oppressor. The Populist movement had seen a remarkable outburst of interracial cooperation; perhaps the Depression could have forged a new coalition.[16]

In December 1932 Maury Maverick, later a liberal Texas congressman, disguised himself as a hobo and traveled from his native San Antonio to Houston to study conditions in the Bayou City. He found crowds of unemployed men gathered in camps along Buffalo Bayou. Blacks and whites mingled freely in the camps; indeed, Maverick wrote that "all race barriers were completely broken down. There was no more difference between a black Negro, than there was with a white graduate of Harvard. . . . There was no race feeling, very little suspicion, and a considerable amount of good will."[17]

A 1933 description of the Harris County Welfare Association Commissary offers further evidence that blacks and whites recognized their mutual interests. "Poverty and hard luck know no color line," the *Informer* observed. The reporter wrote, "If there is any one place, north or south, that gives the appearance of 'brothers under the skin,' it is the bread lines . . . white and black stand side by side. . . . On every available door step, white and colored people sit side by side, sandwiched together discussing current topics. . . . It's just unemployed to unemployed." The sight of unemployed blacks and whites sitting together discussing "current topics" must have sent chills up the spines of men in positions of authority. Early in 1934 the commissary opened a separate entrance for whites. Blacks and Hispanics entered on another street, though two months later Hispanics were allowed to use the white entrance.[18] The Jim Crow laws, set up in the aftermath of the Populist movement, proved useful in preventing a new black-white alliance.

White discrimination in relief contrasted with black relief efforts. While the resources of the black community could not possibly deal with all the unemployed members of their race, the community made a valiant effort. Black contributions to the Community Chest have been noted previously. Women's groups in black churches, with the help of many white businessmen, organized a soup line in the predominantly black Fifth Ward. Women collected food from wholesale grocers and packing houses. From 6:00 a.m. to 8:00 p.m. the black women dispensed food to members of all races. At the same time, white pastors organized a group to collect clothing for poor whites only.[19]

In 1930 the editor of the *Informer* suggested that "In this crisis Negro Houston will either find, or forever lose its civic soul." Earlier in the same year the newspaper had criticized local black churches as places for people to "get happy and shout and forget all about their duty to their fellowman." The newspaper called on churches to become "dynamic factors in the community. . . ." The soup line organized by black churchwomen provides one example of how the suffering brought about by the Depression helped blacks to recognize their common interest and create organizations to further that interest.[20]

The Depression also gave blacks the impetus to organize or revitalize other organizations. Efforts to establish the Urban League in Houston began in 1930. Blacks realized that many of the activities sponsored by the

league, including employment agencies, information gathering, and efforts
to make relief systems more equitable, were badly needed in Houston.
Ministers, no longer as unconcerned as the *Informer* had charged earlier,
led the effort to organize the league in black neighborhoods. In 1933 blacks
held a "great reunion and reorganization meeting" of the National Association for the Advancement of Colored People at the Mt. Corinth Baptist
Church. This successful meeting brought many new members into the organization. The Depression led many blacks to take a more active role
than they might otherwise have taken. The *Informer* criticized "the 'Uncle
Tom' Negro leadership" who tried "to make white people believe that we
are fully satisfied with our lot" and asked instead for "honest, sane leadership from among our own ranks. . . ." The Urban League and the NAACP
had only limited success in Houston from 1929 to 1936. The poverty and
low level of education in the black community and opposition from the
white community hampered their efforts, but they laid important foundations that would bring more significant results in the 1940s and after.[21]

Some Houston blacks carried on a brief flirtation with the Communist
party. In March 1930 Houston police raided a meeting of the Houston Unemployed Council of the Trade Unity League. Most of the league's members were black, but white communists organized and led the group. The
raid did not prevent a demonstration the league planned for March 6,
1930. Over five hundred unemployed men and women marched on City
Hall and presented a list of demands to Mayor Montieth. They demanded,
among other things, emergency unemployment relief, the abolition of Jim
Crow laws, and an end to discrimination against black workers. The communists gained followers in the black community because demands like
these appealed so strongly to those in need.[22]

The *Informer* observed that Houston blacks would lose interest in Communism "in the same proportion that jobs and justice are meted out to Ne-
gores. . . ." Since neither jobs nor justice was immediately forthcoming,
communists continued to attract black support. In March 1933 Houston
communists, mostly blacks, staged a demonstration to coincide with a similar rally in Washington, D.C. The *Informer* wrote that the "pitiable plight"
of blacks led them to search anywhere for a "ray of hope." The *Informer*
and many leaders of the black community opposed the communists, and
the party's influence declined quickly, perhaps because black leaders became more outspoken and black organizations became more numerous.[23]

Radicals could gain support in Houston and across the country because local relief efforts were overburdened and inadequate, but no help
was forthcoming from Herbert Hoover's administration. Though blacks

were traditionally Republicans, the *Informer* supported Franklin D. Roosevelt in his 1932 presidential campaign. In a front-page editorial on October 8, 1932, the *Informer* proclaimed that "Negroes are Tired of Hoover's Words and Solemn Phrases."[24] The editor wanted a man of action in the White House, and when Roosevelt took office in 1933 many Houston blacks looked to Washington with high hopes.

In 1933 the relief of personal hardship was a priority in Washington. The first step in federal relief efforts came in March with the creation of the Civilian Conservation Corps (CCC), designed to provide relief for young men aged eighteen to twenty-five. Blacks were encouraged when Representative Oscar De Priest, a black Republican from Illinois, succeeded in amending the CCC-enabling bill to prohibit discrimination on the basis of race. The *Informer* encouraged men to register for Roosevelt's "afforestation project." In May the newspaper reported that while blacks in some areas of the state were not allowed to register for CCC jobs, they were able to register at several Houston locations. In July the *Informer* published a letter from a young Houston man working at the CCC camp in Canyon, Texas, who reported that twenty-five other Houston blacks worked at the Canyon camp, giving Houston the largest representation there. The CCC program for blacks was never large enough to have any significant impact on Houston blacks. By 1935 the CCC employed only three hundred blacks in the entire state of Texas.[25]

Often it was not the best-known New Deal agencies that had the most positive effect on the lives of blacks but local projects financed by federal funds. In 1933 the Harris County Board of Welfare and Employment opened nutrition centers at three Houston locations. The clinics operated three days each week and provided proper nourishment for black infants and children of preschool age. Both black and white doctors donated their time to the clinics. Praising the centers, the *Informer* wrote: "The results gained from the centers are manifold and border on amazing."[26]

Black businesses, including the *Informer*, eagerly supported the New Deal programs. The newspaper proudly carried the National Recovery Administration's "Blue Eagle" on its masthead. The NRA was to stabilize business with fair-practice codes and generate purchasing power by providing jobs, defining labor standards, and raising wages. Some Houston businessmen reportedly responded to the NRA's wage regulations by firing blacks and replacing them with whites. When the Supreme Court declared the NRA unconstitutional in 1935, it went unmourned by Houston blacks. According to the *Informer*, "Negroes did not get more jobs and either their wages remained the same or they lost their jobs to whites." The

NRA's support of unions also hurt blacks. Most unions, "the proverbial enemy of the Southern Negro," refused to accept black members, and since unions forced more businesses to operate as closed shops, blacks lost even more jobs. The *Informer* agreed with Huey Long—the NRA eagle was actually a "Blue Buzzard."[27]

The Civil Works Administration (CWA) offered more benefits to blacks than did the NRA. Created in November 1933 as the first large-scale work relief agency, the CWA promptly hired Houston blacks at wages of forty cents per hour, five hours a day, and six days every week. In December the *Informer* estimated that the CWA employed nine hundred Houston blacks, but the pattern of discrimination in relief programs was too well established to end quickly. The *Informer* reported that "Open discrimination is beginning to break out in the United States National Employment office in Houston." Blacks who came to the office to register for the CWA were told to come back at a future date while whites were registered in the usual way. Blacks were also discriminated against in wage levels. While hundreds of whites received skilled labor wages above the forty cent minimum, almost no blacks got skilled wages. In February 1934 CWA supervisors at the Negro library, the only blacks in white-collar jobs, were fired. The CWA also employed whites rather than blacks as social workers in black neighborhoods. One branch of the CWA, the classes for the unemployed, won praise from the *Informer*. This branch employed seventy-two black teachers and fifty-nine white teachers, paid blacks and whites the same wages, and provided instruction to thirty-five hundred blacks and fifteen hundred whites. Though the CWA was popular, Roosevelt disliked the program and ended it in February 1934.[28] The CWA was a mixed blessing for blacks. Many blacks got badly needed jobs, but almost always at the lowest level of employment, and discrimination prevented many blacks from getting CWA jobs. The educational program benefited the thousands of black students and the teachers who were hired at a fair rate.

In 1935 Roosevelt proposed a massive emergency employment program and chose Harry Hopkins as head of the Works Projects Administration (WPA). Texas was the only southern state, with the possible exception of Virginia, in which the number of blacks employed by the WPA exceeded the percentage of blacks in the population. The state was 14.4 percent black in 1940 while 15.9 percent of the WPA employees for that year were black. No figures are available for Houston in the 1930s, but the state figures probably indicate the general pattern. While the WPA has been justly praised for its record in Texas, a more significant measure of success would compare the number of blacks in need with the number of WPA jobs. By

this measure the Texas record would look less laudable. While discrimination may have been less prevalent under the WPA, problems did exist.
One black employee missed two days of work because he was too weak to
dig in the hard ground. He had not eaten for two days because his white
foreman carried the time sheets in his pocket for several days instead of
turning them in promptly, thus causing a delay in issuing wages. One
black man who complained about such abuses had four days' pay deducted from his check without explanation.[29]

Early in 1936 Roosevelt began to cut public spending. He ordered
Hopkins to cut WPA rolls as quickly as possible, and Houston felt the WPA
cuts in March 1936. Blacks and whites organized a WPA Workers' Protec-
tive Union in Harris County to protest the layoffs. In April union members picketed City Hall, the civil court building, and the Community
Chest headquarters. The WPA layoffs affected eighteen thousand people
in the city; local relief efforts could not handle the additional load. A mass
resignation from the Harris County relief board resulted. Cuts in federal
aid, the exhaustion of state, county, and city relief funds, and the failure
of private businesses to provide jobs had closed "every door of escape from
actual hunger and suffering. . . ." The degree of suffering among the protestors was illustrated by "one aged and withered woman . . . who . . . has
been removed from the relief rolls and . . . threatened with eviction from
her home in the Fourth Ward."[30]

Relief conditions in 1936 recalled 1929 and the early 1930s. As fall approached, poor blacks once again received an ultimatum—"Pick cotton or
starve." The *Informer* reported that local relief officials cut relief rolls to
force blacks into the cotton fields for whatever wages they could get, usually less than one dollar each day. The *Informer* also charged that WPA officials cut their programs for the same reason.[31]

Many New Deal programs contained provisions that, perhaps unwit-
tingly, prevented many blacks from participating. The Social Security Bill,
for example, excluded domestic and farm workers. The *Informer* estimated
that 75 percent of the black workers in Texas fell into these two categories.[32]

The optimism that the *Informer* displayed when Roosevelt was elected
in 1932 faded by 1936. In September the editor, J. Alston Atkins, wrote,
"Texas Negroes don't benefit much one way or the other whether Roosevelt or Landon is in." In October the newspaper belatedly gave its support to Roosevelt. Atkins grudgingly admitted "that Roosevelt had brought
more benefits to Negroes than any other president," but the benefits fell
far short of the need.[33] Certainly Roosevelt's New Deal benefited blacks

more than any of Hoover's programs had. Unfortunately for blacks, Roosevelt's noble pronouncements against discrimination did not always translate into practice.

The *Informer* was not alone in painting a grim picture of black relief in Houston. From 1933 to 1935 Lorena Hickok, a more disinterested observer, served as Harry Hopkins's "confidential investigator." Traveling across the nation, she gave a firsthand account of conditions in letters to her boss. She traveled through West Virginia, Kentucky, North and South Dakota, Georgia, Florida, South Carolina, and Alabama before reaching Houston in April 1934. Though many of the areas she visited before coming to Houston were supposed to be some of the worst in the nation, she wrote: "At no time previously, since taking this job, have I been quite so discouraged as I am tonight. Texas is a Godawful mess . . . relief in Houston is just a joke." She found that in the city the case load for relief was 12,500 cases with new applications coming in at 1,100 every week. "I haven't figures on how large their Negro load is there," she wrote, "but they were planning to cut it down as low as possible." She had little faith in the city's relief programs. "God help the unemployed," she wrote.[34]

Many blacks placed their faith in God and hoped for a better life in the hereafter; if heaven was to be found, it was not in Houston. Before Roosevelt's election in 1932, relief programs in the city were inadequate and discriminatory. Roosevelt's New Deal brought limited improvements for blacks; but despite federal regulations against discrimination, the practice continued in private, local, and federal agencies. While blacks continued to support Roosevelt, their early optimism was somewhat jaded by 1936. In that year the *Informer* carried a verse from Ecclesiastes above its editorial column: "So I returned and considered all the oppressions that are done under the sun: and behold the tears of the oppressed and they had no comforter; and on the side of the oppressors there was power, but they had no comforter."[35]

NOTES

1. Houston *Informer*, 14 June 1919, 18 January 1930; David G. McComb, *Houston: A History* (Austin, 1981), 115; For examples of "boosterism" and lack of insight into real conditions in Houston see "Prosperity Now," *Houston* (March 1930): 16; "Houston is Sound: Increased Wages and Savings Prove It, Depression Hard Hit," ibid. (December 1930): 11; "Civic Inspiration" and "Frankly, Mr. John Citizen, You Don't Know How Well Off You Are!," ibid. (February 1933): 15; "Let's Go!," ibid. (March 1933): 15; and "Our Brightest Month," ibid. (July 1934): 17.

2. James M. Sorelle, "'An De Po Cullud Man Is In De Wuss Fix Uv Awl': Black Occupational Status in Houston Texas, 1920–1940," *Houston Review* (Spring 1979): 14–26; Jesse

O. Thomas, A *Study of the Social Welfare Status of the Negroes in Houston, Texas . . .* (Houston, 1930), 4; Interview with George T. Nelson, Houston, Texas, 23 March 1984.

   3. Thomas, *Study of the Social Welfare Status,* 12, 18; Houston *Informer,* 18 January, 22 February, 26 April, 8 March 1930; Donald W. Whisenhunt, *The Depression in Texas: The Hoover Years* (New York and London, 1983), 107.

   4. Carl M. Rosenquist and Walter Gordon Browder, *Family Mobility in Houston, Texas, 1922–1938* (Austin, 1942), 29. Whisenhunt, *Depression in Texas,* 137; Houston *Informer,* 5 December 1931. The unemployment rate was higher for blacks than for whites across the nation. See Broadus Mitchell, *Depression Decade: From the New Era through New Deal, 1929–1941* (New York, 1961), 99; Houston *Informer,* 9, 16 September 1933.

   5. Houston *Informer,* 25 October, 20 December 1930.

   6. Thomas, *Study of the Social Welfare Status,* 77.

   7. Houston *Informer,* 20 December 1930.

   8. "Prosperity Now," *Houston* (March 1930): 16. See also the articles from *Houston* cited in note 1.

   9. *Congressional Record,* 72 Cong., 1st Sess., 1932, LXXV, Part 3, 3238 (quotes); "Bright Spot of the Month," *Houston* (July 1934): 23; Houston *Informer,* 22 November 1930; William E. Montgomery, "The Depression in Houston During the Hoover Era, 1929–1932," M.A. Thesis, University of Texas, 1966, 143–46, 150–54.

   10. Houston *Informer,* 20 December 1930; 28 February, 26 September, 5 December 1931.

   11. Ibid., 5 December 1931.

   12. Ibid., 2 January 1932.

   13. Ibid.; Mitchell, *Depression Decade,* 103.

   14. Houston *Informer,* 4 May 1932; 22 February 1936.

   15. Ibid., 7 March, 18 April 1936.

   16. Nelson Interview. For discussions of black and white cooperation in the Populist era see Lawrence Goodwyn, *The Populist Movement* (Oxford, London, and New York, 1978); C. Vann Woodward, *Tom Watson: Agrarian Rebel* (London, Oxford, and New York, 1975), and Woodward, *The Strange Career of Jim Crow* (New York, 1974).

   17. Maury Maverick, A *Maverick American* (New York, 1937), 156.

   18. Houston *Informer,* 30 September 1933; 31 March, 5 May 1934.

   19. Nelson Interview; Houston *Informer,* 5 December 1931.

   20. Houston *Informer,* 11 January, 20 December 1930.

   21. Ibid., 28 November 1931; 11 March, 29 April, 13, 27 May 1933.

   22. Montgomery, "Depression in Houston," 29–31.

   23. Houston *Informer,* 2 April 1932; 18 March 1933; Nelson Interview.

   24. Houston *Informer,* 9 July, 8 October 1932.

   25. Ibid., 29 March, 6 May, 29 July 1933; William J. Brophy, "Black Texans and the New Deal," in *The Depression in the Southwest,* ed. Donald W. Whisenhunt (Port Washington, N.Y. and London, 1980), 120–21.

   26. Houston *Informer,* 16, 23 September 1933.

   27. Ibid., 5 August; 9, 16 September 1933; 1, 8 June 1935.

   28. Ibid., 18 November, 2, 16 December 1933; 6 January, 3 February, 17, 24 March 1934.

   29. Brophy, "Black Texans and the New Deal," 128–29; Houston *Informer,* 7 March 1936.

   30. Arthur M. Schlesinger, Jr., *The Politics of Upheaval* (Boston, 1960), 511; Houston *Informer,* 4 March, 18 April 1936.

   31. Houston *Informer,* 3 October 1936.

   32. Ibid., 24 August 1935.

   33. Ibid., 5 September; 17, 24 October 1936.

   34. Richard Lowitt and Maurice Beasley, eds., *One Third of a Nation: Lorena Hickok Reports on the Great Depression* (Urbana, Chicago, and London, 1981), 216, 228.

   35. Houston *Informer,* 5 September 1936.

"The N.Y.A. at the Sea-Side": A New Deal Episode

JOHN A. SALMOND

The National Youth Administration was created in 1935 to extend the work of the Civilian Conservation Corps. It aimed to provide financial help to high school and college students so that they could complete their education, and it offered job training to those who were neither in school nor employed. The NYA's original policy was not to establish camps or centers like those of the CCC. In 1937, however, because of insufficient population in rural areas "to make locally based projects economically feasible," the agency decided to develop a national system of "resident centers." It was difficult to locate usable buildings for such centers, as this selection indicates. It also shows that ethnic friction was alive and well in the 1930s.

TODAY the southern Californian sea-side community of Hermosa Beach, situated as it is some five miles south of the Los Angeles International Airport, is regarded, and properly so, as merely a part of the greater Los Angeles suburban area. Its citizens are mainly commuters, its values, its interests, are predominantly those of the metropolis. In the 1930s, however, the situation was somewhat different. The commuters were beginning to arrive, but the community nevertheless still thought of itself as something apart from the great city, something away from the mainstream of urban complexity. Its self-image was that of a pleasant, peaceful place with its parks, its public library, its promenades; a community certainly whose pace

From the *Southern California Quarterly*, 55 (Summer 1973), 209–217.

quickened in the summer months when people from the city came for a spell of beach-side holiday living, but a community, nevertheless, where for nine or ten months of the year life could be lived in a leisured style. Hermosa Beach in the late 1930s was still a town where the social problems of the city did not intrude unduly, where the New Deal, to a large extent, was something one read about rather than experienced directly, where property values still held high, where in a changing decade, things had altered little.[1]

Then, in the Christmas season of 1938–1939, the New Deal came to Hermosa Beach. It came in the form of a National Youth Administration residence project, and the furor aroused by its arrival split the small community in such a way as to give us some interesting indications of how national policy decisions could have the most dramatic local effects.

The National Youth Administration was established in June 1935, its purpose being to complement and extend the work of the Civilian Conservation Corps in alleviating the particular problems of unemployed young people in depression America. It worked on two fronts, providing supplementary financial assistance to high school and college students so they could complete their formal education, and attempting to give some measure of job training to those millions who had left school and were unemployed. The N.Y.A. was decentralized in operation, the national office laying down the broadest policy lines only, leaving their detailed implementation to a host of state and local officials. Unlike the C.C.C., the original aim was not to establish camps or centers to which enrollees would be brought, but rather to develop thousands of local training projects, which it was hoped would become truly part of the particular community.[2]

This preference for centering N.Y.A. activities in the locality was never abandoned, but as the agency developed, it had to be modified. It was recognized, in particular, that such a policy tended to discriminate against non-urban youth. There were hundreds of rural communities or sparsely populated counties where young people were in need, but in insufficient numbers to make locally based projects economically feasible. It was decided, therefore, to develop a national system of "residence centers," to which disadvantaged young people could be brought from surrounding counties, and where they could be maintained during training. Training could be given either at the center itself, or in already existing N.Y.A. workshops nearby. From 1937 on, such centers were progressively developed throughout the country.

One of the problems in implementing this new policy, of course, was the difficulty of finding buildings suitable for the N.Y.A.'s needs. Often the agency used vacant college dormitory facilities, sometimes abandoned C.C.C. camps could be converted, occasionally new facilities had to be constructed. The N.Y.A. youth made do with old mansion houses, town halls, school buildings, police barracks; all these and many more similar structures were used at various times for these centers. Anything vaguely suitable which could be bought or leased at reasonable cost was likely to be snapped up as the residence program expanded.

This was how the N.Y.A. came to Hermosa Beach. The drop in summer tourist revenue during the depression years had seriously curtailed the earnings of the town's largest hotel, the aging, 600-room Hermosa Biltmore, owned by the Los Angeles Athletic Club. Indeed, for most of the decade, it had served more as a substitute country club for the local residents, than as a guest house. Consequently, when the N.Y.A.'s California state director, Mrs. Anne Treadwell, approached Frank A. Garbutt, president of the Athletic Club, late in 1938, about leasing the hotel for a residence center, he was more than ready to talk business. As for the N.Y.A., it was just what the agency needed. It was big, it was close enough to the metropolitan area to provide a range of work experiences for the enrollees, yet it also could provide a most attractive living environment for them. Mutually acceptable terms were quickly negotiated, a lease was drawn up for Washington's approval, and preparations to move 500 young men and women into the building were begun.[3]

The news of what the N.Y.A. planned for the Hermosa Biltmore did not become public until the first week in January 1939. When the story broke, reaction amongst local residents was intense. The national N.Y.A. office was deluged with telegrams and letters from Hermosa Beach citizens, generally bitterly critical of the decision. "The young people will be of an undesirable type for association with the young residents of our city," read one such. "We have a high type of residential community of not wealthy citizens, but stable intelligent parents who do not wish to see their own children mingle with the type of young people who will benefit by this N.Y.A. project."[4] Other correspondents, fearing the "deleterious" effect on property values if the project were to eventuate, demanded its immediate termination, as "our town is too small to absorb or control the 500 to 700 youth . . . of all races, colors, creeds, of both sexes, and of various degrees of moral and physical soundness, which it is proposed to handle in this project."[5] At a hastily called public meeting on January 8, a citizens' committee was formed to work for the termination of the project, while both the local member of the House of Representatives, Leland

Ford, a Republican, and the newly elected Democratic senator, Sheridan W. Downey, were absolutely and loudly insistent that it be ended forthwith.[6]

National N.Y.A. officials, completely taken aback by the furor, were initially inclined to panic. Unfortunately, the agency's director, Aubrey W. Williams, a southern liberal and a close friend of both Harry Hopkins and Mrs. Roosevelt, was felled by a severe attack of influenza at the time, and was away from his office. In his absence the man who was left to cope with the controversy was the director of resident projects, David Williams, an idealistic young architect with very little experience of practical policy-making.[7] His instinctive reaction was to cut and run. After consultations with Mrs. Treadwell and the N.Y.A.'s southwestern regional director, Kenneth R. Rowe, he decided to close the project forthwith, without even ratifying the lease agreement. Mrs. Treadwell protested, but with resignation. "If Mr. Downey has to be pleased," she said, she knew there was little she could do about it.[8] Accordingly, she agreed to stop sending young people to the Hermosa Biltmore, and to transfer as soon as possible those already in residence.

The project, however, was not ended. In the first place, Aubrey Williams returned to active duty, full of fight and most reluctant to abandon what he believed to be a thoroughly worthwhile enterprise, without, at the very least, a full investigation of the various complaints against it. Secondly, the tone of the mail from Hermosa Beach was changing slightly. The volume of letters had not slackened, but they were no longer mostly overwhelmingly antagonistic to the scheme. There were, it seemed, at least some citizens who were far from terrified by the prospect of having the N.Y.A. in their midst. Mrs. Mary Dawson Shea, the local postmistress, for example, wrote to Mrs. Roosevelt entreating her assistance to "adjust a great wrong" and claiming that "a limited group of citizens" had "attacked and besmirched the characters of the N.Y.A. students, leaving the unjust impression that a group of 'degenerates, morons, incorrigibles, wards of the courts, communists and unemployables' were taking possession of our community." But most people knew better, she claimed, in begging Mrs. Roosevelt to use her influence to prevent the project's removal.[9]

Kenneth Rowe, who had visited the community on January 13, confirmed this impression. The opposition to the project was "hardly spontaneous," he suggested, but had been manufactured by "property owners along the beach," who feared a fall in values. Though "vigorous and noisy," its numerical strength was small, and there was plenty of support for the N.Y.A. from such groups as the local branch of the Democratic party, the local chapter of the Veterans of Foreign Wars, and the Non-Partisan League. Reversing his earlier position, Rowe now advocated completing the lease, unless it meant, and this he believed most unlikely, the irrevocable loss to the administration of Senator Downey's legislative support.[10]

Aubrey Williams agreed. In a cable replying to a telegram of support from the Hermosa Beach Democratic County Committee he stated that "Procurement Division of Treasury instructed consummate lease yesterday morning, January 16."[11] The project was to go ahead, at least for a time, though in a concession to Downey, Williams asked John Anson Ford, a member of the Board of Supervisors of the County of Los Angeles, and an old acquaintance, to investigate the whole controversy on the N.Y.A.'s behalf.[12]

Williams's decision not to end the project immediately scarcely quieted things down at Hermosa Beach. The last two weeks of January were days of intense activity, as the propagandists on both sides moved into the offensive. Because the opponents of the N.Y.A. had the support of the local press, their views received far wider local coverage. Fearing the effect of this, the project's supporters concentrated their efforts into the production of a series of handbills and pamphlets, coordinated by a hastily formed Citizens' Committee for the N.Y.A. Project. These pamphlets tried to explain in simple terms the function of the N.Y.A. generally, outlined the benefits to the local community the Hermosa Biltmore project would bring, mainly in terms of increased spending in local stores, and appealed for a tangible expression of mass support. Their opponents, in reply, concentrated on their earlier assertions of damage to property values and community morals.[13]

On January 24, the local dispute came to a head. The previous day, those supporting the project learned that its opponents had called a public meeting in the local school hall for the following evening. Moreover, in an effort to get a solid expression of opinion, they had decided not to advertise it widely, but rather to invite only known opponents of the project to attend. Immediately, the pro-N.Y.A. forces went into action. A handbill was quickly produced which vigorously attacked this duplicity and implored those who favored the N.Y.A. to come to the meeting. Forty supporters then distributed it throughout the community to such good effect that, in the words of the Citizens' Committee chairman, Albert E. Axelson, "we packed the hall, never before filled."[14]

The result of the meeting, therefore, was hardly the ringing endorsement of their position for which the N.Y.A.'s opponents had planned. They did most of the talking, but were so clearly outnumbered that the mayor, who chaired the event, decided to adjourn it without taking a floor vote. A card vote was taken after the meeting had formally ended, but as only registered voters or property owners were allowed to participate, fewer than half of those in attendance actually cast their ballots. The result was a narrow win to the "antis," scarcely, in the circumstances, a convincing expression of opinion, as the "pros" were quick to point out to Washington.[15]

By the end of January, the mail from Hermosa Beach reaching the N.Y.A.'s Washington office was divided equally between the "pros" and the "cons." Moreover, the tone of the letters indicated extensive social cleavages in the community, cleavages which the political climate of the decade had exacerbated, and which this particular dispute had brought out into the open. Mrs. Harold A. Bastein, for example, in writing to Mrs. Roosevelt, spoke of the "élite," who had previously used the Hermosa Biltmore for their "wild drinking parties, [their] striptease poker games and [their] *refined* prostitution," and argued that it ill became these people to state that the arrival of N.Y.A. youth would assuredly bring corruption to the community.[16] Mrs. Ada Smith assured Williams that

> It isn't the real worthy, cultural refined citizenry of Hermosa who are fighting this movement. It's that fast-living cocktail drinking group of "wood-Bes" [sic] who think they are somebody who are causing all the trouble . . . there are ever so [sic] many people here who stand solid behind this movement who dare not sign their name to any kind of petition for fear of their jobs.

"The N.Y.A. was a 'wonderful movement,'" she concluded and "will help lift our standard of living here in the United States. . . . The majority of Hermosa people are happy to have the youths here with us."[17] Albert E. Axelson wrote of "a tremendous clash of forces representing conflicting interests, those who favor the New Deal and giving our young Americans some kind of chance, versus the opponents of New Deal, composed mainly of Republicans and a few reactionary Democrats." He went on to assert that "most of the citizens of Hermosa Beach are *not* failures as human beings and will again, if necessary, defeat Republicans and reactionary Democrats attacking any New Deal program."[18]

Mrs. A. L. Stepnick reported that at the meeting of January 24 the opponents of the project "insisted upon denouncing the types of homes and people these N.Y.A. children came from and also the moral question arose." She requested that her name be withheld "as any source of information you have received, as my health is none too [sic] good and I want to retain what strength I have to do my bit towards the good things you people are trying to do and not fighting individually these local people."[19] Clearly the coming of the N.Y.A. to Hermosa Beach had opened up a Pandora's Box of socio-economic and political tensions in the community. It had both politicized and polarized it.

This then was the climate when John Anson Ford submitted his report to Williams. It could hardly have helped the director much, as the document did nothing more than summarize the views for and against the project which Ford had gleaned during a week of reasonably extensive interviewing. These were no different, however, from the views Williams had been receiving daily—via his mailbag. Ford also included in appendices various sample statements, mainly from those who opposed the project, which provide further evidence that the dispute was partly the result of local social divisions. One such was from a Mrs. Horace H. Fulton. She believed that

> there is so much unrest and dissatisfaction in the underprivileged class at present, and then to house them in luxurious surroundings for six months at a time, they cannot be expected to re-adjust themselves to their former meager surroundings without further or more intense dissatisfaction among them after a taste of that which they cannot expect to enjoy after their training period is over—this furthers Communistic tendencies if any are present.

Mrs. Charles P. Taft was particularly concerned about the "sex-mixing" that would inevitably result from housing young men and women from the "lower classes," under the same roof. Moreover, she pointed out, "Our churches will hardly house their own parishioners and I do feel this is a serious problem, for those students should be given every privilege for worship." Mrs. John F. Hopkins was worried about the effect on the summer residents. "The Hermosa Biltmore," she argued, "is located where everyone going to and from their homes are compelled to pass the building, and feel that regardless of the type of youth there, we do not want our small children to have to be in constant contact with that number." Mrs. Hopkins believed too, that "only in one section of town—where the income average is low—was there general sentiment in favour of the project, and that the young people, particularly those with Spanish or Latin blood in them 'would be a menace' to the community."[20] There were other similar manifestations of this particular social viewpoint included in the report, but no recommendation. Ford explained this deficiency, however, in a private letter to Walter Packard, an N.Y.A. aide. He had been worried, he wrote, by his own ignorance of Sheridan Downey's relationship with

Williams, and had decided to confine himself to an impartial report, because to do otherwise would have necessitated implicating the senator's secretary, Delwin Smith. Ford believed that Smith, who was "in close communication with one of the strongest opponents of the project," was clearly influencing the senator adversely. He further believed that the Hermosa project had "splendid possibilities. . . . I feel quite definitely," he said,

> that a tactful handling of the situation will gradually reconcile the community to the presence of this enterprise. In other words, it is partly a problem of skillful internal administration and partly a problem of skillful public relations with a community that is needlessly jittery.

He suggested to Packard that the letter be shown privately to Williams, and this, judging by Williams's own scrawled comments on it, was done.[21]

That was how the situation stood at the beginning of February—vocal opposition to the N.Y.A. continuing from one section of the Hermosa Beach community, but strengthening support for the project from others. Given Ford's privately expressed judgment as well, there seemed no reason whatsoever for Williams to rescind his earlier decision to continue with the project. In a telegram to a supporter, on February 8, he stated that "this Admin. will not close Hermosa Beach Project and will not move it unless more desirable situation and equally good quarters are secured."[22] Senator Downey, not unexpectedly, was far from pleased at Williams's firmness. He still "remained convinced" that the project was "a serious political mistake. . . . As you know," he wrote,

> the burden of holding California in line for the liberal movement and for Democracy is partially, at least, upon my shoulders and the affronting of large numbers of California voters makes this burden just that much heavier. Moreover, I must admit that, in this particular instance, I understand the opposition of the beach residents to have [sic] a large school placed in their vicinity.[23]

Beach residents also continued their protests, but as had been predicted, with somewhat diminished intensity. In a letter to Downey, Tom L. Popejoy, the N.Y.A.'s deputy administrator, was able to allude to "a great many letters from property owners at Hermosa Beach in favor of this project," while assuring the senator that the political consequences of the operation were not likely to be either decisive or disastrous.[24]

Thus the N.Y.A. project at Hermosa Beach survived the initial attacks upon it—but it did not thrive. Those sections of the local community which had fought its establishment so bitterly never became reconciled to its presence. Senator Downey kept up his opposition, and the slow but real expansion of employment opportunities as the great California war boom began rendered its existence less necessary. The lease on the hotel was not renewed after it expired on June 30, 1939, and the young residents were transferred to other N.Y.A. centers in the Los Angeles County area.[25] The residents of Hermosa Beach, having saved their property values, and having prevented the onset of civil disorder, went back about their regular business. The "invasion" of the Hermosa Biltmore must have soon become only a distasteful memory.

From time to time, however, the "memory" surfaced. Congressional opponents of the N.Y.A. found it to be useful ammunition in their various campaigns against the agency. They were able to picture the project as a prime example of the extravagant and illegitimate use of government money in an attempt to bring unwise social change, and incidentally, of the federal government's callous tendency to disregard local views.[26] Much later, when Williams was being considered for the post of rural electrification administrator, a few Hermosa Beach residents protested. "I oppose his [Williams's] nomination because of what the N.Y.A. did to Hermosa Beach," wrote one such. "This screwball and his gang conceived the idea of sponsoring and coddling a lot of foreigners and dregs."[27] On balance, therefore, the Hermosa Beach experiment probably did the N.Y.A. and its administrator more harm than good.

What remains to be said? The Hermosa Beach project was but a minute particle in the totality of New Deal experimentation. Its demise, while regretted by N.Y.A. officials, was clearly not crucial. As the need for trained industrial workers increased with the war boom, the agency was able to develop many more projects in the greater Los Angeles area, projects free from significant community hostility. It is, indeed, the presence of such hostility that makes the Hermosa Beach project worth at least a passing glance. The New Deal has been studied almost solely from the national level. We know much about the way policies were made and the way agencies were created to administer these. We know how things worked in Washington, but we know very little about the translation of such policies to the local level. Until we do, until we study more fully the reaction of local communities to national agencies, until we comprehend how decisions taken in Washington could bisect local interests, and the reasons for these bisections, our knowledge of the New Deal's totality will be far from complete. The Hermosa Beach incident, therefore, assumes some general importance, if only as one signpost along a road which future New Deal scholars could profitably travel.

NOTES

1. This picture of Hermosa Beach in the 1930s has been built up from a file of clippings, reports, and letters dealing with the area found in the Records of the National Youth Administration (henceforth N.Y.A. Records), Group 16 (Correspondence of the Administrator concerning the operation of an N.Y.A. Project at Hermosa Beach, Calif. Jan.–Feb. 1939), in the National Archives, and from talking to former residents of the area, in particular Dr. T. P. Dunning, of La Trobe University, Melbourne, Australia. The author is professor of history at La Trobe University. He thanks the university's council and the American Council of Learned Societies for the financial assistance which made possible the research upon which this paper is based.

2. The fullest and best study of the N.Y.A. is Ernest and Betty Lindley's *A New Deal for Youth: The Story of the National Youth Administration* (New York, 1938), commissioned by the National Advisory Committee of the N.Y.A. as a report to President Roosevelt.

3. See Frank A. Garbutt to Aubrey Williams, Administrator, N.Y.A., January 27, February 1, 1939, N.Y.A. Records, Box 16. In these letters Garbutt recapitulated the negotiations which preceded the leasing of the hotel.

4. Mr. and Mrs. H. Lee Hansen to Aubrey Williams, January 7, 1939, *Ibid.*

5. Loy G. Horn, chairman, Citizens' Advisory Committee, William G. Morn, vice president, Hermosa Beach P.T.A., to Aubrey Williams, January 7, 1939, *Ibid.*

6. Transcript of telephone call between Mrs. Anne Treadwell and David Williams, January 9, 1939, *Ibid.*

7. Williams to Mrs. Edith Foster, January 7, 1939, in papers of Aubrey W. Williams (henceforth Williams Papers), Franklin D. Roosevelt Library, Hyde Park, New York, Box 13.

8. Transcript of telephone call from Mrs. Treadwell and Kenneth Rowe to David Williams, January 12, 1939, N.Y.A. Records, Box 16.

9. Mrs. Mary Dawson Shea to Mrs. Roosevelt, January 14, 1939, *Ibid.*

10. Rowe to David Williams, January 13, 1939, *Ibid.*

11. Aubrey Williams to Albert E. Axelson, January 17, 1939, *Ibid.*

12. Clipping from *Manhattan Beach News*, Manhattan Beach, California, January 27, 1939, in N.Y.A. Records, Box 16.

13. See Albert E. Axelson, chairman, Citizens' Committee for the N.Y.A. Project, to Aubrey Williams, January 31, 1939, *Ibid.*

14. *Ibid.*

15. *Redondo Reflex*, January 27, 1939, Axelson to Williams, January 31, 1939, N.Y.A. Records, Box 16.

16. Mrs. Harold A. Bastein, South Bay Democratic Club, to Mrs. Roosevelt, February 3, 1939, *Ibid.*

17. Mrs. Ada M. Smith to A. Williams, January 29, 1939, *Ibid.*

18. Axelson to A. Williams, January 31, 1939, *Ibid.*

19. Mrs. A. L. Stepnick to A. Williams, January 25, 1939, *Ibid.*

20. John Anson Ford to A. Williams, January 30, 1939, *Ibid.*

21. Ford to Walter Packard, February 1, 1939, *Ibid.*

22. Williams to Robert E. Meachem, member Hermosa Beach Democratic Central Committee, February 8, 1939, *Ibid.*

23. Downey to Williams, January 30, 1939, *Ibid.*

24. Tom L. Popejoy to Downey, February 9, 1939, *Ibid.*

25. Downey to Williams, May 29, 1939, *Ibid. Reduction of Non-Essential Federal Expenditures. Hearings Before the Joint Committee on the Reduction of Non-Essential Federal Expenditures, Congress of the United States,* 77th Congress First Session, Pursuant to Section 601 of the Revenue Act of 1941. Part 1. November 20, December 1, 2, and 4, 1941 (Washington, 1942), (henceforth *Reduction of Non-Essential Federal Expenditures,* Hearings), pp. 262 ff.

26. *Reduction of Non-Essential Federal Expenditures,* Hearings, pp. 262 ff. *Termination of Civilian Conservation Corps and National Youth Administration. Hearings Before the Com-*

mittee on Education and Labor, United States Senate, 77th Congress, Second Session, on S.2295, A Bill to Provide for the Termination of the National Youth Administration and the Civilian Conservation Corps, March 23 to April 17, 1942 (Washington, 1942), pp. 13–49.

27. Forrest Q. Stanton to Senator Kenneth D. McKellar, February 6, 1945, papers of Senator Kenneth D. McKellar, Box 355 Political, 1944, Memphis Public Library, Memphis, Tennessee.

Stitching and Striking: WPA Sewing Rooms and the 1937 Relief Strike in Hillsborough County

JAMES FRANCIS TIDD, JR.

Women in general received limited benefits from the New Deal. They welcomed aid when their husbands were assigned work-relief jobs, but women themselves received disproportionately low percentages of work-relief positions, particularly in the Works Projects Administration. African American women suffered a double handicap: discrimination because of race and gender. Most WPA work for women consisted of sewing projects. The participation in a strike by women in the sewing project in Hillsborough County suggests that active protest is often a recovery phenomenon arising not from utter despair but from hope. African American women did not participate in this strike, but they undoubtedly saw it as a rejection of passive acceptance of inequitable treatment.

On July 8, 1937, a group of women employed in an Ybor City Works Progress Administration (WPA) sewing room instigated a relief worker sit-down strike in Hillsborough County. They laid aside their materials and called for a unified, general relief walkout. Despite economic hardships

From *Tampa Bay History*, 11 (Spring/Summer 1989), 5–21.

created by the Great Depression and faced with possible violence as well as extended unemployment, these women banded together, challenging local and federal authorities to confront numerous problems which plagued WPA efforts, particularly those related to needy female labor. Sewing room work was an important, yet troubled, part of Hillsborough County's WPA undertaking. The experience of sewing women, at work and on strike, reveals much about local support for and criticism of relief activities.

President Franklin Roosevelt's WPA was an attempt to help some of this country's suffering jobless by providing minimum financial assistance to needy people who labored on beneficial community projects. Beginning in 1935, several million workers found employment on government-funded jobs, ranging from toy manufacturing to highway construction. Many aspects of American life were affected by WPA efforts, which aimed to improve institutional and cultural deficiencies, while preserving worker confidence and skills. WPA activities were federally capitalized, approved and supervised, but local sponsoring bodies contributed a portion of expenses, primarily by supplying necessary space, materials, and equipment. Viewed as an innovative method of combating problems too complicated for traditional solutions, WPA was created in 1935 by the Congress and the president in part to thwart the spread of more radical alternatives.[1]

Hillsborough County's economy suffered seriously before and during the depression, and local relief agencies were unable to cope with massive unemployment. Adequate financial assistance to the needy was beyond the ability of Tampa, Plant City, and other smaller communities to provide. Ybor City, Tampa's immigrant quarter, turned "funereal" as slumping cigar sales and factory mechanization forced thousands out of work, inducing many citizens to move north to seek better opportunities. Half of Tampa's employable population stood idle, and Tampa's Cooperative Unemployment Council reported that over 10,000 citizens registered as needy in 1932. By March 1935, 8,746 people (including 2,664 women) were on relief in Hillsborough County.[2] R. E. L. Chancey, Tampa's mayor, wrote directly to Roosevelt, complaining that there was "a very live unemployment problem still in Tampa" and voicing his support for WPA activities.[3]

Officials in Tampa and Hillsborough County applied for and acquired numerous WPA projects from the program's inception in 1935 through its demise in 1943. Roads, sewers, recreation facilities, and other public institutions, including airports, libraries, schools, gymnasiums, and tourist centers, were constructed or improved through federal support. Health care for local blacks improved upon completion of Clara Frye Negro Hospital, and a newly constructed county home and detention hospital served the white populace. Tampa workers replaced the city's battered seawall and repaved Bayshore Boulevard. The Tampa Bay Hotel, city stockade, and fire station were expanded and repaired. Hillsborough's cultural environment was also enhanced: WPA personnel operated an orchestra, theaters, writer and artist programs, education and citizenship classes, surveys, and many other useful community services. By February 1936, sixty-four projects had been started county-wide, employing over five thousand residents. Gloria Jahoda wrote that "had the WPA not come into existence to bring hope to Tampa in 1935, communism would have had impressive success with a substantial portion of blue-collar workers who lived on or near the Hillsborough River."[4]

Tampa's citizens were not unfamiliar with radicalism and often reacted swiftly and violently against those viewed as instigators. Ybor City cigarmakers were experienced agitators, striking against their employers. Tampa officials often used deportation and vigilante violence to quell strikes. Tampa acquired a reputation for anti-socialist violence, and police officers participated in the brutal flogging and murder of Joseph Shoemaker, who was attempting to promote socialist activity in 1935.[5]

Despite Tampa's violent reputation, a group of workers and unemployed organized a local branch of the Workers' Alliance, which promoted socialist solutions to the economic crisis. Eugene Poulnot, who also suffered at the hands of the Shoemaker vigilantes, became local Workers' Alliance president and promoted efforts to persuade elected community leaders to increase relief spending. The Workers' Alliance fought against attempts to close WPA jobs and actively protested worker layoffs. David Lasser, National Workers' Alliance president, predicted a "crisis" as "demonstrations and sitdowns coincided with exhaustion of funds in various states."[6]

Radicals were not the only ones to criticize WPA efforts, not all of which ran smoothly or equitably. A three-week delay in check distribution sparked a small riot in Tampa, as 400 workers clashed with police on September 7, 1935. The *Tampa Tribune* applauded "outstanding" WPA work like Peter O. Knight Airport and Bayshore Boulevard, but criticized "incidental, non-essential" jobs like tree surgery and beautification. A report by Mayor Chancey claimed that only thirty-five percent of those eligible had obtained WPA work during May 1937.[7]

Most WPA projects were labor-intensive construction, beautification, and road work, which predominantly utilized men. Women accounted for only twelve to eighteen percent of those on WPA jobs, a rate far lower than their overall participation in the work force. Despite Roosevelt's interest in employing and training women through the relief agency, men dominated relief ranks in Tampa as elsewhere. Finding suitable employment for females was difficult, particularly for those with limited skills. While many women obtained WPA positions as teachers, librarians, nurses, and clerks, and a few ladies were appointed to high management positions, most women were placed in handicraft work. Officials argued that sewing was easier for ladies because they usually had some experience, picked up additional skills quickly, and required less supervision. During the week of April 2, 1938, fifty-six percent of women employed on WPA jobs in the United States were engaged in sewing or other goods production, while another forty-one percent were in white collar positions; eighty-seven percent of workers occupied in sewing rooms were women. Nationally, sewing ladies produced 117,800,000 household and hospital items, and 382,800,000 family wear garments. When WPA's emphasis shifted to defense preparation prior to World War II, WPA sewing ladies repaired uniforms and other armed services material.[8]

Women in Florida found themselves in jobs similar to those of their WPA sisters nationwide. They were predominantly placed in fields considered acceptable for females, like nursing, teaching, laundry work, and domestic service; there were very few women in skilled or semi-skilled construction. Florida's WPA sewing ladies produced a large amount of goods as well, accounting for 10,008,506 garments and 2,528,124 other articles.[9]

WPA sewing rooms were activated in Hillsborough County on October 28, 1935, and were co-sponsored by Florida's State Board of Social Welfare, Hillsborough's Board of County Commissioners, and the City of Tampa. During most of WPA's tenure, sewing rooms were decentralized, with seven locations established early in the program. By September 1936, 375 women were employed, and they had produced 70,847 articles. Ten units were in operation by July 1938. Throughout WPA's duration, the number of women employed in sewing rooms fluctuated according to financial and policy considerations. One report claimed 1,476 ladies were actively engaged in sewing by September 1936. In December 1937, however, only 1,224 women were busy producing cloth items. They labored at sixteen sites, including one which supported eighty black women. By September 1940, with a small Plant City operation the only exception, the projects had been centralized with all sewing women concentrated at a high-speed, modernly equipped facility in Ybor City.[10]

A variety of associations benefited from products supplied by WPA sewing efforts, and it was these local organizations which dispersed WPA materials to needy citizens. They included the American Red Cross, Girl and Boy Scouts, Hillsborough's Children's Home, Family Service Association, Old People's Home, Salvation Army, Women's Home, Tampa Day Nursery, Traveler's Aid Society, YMCA, YWCA, Urban League, PTA, civic clubs, orphanages, and churches. Hillsborough County's Health Unit received gowns, aprons, instrument cases, and uniforms for nurses. Graduation dresses and outfits were provided to sixty-five high school seniors. Cushion pads were fashioned for army truck seats, and an Ybor City unit repaired and manufactured dolls. Ladies in the Plant City sewing room stitched pillow cases, sheets and obstetric pads and provided quilts for an Arcadia orphanage and Plant City's jail.[11]

Sewing rooms served more functions than simply a place for emergency employment, where women could earn a small wage while producing valuable articles needy citizens could not afford to purchase. Some sites provided educational opportunities and recreation through a number of small libraries. For a few women they provided a chance to learn a new, marketable skill, which could help them obtain outside income. Rivalries among units produced a spirit of competition, and products were proudly displayed at fairs and exhibits. Christmas parties were staged, and presents were distributed to workers' children. Health instruction was given; some nurses actively tried to discourage women who were "adicted [sic] to the use of snuff."[12] Sewing rooms probably served another important function, that of a gathering place where women could communicate and exchange ideas and establish new social contacts and relationships.

Notwithstanding positive reports and productive sewing units, some people voiced criticisms of the projects. One lady complained that favoritism was being shown supervisors and that some women did not qualify for their positions. Another charged that white collar workers received special favors. Some WPA officials were accused of protecting cushy positions for their friends, while sending more qualified women to sew. One writer claimed that "society girls" and recent high school graduates obtained desirable nursery school slots, while teachers with experience sat in sewing rooms. A Family Service Association official complained that WPA sewing room workers seemed "indignant" when questioned about production. Some complaints were rooted in men's prejudice against women working at all. One particularly harsh critic asserted that the "sewing room project is merely a modified form of direct relief. Practically none of the women employed on this project are qualified workers. Many of them have never been employed prior to the opening of the sewing room projects. However, as these women all have dependents and are entitled to relief, we feel that the proper solution would be to give them direct relief so that they could stay at home with their dependents, where they are needed."[13]

Black women were attacked even more severely than whites for opting to work on WPA sewing projects. Southern white men disliked seeing Negro women receive government money because it strengthened black demands for federal intervention, raised their standard of living, and provided them an opportunity to escape low-paying menial labor positions. A Tampa doctor angrily complained to U.S. Senator Claude Pepper that a black girl made more in a sewing room than as a maid for his daughter, and he inquired, "How long will the solid south remain solid when the negro is permitted to insult our white citizens believing that they have the backing of our government?"[14] Surely black sewing room women realized their precarious position and must have feared that funding could quickly dry up in response to such attacks.

In addition to charges of corruption, waste, and mismanagement, sewing rooms were constantly plagued with funding difficulties and relief policy changes. Funds often ran low, forcing closings and layoffs. When money was appropriated, it frequently was insufficient to re-employ large contingents of women. This chronic problem inflamed worker discontent and focused it on existing WPA regulations. Rumors that a strike was brewing circulated for weeks in 1937, and when eighty-eight women were laid off in an economy move, the stage was set for a confrontation between female sewing workers and local officials.[15]

Four hundred women were employed at the WPA sewing facility on Twelfth Avenue and Twentieth Street in Ybor City on July 8, 1937. Formerly home of the La Flor de Cuba cigar factory, the three-story brick structure had now become federal property and housed a sewing unit which employed both Anglo and Latin women. On a Thursday, weeks of concern crystallized when Mabel Hagen, head of the local Workers' Alliance women's committee, declared that a sitdown strike had been called.[16] The decision to stage a sitdown strike was undoubtedly influenced by the recent wave of factory seizures that had begun in December 1936 with the successful sitdown strike by General Motors workers in Flint, Michigan. In the months that followed, various protestors around the country resorted to the sitdown technique because it proved effective in gaining publicity and winning demands.[17] In Tampa Mabel Hagen reportedly called for her fellow workers to "stand together like they do in the

North," and WPA forewomen at the site immediately ordered work to stop.[18]

Unfortunately, little is known about Hagen or her fellow strike leaders, Adela Santiesteban and Elsie Seth. Although Tampa's branch of the Workers' Alliance was active in petitioning local community leaders for increased relief funding, records do not exist which might detail particular women's roles within the organization. Hagen was described by some as a likeable woman, and she must have had considerable leadership qualities. Two years after the strike, however, another local resident described Hagen in less than glowing terms, accusing her of continued radical activity, thievery, and loose morals.[19]

Whatever her position or personality, Hagen inspired her co-workers. A strike committee was quickly established, and a call went out for reinstatement of the released women. Strikers also demanded a twenty-percent increase in wages, a two-week notice of future layoffs, and formation of a board which would handle complaints against WPA decisions. They wanted to see this three-person board include representatives from the Workers' Alliance, the WPA, and a mutually acceptable third party. They emphasized that their actions were not directed at local administrators or unit supervisors.[20]

W. E. Robinson, district WPA supervisor, and Hillsborough County Sheriff J. R. McLeod, first WPA district director for the area, arrived to negotiate with the strikers. Robinson claimed that he had no alternative other than to release the women because he had received direct instructions from Washington to do so. He expressed his regret for the lack of notice, arguing that he had allowed them to continue in their positions long beyond initial directions to reduce payrolls. He protested that he had no authority to establish a grievance committee and that problems should instead be brought directly to him or a representative of the labor department. The women remained firm in their demands, despite Robinson's assurance that he would review each case and that he had been informed that wages would be increased soon.[21]

Sheriff McLeod, showing sympathy and restraint, sought to avoid violence, proclaiming, "I have left my badge and gun at the jail." However, McLeod demanded that any women who wished to leave be allowed to do so, promising that they would receive protection from him. Almost three-fourths of the workers opted to accept his offer and left the factory at day's end, although many may have planned to return later. Approximately 100 to 130 women chose to remain. McLeod's promise of nonviolence was realized. The protest drew a gathering of nearly five hundred family mem-

bers and curious onlookers, many of whom expected law officers to evict
the women. Deputies and police were held back from clearing the facility, however, because it was considered a federal site and their authority to
take such an action was questioned.[22]

Clearly, Tampa's Workers' Alliance hoped to use the strike to promote
their activities. Hagen later charged that Eugene Poulnot had talked her
into calling the strike, and Poulnot did not seem ready to take a leading
role by calling a general walkout from all WPA projects in support of the
women. He argued that the sewing ladies could not support their families
on thirty-four dollars a month. Although no evidence points to prior knowledge of the strike by national Workers' Alliance leaders, David Lasser sent
a telegram which arrived before midnight, immediately approving the sit-
down.[23]

Despite rejection of the action by a majority of those working at the
site, the remaining women sang and smoked, and they cheered the arrival
of food and supplies brought in by family members and other supporters.
The Workers' Alliance sent guava pastries, bread, cookies, and coffee. The
strikers who chose to stay included "girls of eighteen and grandmothers of
sixty-five, most of them of Latin descent and most of them wearing yellow
Workers' Alliance badges." They bedded down for the night, amidst rumors that the lights would be shut off, which proved groundless, and
waited for the following day's activity.[24]

On Friday morning it was clear that police intended to maintain control of the situation. Strikers were confined to the first floor of the factory,
and adjacent streets were roped off. Police and deputies stood guard, but
allowed food, mail, newspapers, bedding, and clothes to be delivered.
Most disturbing for the strikers was the arrival of over two hundred workers who had refused to join in the strike. They were allowed to occupy the
top two floors of the factory and continue with their work, effectively undercutting the strikers' efforts.[25]

Countywide support for the strikers by fellow WPA workers also failed
to materialize. Although approximately 250 men walked off their jobs on
mosquito ditching and road paving projects, 3,500 others remained at their
positions on thirty-nine WPA jobs countywide. Pickets tried to influence
workers at other sites but met with little success. Failure of native-born
workers to support the predominantly Latin strike deeply disturbed writers
at *La Gaceta*, Ybor City's premiere newspaper. They claimed that Americans started the strike, then failed to support it, leaving Latin workers
vulnerable and holding the bag.[26]

Black sewing room workers also failed to stand behind their Latin sisters, though probably for somewhat different reasons. One story reported that women at a black sewing room "chanted derisively" in response to the strike. Reportedly adopting a refrain from a popular black movie, they sang "Lawd no, I cain't sit down! I just got to heaven and I got to look around. No lawd, I just cain't sit down." Even when sixty-four women were released from the Morgan Street sewing room, they failed to join the sit-down.[27] Undoubtedly, black women on local WPA projects were reluctant to jeopardize such an important source of income, particularly when positions for blacks were few. Their sense of solidarity with striking workers may also have been weakened by their residential, social, and occupational segregation from Anglo and Latin communities.

When Frank Ingram, Florida's WPA director, arrived on the scene, he said he would not cooperate with the Workers' Alliance, claiming that there were plenty of people willing to take the strikers' places. He argued that Florida had received a good deal in not having to suffer as many cuts as neighboring states, and he offered to refer complaints to Washington. He gave Robinson permission to close any projects that had insufficient numbers of workers present. Consequently, a number of projects were closed down, and Monday's scheduled activity cancelled.[28]

A mass meeting, sponsored by the Workers' Alliance, was held in Ybor City's Labor Temple on Friday night. Cigar workers were asked to show support for the women by sponsoring a fifteen-minute work stoppage. Speakers pointed out the injustice caused by American women refusing to back their Latin sisters. Police were in attendance, and calm was maintained. Meanwhile, the striking women stayed put in the factory, despite rumors that police violence would occur during the night. However, local authorities continued to show restraint, and the night passed quietly.[29]

On Saturday, July 10, Tampa city officials tried a different approach by sending Tampa's health officer to inspect the facility. He reported that the women were sleeping on tables and chairs and that although their floor was being kept clean, the building lacked proper toilet facilities, which was ironic since a larger number of women had been using the same facilities before the strike. He also claimed that one woman had become ill.[30] However, the city's attempt to scare the women into giving up their sitdown with health warnings failed.

Although Poulnot asserted that more workers would be striking, he was able to produce only a small number of pickets, who generated little support. A group of seamen off the ship *Cuba*, who had been arrested and thrown off the ship when they staged a sitdown strike a month earlier, sent milk to the striking women. Otherwise activities quieted down considerably during the weekend, though only a couple of women chose to give up the strike. The "pastoral" setting, complete with picnics and cows grazing on factory grounds, persuaded local officials to replace police with deputized WPA foremen. Family members of the strikers brought food, clothing, soap, and pillows, and they were allowed to visit with the women.[31]

The Workers' Alliance continued to promote support activities and prepared to expand the strike during the following week. They called for unity and asked for help from cigar makers and bakers, claiming the women had shown class consciousness, and they published a manifesto arguing against rampant favoritism within Hillsborough's WPA ranks. West Tampa and Ybor City residents were solicited for contributions to help the women, and over $150 was raised. However, all did not go well with the collections. Workers' Alliance Finance Secretary M. Salazar asked that no money be given unless an official Alliance seal was affixed to the letter of introduction, because someone had been taking advantage of the situation to con unwary supporters.[32]

Even this limited activity led Sheriff McLeod to request additional deputies to manage expected Alliance demonstrations when projects reopened on Tuesday, July 13. Hillsborough County's commissioners shied away from any action which might prove a political liability and placed the decision back in McLeod's lap. McLeod already had the right to deputize citizens if necessary, but claimed he wanted to have a show of support from county officials. Ingram ordered that closed operations be resumed, and warned strikers of a WPA regulation which allowed for workers to be released from their jobs if they stayed away for more than four days. Strikers were officially absent for the third day on Tuesday.[33]

Tuesday morning the projects reopened, and violence was avoided everywhere except at the factory site. There a scuffle broke out between a picket and a police officer. Peter Riscile, reported to be an Alliance lookout, was charged with assault and resisting arrest. Riscile was accused of trying to cross a police line, and a police officer reportedly hit him with his own sign. The Workers' Alliance protested the fight, claiming that pickets were being beaten, but WPA officials claimed ignorance of the entire incident. Riscile later received a suspended sentence, and the Alliance paid his fine.[34]

Further confrontations were avoided when the sitdown collapsed on Wednesday. On that day, ninety-six women left the factory, throwing their belongings to family members and giving up, although a dozen women held out until after nightfall while strikers' families pressured Alliance officials to call off the strike. Ingram's warning that they stood to lose their positions if they held out longer than four days probably provided the greatest incentive, and the final decision came at 10:15 p.m. Although Poulnot and other Alliance officials claimed that they stopped the strike in order to avoid "bloodshed," it seems more likely that they just never received the level of support they expected. The remaining strikers left the factory and marched to the Labor Temple to join their families and friends. Arriving to grand applause and cheering, strike leaders took center stage. Mabel Hagen, one of several who gave speeches, said she had no regrets, and claimed "it was not pleasant, but we would do it over again." A large gathering of police, detectives, and deputies watched the proceedings behind Sheriff McLeod, who reportedly made sure his presence was acknowledged.[35]

WPA activities continued well into 1943, and little changed as a result of the strike. Poulnot, Hagen, Santiesteban, and four other Alliance leaders were fired from their WPA positions. Poulnot and Hagen were forced to ask Tampa's Family Service Association for aid, and their involvement in the strike almost cost them aid from even this agency of last resort. "It looks like I am between the devil and the deep blue see [sic]," Poulnot reflected privately in November 1937. Hagen later turned on Poulnot in an effort to obtain work, and reportedly begged for reinstatement. The Workers' Alliance collapsed in the 1940s, after the group was tainted by charges of communist involvement. Poulnot lost his position in an internal purge by local Alliance leaders.[36]

Two months after the brief sitdown strike, many Latin women permanently lost their WPA jobs when aliens were eliminated from the relief agency's rolls. Ybor City was hard hit by this federal ruling, and hundreds of Latins turned to the Family Service Association (FSA) for help. Many of those released had lived in Ybor City most of their lives but had failed to become citizens. The FSA complained that "the law recently passed by Congress, practically barring aliens from WPA employment, has directly affected many families in Tampa. In many cases, the disbarred fathers are the sole support of American born wives and children." By September, 106 of 162 cases receiving aid from the FSA were aliens who were "very bitter and resentful toward the government because of their recent layoff from WPA rolls."[37] Such actions further damaged the image of the WPA, placed a greater burden on overtaxed relief agencies, and gave additional ammunition to radical groups.

Many editorials called the strike "foolish," because of lost jobs and prestige. Poulnot's attempt to widen the strike backfired and hurt the Alliance's ability to press for improvements and additional funds. The *Tribune* claimed that "undoubtedly the futile and foolish conduct of these strikers was prompted by the influence of agitators who are continually stirring up dissatisfaction among relief workers." A "slight feeling of unrest in some areas of the district, particularly Tampa," remained a month after the strike's conclusion because of its unfavorable outcome.[38]

Ybor City's relief strike failed for a number of reasons. Native-born American and black women were not sufficiently radicalized to join their Latin sisters, who had a longer, deeper experience with worker protest in the cigar industry. Quick, effective action by WPA officials and local law enforcement agencies, in undercutting and isolating the strikers, dealt a death blow to the strikers' effort. A calm, non-violent approach avoided incidents which might have otherwise increased support for the strikers, and threat of discontinued projects and lost jobs lessened the strikers' resolve.

Tampa was not ready for widespread radical agitation, particularly outside of Ybor City. The sitdown strike of 1937 revealed a deep chasm in experiences and expectations between Tampa's Latin and Anglo communities. However, despite a violence-filled past and a poor record in handling labor agitation, local law enforcement showed it could handle this potentially explosive situation calmly and firmly. That the protest began in a woman's sewing center and was led by women may have caused civic leaders to downplay the necessity for a more forceful response, but at the same time, it showed that women did not always accept their place quietly and that some women were ready to exert pressure to improve working conditions. Finally, the failure of the strike shows that most Hillsborough County residents, although hurt by economic hardship, were more willing to accept reforms in the economic and social system than to embrace more radical activity.

NOTES

1. Works Progress Administration (WPA), "Final Report on the WPA Program, 1935–43" (December 18, 1946), 7–15; Donald S. Howard, "As WPA Goes On," *The Survey*, 72 (October 1936): 297–98; Nels Anderson, *The Right to Work* (New York: Modern Books, 1938), 19; WPA, "Report on Progress of the Works Program" (March 1937), 25; "WPA Funds Still Available," *American City*, 50 (November 1935): 5; William E. Leuchtenburg, *Franklin D. Roosevelt and the New Deal* (New York: Harper and Row, 1963), 122–28.

2. Gloria Jahoda, *River of the Golden Ibis* (New York: Holt, Rinehart and Winston, 1973), 311; WPA, Federal Writers Project, "Seeing Tampa" (1935), 67, University of South Florida Special Collections; Charles W. Tebeau, *A History of Florida* (Coral Gables, Florida: University of Miami Press, 1971), 398; Hillsborough County Commission Minutes (HCCM), May 21, 1937, #4, p. 211, Hillsborough County Courthouse; Tampa Cooperative Unemployment Council, "Operations of the Tampa Cooperative Unemployment Council," June 24, 1932, R. E. L. Chancey Papers, box 3, file 20, City of Tampa Records and Micrograph Cen-

ter (CTRC); Philip A Hauser, "Workers on Relief in the United States in March 1935, A Census of Usual Occupations," vol. 1 (WPA Division of Social Research, 1938), 281.

3. R. E. L. Chancey to Franklin D. Roosevelt, March 12, 1936, Tampa Board of Representatives Files (TBRF), box 8-3H-4, file E-2625, CTRC.

4. Jahoda, *River of the Golden Ibis*, 315 (quotation), 317–18; Karl H. Grismer, *Tampa, A History of Tampa and the Tampa Bay Region of Florida* (St. Petersburg, Florida: St. Petersburg Printing Company, 1950), 272–73; Proceedings of the Tampa Board of Representatives (TBR), August 27, 1935, #20, 72, CTRC; *Tampa Tribune*, February 9, 1936.

5. George E. Pozzetta, "¡Alerta Tabaqueros! Tampa's Striking Cigar Workers," *Tampa Bay History*, 3 (Fall/Winter, 1981): 19–29; Gary R. Mormino and George E. Pozzetta, "Immigrant Women in Tampa: The Italian Experience, 1890–1930," *Florida Historical Quarterly*, 61 (January 1983): 305–06; Robert P. Ingalls, *Urban Vigilantes in the New South: Tampa, 1882–1936* (Knoxville: University of Tennessee Press, 1988).

6. Tampa Workers' Alliance, Executive Board Resolution, May 12, 1936, TBRF, box 8-3H-4, file E-2766; *Tampa Tribune*, August 18, 1935; *El Internacional*, June 18, 1937.

7. *Tampa Tribune*, August 1, September 8, 1935, May 7, 1937.

8. WPA, "Final Report," 41–45; James J. Kenneally, "Women in the U.S. and Trade Unionism," *The World of Women's Trade Unionism*, ed. Norbert C. Soldon (Westport, Connecticut: Greenwood Press, 1985), 76; Philip S. Foner, *Women and the American Labor Movement* (New York: Free Press, 1980), 293; Martha H. Swain, "The Forgotten Woman: Ellen S. Woodward and Woman's Relief in the New Deal," *Prologue*, 15 (Winter 1983): 201–13.

9. WPA, "Usual Occupations of Workers Eligible for Works Programs in the United States" (January 15, 1936), 24–25; WPA, "Final Report," 134.

10. WPA, Division of Women's and Professional Projects, "State Report: Florida, Alachua to Washington #29, Hillsborough" (September 14, 1936), 1, WPA Papers, Record Group 69, National Archives, Washington, D.C.; Florida WPA, Division of Women's and Professional Projects, "Narrative Reports" (July 1938), 2, (December 1937), 3, 9, (September 1936), 2, ibid.; *Tampa Tribune*, September 29, 1940.

11. HCCM, November 3, 1939, #7, p. 486; Florida WPA, "Narrative Reports" (April 1937), 17, (May 1937), 30; *Tampa Tribune*, December 12, 1937, October 30, 1938; Tampa Children's Home Minutes, October 8, 1940, USF Special Collections.

12. Florida WPA, "Narrative Reports" (October 1936), 3, (November 1936), 5, (December 1936), 4, (January 1937), 4, 8; HCCM, April 16, 1937, #4, p. 170.

13. *Tampa Tribune*, April 8, September 28, 1936; Tampa Children's Home Minutes, April 9, 1940; Plant City, "Community Improvement Appraisal" (March 8, 1938), 4, box 186, file 1922, WPA Papers.

14. James T. Patterson, *Congressional Conservatism and the New Deal* (Lexington: University of Kentucky Press, 1976), 145; W. M. Rowlett to Claude Pepper, November 2, 1938, box 1086, file 642, WPA Papers.

15. *Tampa Tribune*, April 18, May 10, July 18, 1936; *Florida Labor Advocate*, July 2, 1937; HCCM, May 1, 1936, #2, p. 460; Lillian Dasher to C. W. Lyons, April 7, 1937, Florida Service Association Minutes, Family Service Association Papers, USF Special Collections; Hattie McKeel, "Tampa Narrative Report for July 1937," in Florida WPA, "Narrative Reports" (July 1937).

16. *Tampa Tribune*, July 9, 1937; *La Gaceta*, July 8, 1937; McKeel Report.

17. Irving Bernstein, *Turbulent Years: A History of the American Worker, 1933–1941* (Boston: Houghton Mifflin, 1971), 499–501.

18. *Tampa Tribune*, July 9, 1937.

19. J. R. McLeod, telephone conversation, October 1987; Bessie Phinney to Franklin D. Roosevelt, May 18, 1939, box 1086, File 642, WPA Papers.

20. *Tampa Tribune*, July 9, 1937; McKeel Report.

21. *Tampa Tribune*, July 9, 1937.

22. Ibid., July 15, 1937.

23. *La Gaceta*, July 9, 1937; *Tampa Tribune*, July 11, August 21, 1937; *Florida Labor Advocate*, August 27, 1937.

24. *La Gaceta,* July 9, 1937; *Tampa Tribune,* July 11, 1937.

25. *Tampa Tribune,* July 10–11, 1937.

26. *La Gaceta,* July 10, 1937; *Tampa Tribune,* July 10, 1937.

27. Florida WPA, "Narrative Reports" (July 1937), 23; *Tampa Tribune,* July 21, 1937.

28. *La Gaceta,* July 10, 1937; *Tampa Tribune,* July 10, 1937.

29. *Tampa Tribune,* July 10–11, 1937.

30. Ibid., July 11, 1937; *La Gaceta,* July 12, 1937.

31. *Tampa Tribune,* July 10–14, 1937; *Miami Herald,* July 12, 1937; McKeel Report; McLeod conversation.

32. *La Gaceta,* July 13, 1937.

33. *Tampa Tribune,* July 13, 1937.

34. *La Gaceta,* July 14, 1937; *Tampa Tribune,* July 14, 1937.

35. *La Gaceta,* July 15, 1937; *Tampa Tribune,* July 15, 1937.

36. *Tampa Tribune,* August 21, 1937; *Florida Labor Advocate,* August 27, 1937; FSA Minutes, nd (probably August 13, 1937); Poulnot to Aron S. Gilmartin, November 12, 1937, box 143, Worker's Defense League Papers, Archives of Labor History, Wayne State University, Detroit; Steve Lamont to Tampa Board of Representatives, August 10, 1940, TBRF 8-3H-3, file 5076; James E. Sargent, "Woodrum's Economy Bloc: The Attack on Roosevelt's WPA, 1937–39," *Virginia Magazine of History and Biography,* 93 (April 1985): 175–207.

37. *Tampa Tribune,* September 12, 1937; FSA Minutes, September 20, October 15, 1937.

38. *Tampa Tribune,* July 16, 18, 1937; *La Gaceta,* July 15, 1937; *Florida Labor Advocate,* July 16, 1937; Florida WPA, "Narrative Reports" (August 1937), 16.

DAWSON COUNTY, NEBRASKA

Dawson County Responds to the New Deal, 1933–1940

JEROLD SIMMONS

For many farmers the Great Depression began in the twenties. A "farm relief" movement throughout that decade sought help against a chronic surplus acting as a depressant on farm prices. There were many proposals for some kind of government-sponsored price-support program; the question of production controls was hotly disputed. The Roosevelt administration finally emphasized a Voluntary Domestic Allotment Program under which staple farmers (producers of crops such as corn, wheat, cotton, tobacco, and rice) would receive subsidies for reducing production to the demands of the domestic market—seemingly an anomaly when many Americans did not have enough food, though the administration created the Surplus Relief Corporation to deal with this problem. Losses incurred by farmers in sales in foreign markets would not be subsidized. The administration argued that without production controls, any subsidy fund would be quickly exhausted. An important aspect of the following selection is its delineation of a gap between farmers' profession and practice: in line with their traditional ideology they deplored government programs, but they were willing to accept subsidy payments. Looking beyond the 1930s, we see irony in history. Designed largely to aid family farms, over time the subsidy program dispensed a high percentage of its funds to large corporate farms.

From *Nebraska History*, 62 (Spring 1981), 47–72.

Franklin Roosevelt's New Deal may well be the most popular political program of the 20th century. This array of new reform programs, regulatory agencies, and recovery measures won widespread public approval and attracted vast numbers of new voters to the Democratic Party. Yet, the voters of the Great Plains, particularly those of central Nebraska, refused to commit themselves permanently to the emerging New Deal coalition. In 1932 with the nation paralyzed by depression, central Nebraskans voted for Roosevelt out of desperation, and for a year following his inauguration in 1933, they seemed pleased with the activism of the new administration. But as the decade wore on, their enchantment with the New Deal began to fade, and by 1940 they had returned overwhelmingly to their traditionally Republican voting habits. In light of the substantial benefits which New Deal programs brought to central Nebraska, this voting pattern is puzzling. Why should voters who received so much reject the New Deal so completely? While there is no simple answer to this question, some insights can be gleaned through a detailed examination of one county's response to the New Deal.

Dawson County is an excellent vantage point from which to view the response of central Nebraskans to the New Deal. Its geography, economy, and population are characteristic of the region, and its 20th-century voting patterns have mirrored those of surrounding counties and the state as a whole.

Astride the Platte River in the center of the state, Dawson County lies at the extreme western edge of the corn belt in a transitional zone between the eastern corn-producing and western wheat and grazing regions of Nebraska. The Platte Valley, which crosses the county from northwest to southeast, includes nearly one-half of the county's total land area, the remainder being composed of rolling hills which merge into a broad tableland. At the end of the 1920s, Dawson's agriculture was reasonably diversified with roughly 50 percent of the cropland in corn, 12 percent in alfalfa, and 17 percent in wheat and other grains. While corn was cultivated throughout the county, alfalfa was limited primarily to the valley, and wheat to the western half. Livestock was raised on most farms, with the lush prairie grasses of the hills and the corn and alfalfa of the valley providing the cattleman and hog producer with a ready supply of local feed. Prior to the development of extensive irrigation facilities, the valley farmer held a distinct advantage over his upland counterpart, benefiting from a modest system of ditch irrigation and an unusually high water table, which the deep-rooted alfalfa could reach even in the driest years.

Upland farmers were almost totally dependent upon fickle mother nature for their moisture, leaving them more vulnerable during the drought-ridden 1930s.[1]

Unlike many Nebraska counties, Dawson had no central town which dominated county life. Instead, three communities shared the role. Lexington in the east-central part of the county was county seat and the largest town, with a 1930 population of 2,962. Cozad, located 12 miles west of Lexington, had a population of 1,813, and Gothenburg, near the county's western border, had 2,322.[2] The fact of major trading centers adds to the county's usefulness as a model for studying central Nebraska attitudes. Each community had its own newspaper, and each paper reflected a slightly different political perspective. The *Gothenburg Times* was edited by a moderate Democrat, who rarely engaged in political commentary; the *Cozad Local* by an intensely partisan conservative Republican, who constantly expressed his views; and the *Lexington Clipper* by a more moderate Republican who was less inclined to exhibit his partisanship in print.[3] Read together the three papers afford insights into the way the New Deal was perceived locally because the two-to-one Republican-over-Democrat affiliation by local editors roughly mirrored the partisan alignment among county voters at the onset of the New Deal.

Since its organization in 1871, Dawson County had shown a strong preference for the Republican Party in presidential contests. Prior to the New Deal, only Woodrow Wilson and Nebraska's William Jennings Bryan had been able to break this Republican pattern, and Bryan's margins of victory were slim. During the 1920s Republican strength was overwhelming. Both Harding in 1920, and Hoover in 1928 carried the county by more than two-to-one majorities, and Coolidge in 1924 attracted more voters than his Democratic (John W. Davis) and Progressive (Senator Robert M. LaFollette) opponents combined. Even after economic conditions began to deteriorate at the end of the decade, the Republican attachment persisted, as was evident in the 1930 primaries when over 80 percent of voters selected Republican ballots.[4] The county's two Republican newspapers reflected and reinforced this attachment. Both consistently praised the Republican commitment to limited government and expressed suspicion of proposals calling for federal regulation or financial assistance. The *Gothenburg Times*, however, perhaps reflecting the views of the county's western precincts, which included a higher percentage of marginal farmers, evidenced less fear of big government and as the decade progressed, a growing desire for an effective program of assistance to agriculture. But throughout the 1920s, the *Times* could only speak for a small minority of the county's voters. Faith in the Republican Party and its principles held firm. Only the Great Depression could shake that faith.

The depression did not reach the central portion of Nebraska until 1931. While farm prices did begin to sag late in 1929 and dropped sharply the following fall, it was not until the harvest of 1931 that the disheartening effects of the decline were fully felt, and the continued price descent through 1932 placed an already weakened farm economy in a state of utter collapse. By the autumn of 1932, corn, the county's chief crop, had dropped from a high of 71¢ per bushel in 1928 to 13¢ and wheat from 94¢ to 27¢. Alfalfa, the county's second-ranking crop, declined from $10 per ton to $4.10. Livestock prices took a similar slide, as cattle, which had sold for $12.60 per hundred-weight in 1928, went to $4.10 in 1932, and hogs from $11.50 to $2.30.[5]

The decline in farm prices affected the county in varying degrees of severity. While corn prices caused individual farmers considerable grief, their effect on the county's overall economic health was relatively moderate because local livestock consumed most of the corn. The decline in alfalfa and livestock prices, however, caused severe economic dislocations. These commodities were responsible for bringing substantial outside income into the county. The sale of livestock alone ordinarily accounted for over 70 percent of local farm revenue, and alfalfa production, about half of which was normally shipped to Wisconsin dairy farmers, generated much of the rest. Consequently, the price slump in these commodities undermined the entire local economy. The result was a doubling of the annual number of farm foreclosures and a dramatic increase in local business failures and unemployment.[6] In response, both Lexington and Cozad were forced to create special welfare committees to collect and distribute essentials to the local unemployed and the never-ending stream of transients passing through the county in search of work. The Lexington committee created a special "woodpile" where unemployed men could saw logs to stove-size lengths. They were paid in scrip, meals, or wood. By March, 1933, this woodpile was employing 121 men, and the welfare committee was providing relief to another 137 families in Lexington alone.[7] Fortunately, however, the banking crisis which brought widespread chaos throughout the nation in 1932, was not felt so strongly in Dawson as in surrounding counties. Custer County, Dawson's northern neighbor, suffered 15 bank failures between 1930 and 1933, but Dawson had none. Apparently the banks of Dawson County were well managed, and residents retained their faith in those institutions. As late as July, 1932, the directors of the Cozad State Bank could boast that there had been "no withdrawals of large deposits by customers in late months. . . . Confidence in banks appears to prevail in this community."[8]

But the confidence expressed by these Cozad bankers and frequently echoed in the county press could not hide the growing desperation generated by the depression. Dawson County needed help, and its voters had nowhere to turn but to the federal government. Prior to 1933 they were disappointed in Washington's response. The Hoover Administration's farm program proved to be "wholly inadequate and doomed to failure from the beginning," and its efforts to relieve unemployment and restore prosperity appeared equally ineffective.[9] By November, 1932, the voters of Dawson County, like those of the rest of Nebraska, had concluded that it was time for a change. The result was "the most substantial protest vote in the history of the state."[10] Franklin Roosevelt carried all but two of Nebraska's 93 counties and won 63 percent of the popular vote in the state. His totals in Dawson County were only slightly less impressive: 60 percent of the popular vote and majorities in 20 of the county's 22 precincts.[11]

The Roosevelt landslide of 1932 was based in large part on a recognized need for federal action to end the depression, and once in office the new administration responded with a vast array of new legislative proposals and executive actions. This flurry of activity in Washington had a dramatic impact across the country, generating new hope and confidence in the president. That optimism was apparent in Dawson County. Three weeks after Roosevelt's inauguration, some of the county's most ardently Republican editors were impressed. The editor of the *Cozad Local*, who during the 1932 campaign had expressed the opinion that Roosevelt's infirmities (crippled legs, polio ravaged) and his East Coast perspective would impair his ability to lead the country, now praised "the vigorous manner with which he is attacking our national problems" and expressed "confidence in the wisdom of his programs." The editor of the *Lexington Clipper*, co-chairman of the county GOP, was similarly impressed, noting that local residents had "unbounded confidence in President Roosevelt as a leader and all are radiating that confidence."[12] That spirit of optimism and trust in the Democratic Administration pervaded news stories throughout the spring and summer of 1933 and was evident whenever its editors discussed New Deal measures. For example, the Bank Holiday and subsequent banking reform legislation were given credit for bringing money "out of hiding" and putting the nation's banks on a "sound basis."[13] The Economy Act, which provided for sharp cutbacks in government salaries and veterans' pensions, was also warmly received, as was the far more important Agricultural Adjustment Act. For over a decade farmers had demanded a comprehensive program to bolster farm prices, and while many remained suspicious of the system of commodity controls employed by the AAA, most seemed pleased that the new administration had acted with dispatch.[14]

The New Deal's honeymoon in central Nebraska extended well beyond the famous first "100 days." In fact, its popularity did not peak until the fall and winter of 1933–1934. Surprisingly, that extended popularity seemed to stem less from the New Deal agricultural program than from two new agencies oriented toward urban America, the Civil Works Administration and the National Recovery Administration. Both agencies became active in the county during the final six months of 1933 and quickly generated new support for the New Deal. The CWA was created on November 8, 1933, as a temporary work-relief agency to ease the economic distress of the unemployed during the approaching winter. Its impact was immediately felt in Dawson County. Within days of its creation, the county welfare committee reconstituted itself as a local CWA committee and began hiring workers. By the end of January, 1934, the committee was employing over 350 men on projects ranging from street improvements to the removal of weeds and debris from county roads, and its efforts were winning the support of the local press. As the *Pioneer* put it, "The CWA has been doing a great job for the unemployed, and right here in Lexington it has relieved a great many households."[15]

The impact of the National Recovery Administration was even more dramatic. Created by the National Industrial Recovery Act of June, 1933, the NRA, symbolized by a Blue Eagle emblem, was the linchpin of the New Deal's program for economic recovery. It was designed to reform the American economy through codes of competition which would establish wages, hours, and other standards for each industry. The scope and complexity of the program dictated that the NRA rely primarily upon voluntary public compliance to achieve its objectives. To win this compliance NRA officials launched a major propaganda campaign in August, which quickly won widespread support in central Nebraska. The Dawson County press cooperated fully. From August through October, NRA news handouts were displayed prominently, and on one occasion an entire edition was devoted to spreading the NRA word.[16] Initial results were impressive. As early as August 4, 75 county businessmen met in Lexington to establish a code covering working hours and wages. Within a month the local press had credited the NRA with increasing employment and predicted a rise in farm prices due to improved consumer purchasing power.[17]

While the NRA later became the most universally despised of the New

Deal programs, during the fall of 1933, it was among the most popular. The great enthusiasm which its campaign engendered brought the zenith of New Deal popularity in Dawson County. Other New Deal agencies contributed to that popularity, but it was the NRA campaign which molded public enthusiasm into a spirit of unity behind the president. By the end of the year, after the first AAA checks had arrived and the CWA had begun hiring laborers, Roosevelt's popularity could not be ignored. From the perspective of central Nebraskans, the New Deal appeared to be off to a marvelous start. It was responding to Midwestern needs and seemed to have the entire area moving toward prosperity. But there was always a significant number of standpat Republicans.

The Roosevelt Administration was not destined to maintain the high level of popular approval reached during the final six months of 1933. Gradually Dawson County began to return to the Republican fold. While it is difficult to say exactly why or when this process began, it is apparent that by mid-1934 the enthusiasm generated by the NRA campaign had dissipated. Unfortunately that agency's local activities never went much beyond the initial ballyhoo, and nationally it began to attract considerable criticism. In tune with this shifting sentiment, the Dawson County press stopped urging compliance with the Blue Eagle codes and ceased its predictions of rapid recovery.

The termination of CWA activities in March also diminished the New Deal's local popularity. While that agency had been created merely to see the nation through the winter, the soaring unemployment which followed its dissolution revealed that the depression was far from over. By mid-June nearly one-fifth of the county's work force had registered as unemployed, and local welfare agencies were once again swamped.[18] Clearly, Roosevelt's "quick fix" had failed to materialize.

Evidence of disenchantment was quickly apparent. In the primary elections of April, 1934, barely 50 percent of the local voters selected Democratic ballots, a decline of 11 percent from 1932, and the congressional contests in the fall witnessed a similar softening of New Deal support.[19] But central Nebraskans had not yet completely rejected the New Deal. Many were still impressed with its efforts. Yet, the enthusiasm of 1933, which followed the administration's vigorous assault against the depression and had provided almost unquestioning approval of each new measure adopted, was gradually giving way to a more cautious and critical mood. In effect, Dawson County was entering a period of watchful waiting. From now on the New Deal was to be judged on how well its individual programs met the needs of central Nebraska.

By mid-summer, 1934, it was becoming increasingly apparent that those needs were changing. Over the preceding decade the paramount economic concerns of central Nebraskans revolved around the problems of surplus production and the consequent low farm prices. In 1934 the problems were scarcity and drought. Rainfall for the entire year totaled less than 11 inches, roughly half that normally received in the county and well below the minimum necessary to produce a reasonable harvest. High temperatures added to the devastation. In July local gauges rose above 100 degrees for 16 consecutive days. The results were disastous. Between 70 and 80 percent of the county's wheat and nearly 30 percent of its corn crop produced nothing, and the rest was substandard.[20] The short corn crop created additional problems for local cattle feeders. With hill grasses burning under the July sun and without substitute forage to take up the slack, cattlemen faced a critical feed shortage which threatened to destroy their herds. The one bright spot in the county's economic picture was alfalfa. That crop's unique root structure, enabling it to take advantage of the high water table near the Platte, meant valley farmers could produce near normal harvests, and because the drought destroyed most other forms of livestock feed, the price of alfalfa soared. By the end of the year, it was selling for nearly $20 per ton, almost five times its 1932 price.[21] Yet, in 1934 the prosperity generated by alfalfa helped only the relatively few valley farmers who had large, well-established stands of the crop. The rest of the county was in dire straits.

In response to these new needs, the Roosevelt Administration provided emergency feed and seed loans to those hardest hit and a special program of hog and cattle purchases. These programs afforded only minimal relief. The feed and seed loans averaged less than $100 per recipient, and the purchase price for cattle averaged only $13.74. Even the more substantial AAA payments and crop loans and the extensive refinancing activities of the Federal Land Banks could not stem the growing tide of farm foreclosures. Many smaller farmers, already weakened by successive years of low prices, simply went bankrupt under the weight of the drought.[22]

In 1935, however, central Nebraskans regained some of the optimism and confidence which the drought had withered. County papers once again predicted imminent prosperity as ample spring rains and a sharp increase in farm prices bolstered local spirits. Paradoxically, it was during this period of renewed optimism that the first direct criticism of the New Deal appeared in the county press. Not surprisingly, the agency criticized was the NRA. By the end of 1934, the NRA had lost much of the support its 1933 campaign had generated. The complexity of its codes of competition, the increasing burden of red tape, and a growing resentment of bureaucracy all combined to undermine faith in the NRA experiment. By April, 1935, Dawson County papers had ceased all positive reference to the NRA and dropped the Blue Eagle symbol from their mastheads. Increasingly, local businessmen disregarded code provisions, causing one editor to observe that "the only reason we can see for the statement that the NRA is better liked is because fewer people are adhering to it." When the U.S. Supreme Court invalidated the NRA the following month, the same editor exclaimed: "Now that the American Eagle has triumphed over the Blue Eagle, we are all a darned sight better off."[23]

The spurt of legislative activity which followed the invalidation of the NRA received only modest comment in the county press, much of it negative. The Social Security Act, National Labor Relations Act, and the banking reform legislation of 1935 drew mild criticism, and the new work-relief program established under the Works Progress Administration was less popular than that conducted under the CWA in 1933. In each case local criticism reflected a growing concern about big government, unbalanced budgets, and excessive federal regulation. The new farm credit act and rural electrification program, however, were more warmly received, indicating that opposition to federal growth could be selective.[24]

By the end of 1935, the most popular New Deal program in Dawson County was the AAA. In this respect farm opinion had shown a dramatic reversal within one year. In a special referendum conducted as part of the AAA's corn-hog program in October, 1934, local farmers had voted better than two to one against continuation of that program and five to one in favor of scrapping the entire AAA. While the county agent attributed the negative vote to low hog quotas and irritating mid-year alterations in the program, it nonetheless represented a dramatic rejection of the initial New Deal farm program. One year later, however, the corn-hog farmers voted to continue their program by better than a three-to-one margin, and wheat growers endorsed theirs by nearly six to one.[25] Since there was no appreciable alteration in the program, the only plausible explanation for this change in attitude stems from the fact that by October, 1935, Dawson County farmers were convinced that the AAA was working. They had seen commodity prices rise modestly in 1934 because of scarcity but were surprised and pleased when in 1935 with production back to near normal, prices remained relatively high. The New Deal program along with the drought seemed to be solving the basic problem that had plagued agriculture since World War I.

Although the AAA was invalidated by the Supreme Court the following January, the gradual return of farm prosperity continued into 1936. The Soil Conservation and Domestic Allotment Act, which replaced the AAA in February, continued to reward farmers for reduced production, and prices continued to rise with both corn and wheat ultimately exceeding $1.00 per bushel.[26] One aspect of the new program, however, caused local concern. Under the Soil Conservation Act, farmers received payments for converting land to soil-conserving crops, including alfalfa. While local farmers favored soil conservation, many feared that this inducement would cause overproduction and destroy alfalfa's value as a cash crop. In March local farmers and businessmen gathered to send a protest to Washington, but aside from a disdainful reply from Senator George Norris, their efforts achieved nothing. The feared price decline did not materialize, and ultimately most of the county's farmers signed up under the new program.[27]

While high farm prices insured the continued popularity of the crop reduction program in 1936, low rainfall, high temperatures, and the hordes of grasshoppers which ravaged local farmers in July and August brought increased awareness of New Deal emergency assistance programs. By late summer the *Gothenburg Times* estimated that at least 220 farm families would need federal assistance to maintain their farms. Most of them resided in the marginal hill and tablelands in the western half of the county.[28] For these families the crop reduction program was far less important than the emergency grants and feed and seed loans administered by the county agent and the rehabilitation and resettlement loans provided by the recently created Resettlement Administration. The various branches of the Farm Credit Administration also "assisted materially in carrying Dawson County farmers through the crucial period" by providing the credit necessary to continue production and refinance mortgages.[29] By September, 1936, the Federal Land Bank had made 544 loans and accounted for roughly 66 percent of all farm mortgage credit in the county.[30]

As the 1936 election approached, central Nebraskans began judging the New Deal on its merits. The campaign waged by Governor Alfred Landon of Kansas seemed to bring "to the fore the whole New Deal conception of government," forcing Nebraskans, like other Americans, to choose between competing philosophies.[31] Landon, while not advocating complete eradication of the New Deal, seemed to promise a return to the Republican virtues of fiscal responsibility and laissez-faire. The Roosevelt record promised continued federal programs and spending. In light of the intense partisan interest in the campaign, it is surprising that only one of the local newspapers endorsed either candidate. The *Gothenburg Times* and *Lexington Clipper* remained neutral during the campaign, perhaps reflecting the uncertainty with which voters faced the election. The *Cozad Local*, however, was far from neutral. Its editor came out strongly for Landon and throughout the summer devoted increasing space to a critique of the New Deal. The *Local*, speaking of the concerns of county conservatives, expressed its growing skepticism of huge expenditures, mushrooming federal bureaucracies, and government paternalism. Rarely did its editor condemn specific New Deal agencies, preferring to protest their impact on the American system as they had known it. The NRA, by then defunct, was a major exception to this rule of general rather than specific condemnation because it seemed to offer a clear example of New Deal regimentation. The Trade Agreements Act of 1934 was another. It was condemned for allegedly allowing price-depressing farm imports. By the end of August, the *Local* shifted its emphasis from the New Deal to President Roosevelt, using political cartoons to draw attention to his East Coast origins, broken campaign promises, and attempts to buy votes with so-called give-away programs.

The election results, however, clearly demonstrated that the *Cozad Local* did not speak for Dawson County. Roosevelt won a majority of the county's votes just as he had in 1932. Yet the returns also demonstrated that approval of the New Deal was far from universal in central Nebraska. Compared with the overwhelming landslide which Roosevelt received nationally and in Nebraska, his margin of victory in Dawson County was modest, less than 6 percent of the total vote. The president had indeed lost ground since 1932. His share of the popular vote dropped from 60 to 52 percent, and his support declined in 21 of the county's 22 precincts.[32]

County precinct returns provide only general indications as to which local groups were most inclined to turn away from Roosevelt. Cattlemen were moving in this direction, as the five precincts showing the largest Republican gains in 1936 all contained sizeable portions of pastureland and large numbers of cattle. Large-scale alfalfa growers followed a similar pattern, as the three strongest Landon precincts were large producers of alfalfa, while the strongest Roosevelt precincts grew little. Since these cattle and alfalfa precincts had provided the coolest reception to the New Deal farm program in the AAA referendums of 1934 and 1935, it is logical to assume that their return to Republicanism was prompted in part by their dissatisfaction with that program. Many cattlemen resented the fact that the AAA had driven up the price of corn and other sources of livestock feed more rapidly than the price of cattle, thus putting them in a cost/price bind. They also resented the administration's efforts to admit Argentine beef into the American market via the ill-fated U.S.-Argentine Sanitary

Convention of 1935.[33] Alfalfa growers were worried about the new competition promised by the 1936 conservation act.

But more significant than the defection of the cattleman and alfalfa
grower was the fact that the farmer in trouble tended to remain with Roosevelt. Seven precincts showed only minor or no Democratic losses in
1936, and all of these contained a significant percentage of upland marginal farms. In each case the precinct had been the site of many foreclosures, and farmers there were probably more appreciative of the New Deal
emergency drought and farm credit programs than were more prosperous
valley farmers. Because six of these precincts also ranked at the top of the
county in wheat acreage, the relative popularity of the AAA wheat program
and high wheat prices in 1936 may also have contributed to Roosevelt's
strength.[34]

The town vote is much more difficult to gauge because each town
ward included a large number of rural voters. Nonetheless, one obvious
conclusion can be drawn—the town vote shifted far less than the rural
vote. While Roosevelt's percentages declined in each town, in no instance
was the shift substantial. He retained strong majorities in both Cozad and
Gothenburg and lost Lexington by only 17 votes, thus indicating that Main
Street opposition to the New Deal had not yet fully materialized in Dawson County.[35] Town voters like their rural counterparts had not yet arrived
at a consensus on the merits of the New Deal. Many were still pleased
with Roosevelt's eclectic reform program; others were frightened by the
changes it brought, but most were simply uncertain.

After 1936 the division and uncertainty reflected in that election disappeared. Over the next four years, the vast majority of Dawson County
voters came to reject the New Deal and the leadership of Franklin Roosevelt. The initial phase of that rejection began early in Roosevelt's second
term when he announced his controversial plan to reform the federal
court system. This "court-packing" proposal was clearly Roosevelt's greatest single political mistake. It met with intense resistance in Congress and
afforded the president's critics new evidence of his disdain for constitutional government. Within Dawson County it generated new and more intense criticism of the New Deal. Prior to the election of 1936, only the
Cozad Local had been vigorous or consistent in its condemnation of Roosevelt, but with the announcement of the court-packing proposal, the *Lexington Clipper* joined in directing increasing criticism at the Roosevelt
Administration and its philosophy.

The two papers gained new ammunition for their anti–New Deal offensive during the spring of 1937 with the outbreak of labor strife in the

auto and steel industries. The editors of both papers condemned the new sit-down technique employed by the strikers and blamed the Roosevelt Administration for promoting industrial conflict. They argued that the National Labor Relations Act had given organized labor too much power and should be amended before labor militants destroyed the industrial order and drove the cost of living out of sight.[36] From the specific issues raised by the court-packing plan and labor unrest, conservative criticism moved to condemn spending programs, growing taxes, and federal regimentation. In August the *Cozad Local*'s editor praised business leaders for expanding production facilities in the face of "higher labor costs, increased taxation, and harassment by a multiplicity of governmental regulatory agencies."[37] Such criticism, however, could hardly be telling as long as the economy continued to improve, as it did throughout most of 1937. But in the fall the prosperity bubble burst. Unemployment jumped to near 1932 levels and farm prices collapsed. Corn, which had sold for $1.20 per bushel as late as July, plummeted to 51¢ by the end of the year, and other farm commodities followed suit.[38] This, combined with the twin ravages of drought and grasshoppers which once again visited the state in 1937, left local farmers in straitened circumstances. The conservative critique of the New Deal began to take on new meaning. Now New Deal experimentation and regimentation could be blamed for the recession, and the plight of local farmers could be used as evidence of the Roosevelt Administration's failure.

As the recession worsened, federal programs were directed toward assisting the hard-pressed marginal farmer. His plight was the primary concern of the newly created Farm Security Administration, which through 1937 and 1938 was the most active federal agency in Dawson County. The FSA provided small loans and direct monthly grants to over 300 families who were in dire need, organized a volunteer debt adjustment committee which arranged 30 mortgage readjustments, and administered special loans to assist tenants in acquiring their own land. These actions in conjunction with the continued efforts of local lending institutions and the Farm Credit Administration prevented the anticipated rash of farm foreclosures.[39] The continued subsidies for crop reduction also provided assistance. By 1937 virtually every farmer in the county had signed up under the conservation act and was receiving payments. Participation declined the following year because of the uncertainty created by the new Agricultural Adjustment Act of 1938, but within a year the advantages of enrolling under the new program became clear, and sign-ups returned to near 1937 levels.[40]

The activities of the FSA and AAA, however, did not generate economic recovery. Farm prices remained low for the remainder of the decade, and unemployment continued to plague the towns. Even with the work-relief activities of the WPA, which employed as many as 400 workers when funds were available, the county's rate of unemployment was still at 8 percent as late as the spring of 1940. The persistence of the recession was obvious in the results of an economic survey conducted in 1939 by the county agent. It revealed that 55 percent of all families in the county earned less than $1,000 per year.[41] Given these conditions, it is not surprising that the Democratic Party continued to lose ground in Dawson County. In the 1938 primary elections less than 43 percent of local voters selected Democratic ballots, and in November county voters supported Republicans in five of the six state contests and an anti–New Deal Democrat, Harry B. Coffee, for Congress.[42]

After the elections the "Roosevelt recession" continued, and local criticism of the president intensified. As in the past, criticism focused upon the broad consequences of the New Deal rather than on specific agencies. In fact, the local press normally expressed approval of the agencies it mentioned. The Public Works Administration won strong approval for its contribution to the development of local irrigation, as did the Rural Electrification Administration for its grants which assisted in bringing electric power to the farm. Other New Deal efforts to assist the nation's farmers through the credit programs of the FCA, the emergency relief activities of the FSA, and the direct subsidies of the AAA also received praise from the local press.[43]

Even the Works Progress Administration, frequently condemned elsewhere as a classic example of government paternalism, received only limited criticism in Dawson County.[44] While the Cozad Local occasionally referred to the WPA in scornful terms, the other local papers were more likely to offer praise. Much of that praise was directed at the many WPA projects completed in the county. From the standpoint of the Lexington Clipper, the construction of 42 miles of county road, 2 miles of street improvements, 2,940 feet of sidewalk, 18 culverts, five new buildings, improvements on eight existing structures, one new park, three new wells, a water pumping station and 27,339 feet of water main, 10,924 feet of new or improved sewer lines, and the cataloguing of 1,200 library volumes constituted a "gigantic face lifting" which deserved the county's applause.[45]

The more liberal Gothenburg Times seemed less impressed with WPA construction than with its efforts to ease the burden of the unemployed. Its editor wrote several editorials which praised the agency for making it possible for "needy people to obtain employment and honorably support themselves and their loved ones by constructive labor."[46]

While most specific agencies received praise or at least grudging approval from the county press, the assault on the New Deal philosophy continued. Much of the criticism echoed the concerns voiced by the *Cozad Local* during the 1936 campaign—in particular, federal spending. The *Clipper*'s editor claimed the nation was moving toward financial ruin "not only because of debts and deficits themselves but because there has been no serious inclination to chart a course that will ultimately bring government spending under control."[47] The *Local*'s editor directed his ire at New Deal experimentation, citing 39 national emergencies declared by the president since 1933, all of which were used as "springboards for some new fangled experimenting or planning."[48]

After August, 1939, the war in Europe began to take people's minds off their economic woes. Surprisingly, while all three papers advocated nonintervention, none directed criticism at President Roosevelt. Even after the famous destroyers-for-bases deal, in which Roosevelt took the first step toward aligning the United States with the Allied cause and thereby attracted censure from other Midwestern newspapers, the Dawson County press remained silent on the president's actions. Its editors seemed far more concerned with internal problems—with what they saw as an increasing tendency toward internal decay in America. From their perspective that decay was the inevitable product of excessive government paternalism which promoted an increasing "gimme" influence" among American voters. The *Clipper* editor expressed his growing concern in a series of editorials in August, 1940. He drew a parallel between the collapse of France the preceding spring and conditions in the United States:

France carried "social reform" to the point of national decay. Politically we have been following a parallel path. We too have been chasing rainbows of unreasoned reform surrounded by burgeoning bureaucracy, skyrocketing debt, and crumbling initiative.

He blamed these problems on professional politicians who "talk much of sacrifice, in noble words," but refused "to sacrifice one thin dime of patronage . . . to support a principle." He said the result was that

money still goes out for farm relief schemes foredoomed to failure—for unnecessary tax-built and tax-subsidized government electric plants, for government credit schemes of all kinds, and for a thousand and one purposes which are in no way a true function of government but which are prolific sources of votes and power.[49]

Closely allied to this fear of paternalism and internal decay was a growing sense that the New Deal had lost touch with the Midwest, that it had become an essentially urban and eastern political phenomenon with little concern for rural America. Much of this perception was based upon the emerging alliance between the New Deal and organized labor which was most visible in the increasing political action of the CIO. But it was also based upon the assumption that the New Deal's relief and reform programs were designed to appeal to an urban population perceived to be unthrifty. In that sense the growing urban character of Roosevelt's support revived rural distrust of the city and caused it to be directed at the Democratic Party.[50]

One final concern emerged as the 1940 election approached—Roosevelt's tradition-breaking quest for a third term. While the local press made few direct references to this development, subtle comments, such as the inclusion of the text of Jefferson's refusal to accept a third term, were frequently featured. While never condemned by local editors, Roosevelt's decision to ignore the two-term tradition seemed to heighten local fears that he was aspiring to excessive power. When viewed in conjunction with his effort to pack the Supreme Court in 1937 and his attempt to purge the Democratic Party of anti–New Deal congressmen in 1938, Roosevelt's quest for a third term appeared ominous. They reasoned that since 1937 he had seemed bent on destroying the traditional separation of powers which limited executive authority; now he wanted to hold that authority even longer.[51]

Given these perceptions, the outcome of the 1940 election in Dawson County was never in doubt. The election returns merely confirmed what was already evident in the county press—that central Nebraskans had rejected Roosevelt and had returned to the Republican Party. Only the scope of Wendell Willkie's victory was surprising. He carried the county by a two-to-one margin, winning 66 percent of the popular vote and carrying every precinct. His margin of victory was thus nearly 7 percent greater than Roosevelt's in 1932, when the county was wallowing in the depths of the depression, and 13 percent higher than Roosevelt could muster after four years of providing relief. Willkie's victory also meant doom for the few remaining Democrats who held state offices. Dawson County voters gave strong majorities to Republican candidates with the single exception of

Representative Harry Coffee, who had openly opposed Roosevelt's third-term bid.

The rejection of Roosevelt was consistent throughout the county. Precinct returns showed no appreciable variation between town and rural voting and only slight differences between commodity groups. Precincts with significant numbers of marginal farmers or with a higher percentage of wheat growers did support Willkie less completely than the rest of the county. But even there, where Roosevelt's strength had been greatest in 1932 and 1936, Willkie's margins were close to 60 percent, and in two of these precincts exceeded 75 percent. These two precincts showed by far the most dramatic Democrat-to-Republican shift in the county, and their behavior suggests one clue toward understanding the Roosevelt-to-Willkie shift which was not evident in the county press—the German-American vote. The two precincts in question contained high concentrations of ethnic Germans whose dramatic rejection of Roosevelt was a statement of their disapproval of his assistance to Britain in 1940. While the president's actions attracted little criticism in the press, they may well have decreased his popularity among the 10 percent of the county's German-Americans, turning what would have been a substantial Republican victory into a rout.[52]

In spite of this ethnic variation, the election of 1940 in Dawson County represents the culmination of a conservative reaction to the New Deal which began as early as mid-1934. From that point through the end of the decade, opposition to the Roosevelt Administration grew. At first anti–New Deal sentiment evolved slowly, but in the closing years of the decade it seemed to snowball, culminating in the overwhelming rejection in 1940.

Why did Dawson County reject the New Deal? The answer involves complex factors, but one conclusion can be drawn with some certainty: the voters of Dawson County were never fully comfortable with the New Deal brand of government. Undeniably in the autumn of 1933, under the influence of the NRA campaign, a new farm program, and the obvious vigor of the administration, the president won broad-based approval in the county. But that approval was built more upon the belief that spirited action would cure economic ills rather than upon any conscious agreement on approach or philosophy. By early 1935, as the effects of the NRA campaign wore off and the worst of the depression passed, central Nebraskans began to judge the New Deal on its merits. While most approved of the specific New Deal agencies at work in the county, a growing number evidenced concern about the impact of the New Deal, and although Roosevelt carried the county in 1936, his margin was substantially narrowed from 1932. After 1936 in the wake of economic recession, the court-packing scheme, and a series of labor upheavals, those concerns intensified. By 1940 county voters seemed convinced that the New Deal had gone too far—that its experimentation and increased spending had become harmful to the economy, that its magnification of presidential power weakened the constitutional system, and that its attempt to appeal to urban voting blocs through paternalistic programs threatened the America they had known. In that sense the rejection of the New Deal in central Nebraska represents a return to the political ideology which characterized the region in the 1920s. Central Nebraskans, like most Midwesterners, had never really abandoned their philosophy of rugged individualism, limited government, and unfettered free enterprise; they had merely been forced by an economic catastrophe to compromise. When the crisis had passed, they returned to those ideals and found the New Deal wanting.

Yet the return to the Republican Party did not mean that central Nebraskans had rejected all aspects of the New Deal. Their disenchantment was selective. Farm subsidies, the expanded system of agricultural credit, federal support for irrigation and rural electrification, and the many other New Deal programs which were improving the quality of rural life all retained their popularity in central Nebraska well beyond 1940, and any candidate seeking political support in that region dared not threaten those gains of the 1930s.In that sense the traditional ideals to which central Nebraskans returned in 1940 had been profoundly influenced by the New Deal and the depression experience. The conservatism which reemerged in that election and guided their political choice thereafter was more pragmatic and far more tolerant of federal power than it had been in 1930. But it was, nonetheless, a conservatism which fit much more comfortably into the Republican than the Democratic fold. After 1940 the pattern was set. Over the succeeding decades, central Nebraskans consistently provided GOP presidential candidates with landslide majorities. They had returned to the Republican Party to stay.

GLOSSARY OF MAJOR NEW DEAL AGENCIES ACTIVE IN DAWSON COUNTY

Agricultural Adjustment Administration (AAA): Created under the Agricultural Adjustment Act of May, 1933, this agency was responsible for administering the New Deal farm program. Its county and precinct committees arranged and monitored reduction agreements with local farmers in line with guidelines established by the AAA, and the county agent directed other AAA programs including the emergency purchase of cattle and hogs and the distribution of emergency loans.

Civilian Conservation Corps (CCC): Created under the Civilian Conservation Corps Reforestation Relief Act of March, 1933, the CCC provided work for jobless males between the ages of 18 and 25 in reforestation, road construction, and the prevention of soil erosion. Approximately 220 Dawson County boys were employed in CCC work camps between April, 1933, and April, 1940.

Civil Works Administration (CWA): An emergency relief program created in November, 1933, to provide work for the unemployed during the coming winter. It was terminated in March, 1934.

Commodity Credit Corporation (not to be confused with Civilian Conservation Corps; see above): An agency created under the AAA in October, 1933, to extend crop loans to farmers, thereby allowing them to withhold their products from the market until prices improved.

Farm Credit Administration (FCA): Created by executive order in March, 1933, the FCA was designed to bring all federal farm credit operations under centralized direction. It assumed supervision of the Federal Land Banks, Federal Intermediate Credit Banks, Production Credit Corporations, and Banks for Cooperatives.

Farm Security Administration (FSA): Created under the Bankhead-Jones Farm Tenant Act of July, 1937, the FSA assumed most of the functions of the Resettlement Administration including the administration of low-interest loans to farm tenants and laborers for the purchase of land and equipment and to small farmers for operating expenses or the refinancing of farm mortgages.

National Recovery Administration (NRA): The agency created under the National Industrial Recovery Act of June, 1933, to administer the complex codes of competition designed to regulate wages, hours, prices, and standards in each industry.

Public Works Administration (PWA): Created under Title II of the National Industrial Recovery Act, the PWA was designed to stimulate employment and business activity through grants to local governmental bodies for the construction of roads, public buildings, and other major projects.

Resettlement Administration (RA): Established by an executive order of May, 1935, the RA was created to improve the lot of farmers who had not been aided by the AAA. It was authorized to resettle destitute farm families, grant loans for the purchase of farms and equipment, and establish

240 HOPE RESTORED

subsistence homestead communities. Its functions were absorbed by the Farm Security Administration in 1937.

Rural Electrification Administration (REA): Created by an executive order of May, 1935, the REA administered loans for the purpose of generating and distributing electricity to rural areas.

Works Progress Administration (WPA): Established under the Emergency Relief Appropriation Act of April, 1935, the WPA directed a massive work program to employ the nation's jobless. It was administered through local WPA committees which designed projects and employed the workers.

NOTES

1. Harold Stevens and John Stuart, "Report on the Overall Economic Development Program for the Dawson County Redevelopment Area: Dawson County, Nebraska" (Extension Service, University of Nebraska, 1964), 20–26, 32–49; James C. Adams, "Annual Report of Cooperating Work in Agriculture and Home Economics, Dawson County, State of Nebraska, 1940," (Office of the Extension Agent, Dawson County Courthouse, Lexington), 45, 52a. Hereafter cited as Adams, "County Agent's Report." For a more detailed description of the county, see Jerold Simmons, "The New Deal in Dawson County, Nebraska" (unpublished master's thesis, Department of History, University of Nebraska at Omaha, 1967), 1–11.

2. U.S. Bureau of the Census, *Fifteenth Census of the United States: 1930. Population,* I, 671.

3. In a comment following the 1936 election, the editor of the *Times* admitted that he had long been a Democrat. The *Clipper's* editor announced his party preference before that election and also served as co-chairman of the Republican county committee through most of the decade. *Gothenburg Times,* November 11, 1936; *Lexington Clipper,* August 27, 1936.

4. W. Dean Burnham, *Presidential Ballots: 1836–1892* (Baltimore: The Johns Hopkins University Press, 1955), 607; Edgar Eugene Robinson, *The Presidential Vote, 1896–1932* (Stanford: Stanford University Press, 1934), 32, 263; Dawson County Abstract of Votes (Office of the County Clerk, Dawson County Courthouse, Lexington), II, 96, 103. The party percentages in Dawson County through the first three decades of the 20th century were similar to those of most counties in the corn and livestock producing region of the state. See Charles J. Knibbs, "The Political Map of Nebraska, 1900–1934" (unpublished master's thesis, Department of History, University of Nebraska at Lincoln, 1935), 145.

5. *Nebraska Agricultural Statistics: Annual Reports, 1928 and 1932* (Lincoln: State Federal Division of Agricultural Statistics, 1928 and 1932), 118–20, 3. For an excellent description of the impact of the depression on central Nebraska, see Lloyd Glover, Jr., "The Economic Effects of Drought and Depression on Custer County" (unpublished master's thesis, Department of Economics, University of Nebraska at Lincoln, 1950).

6. Adams, "County Agent's Report, 1930," 52; "1940," 52a. Farm foreclosure sales totaled 12 in 1930, 15 in 1934, and 34 in 1932. Sale Docket of Dawson County, Nebraska (Office of the Clerk of the District Court, Dawson County Courthouse, Lexington), III, 108–201.

7. *Dawson County Pioneer,* October 7, 1932; March 10, 1933; *Cozad Local,* September 30, 1932. The *Pioneer* was a Lexington weekly absorbed by the *Lexington Clipper* in 1934.

8. Minutes of the Directors, Cozad State Bank, July 30, 1932; Glover, "Drought and Depression in Custer County," 10; *Lexington Clipper,* May 23, 1935.

9. Murray R. Benedict, *Farm Policies of the United States, 1790–1950* (New York: Twentieth Century Fund, 1953), 257.

10. James C. Olson, *History of Nebraska* (Lincoln: University of Nebraska Press, 1955), 300.

11. Dawson County Abstract of Votes, II, 147.

12. *Cozad Local,* March 24, 1933; *Lexington Clipper,* March 16, 1933.

13. *Cozad Local,* July 18, 1933.

14. An excellent description of the New Deal's efforts on behalf of Midwestern agriculture is by Kearney State College Professor Michael W. Schuyler, "The Dread of Plenty: Agricultural Relief Activities of the Federal Government in the Middle West, 1933–1939" (unpublished manuscript loaned to the author).

15. *Dawson County Pioneer,* January 5, 1934.

16. See especially the *Gothenburg Times,* August 9, 1933, or the *Cozad Local,* August 15, 1933.

17. *Dawson County Pioneer,* August 4, 1933; *Lexington Clipper,* September 7, 1933.

18. *Dawson County Pioneer,* June 29, 1934.

19. Dawson County Abstract of Votes, II, 156, 160, 169–71. For a detailed discussion of the 1934 election results, see Simmons, "The New Deal in Dawson County," 60–63.

20. *Cozad Local,* July 27, 1934; *Lexington Clipper,* May 23, 1935; Arthur C. Schmieding, "Geographic Patterns of Failure of Wheat and Corn in Nebraska, 1931–1952" (unpublished master's thesis, Department of Geography, University of Nebraska at Lincoln, 1954), 26–27.

21. *Nebraska Agricultural Statistics,* 1934, 3.

22. Adams, "County Agent's Report, 1934," 72–74; Sale Docket of Dawson County, Nebraska, III, 248–310.

23. *Lexington Clipper,* April 4, 1935; May 30, 1935.

24. *Cozad Local,* June 7, 1935; *Lexington Clipper,* June 27, 1935; September 26, 1935.

25. Adams, "County Agent's Report, 1934," 72; "1935," 21, 28. Interview with James C. Adams, Brady, Nebraska, August 24, 1966.

26. *Nebraska Agricultural Statistics,* 1936, 3.

27. *Cozad Local,* March 10, 1936; *Lexington Clipper,* March 12, 1936. Norris chided local farmers for asking Congress "to keep anybody from planting or producing a crop which will come into competition with anybody else who is now producing similar crops." *Cozad Local,* March 17, 1936; Adams, "County Agent's Report, 1936," 22.

28. *Gothenburg Times,* August 19, 1936.

29. Adams, "County Agent's Report, 1936," 46.

30. *Gothenburg Times,* September 23, 1936.

31. Dixon Wecter, *The Age of the Great Depression, 1929–1941* (New York: The Macmillan Company, 1948), 101.

32. Dawson County Abstract of Votes, II, 192.

33. This trade agreement died in the Senate Foreign Relations Committee due in large part to the protests of cattle feeders. John T. Schlebecker, *Cattle Raising in the Plains* (Lincoln: University of Nebraska Press, 1963), 147.

34. Dawson County Abstract of Votes, II, 192; Adams, "County Agent's Report, 1940," 32–33.

35. Dawson County Abstract of Votes, II, 192.

36. See especially the *Lexington Clipper,* March 11, 1937, and the *Cozad Local,* July 23, 1937.

37. *Cozad Local,* August 31, 1937.

38. *Nebraska Agricultural Statistics,* 1937, 3.

39. Local farm foreclosures increased by only seven between 1937 and 1938. Sale Docket of Dawson County, Nebraska, III, 445–642; IV, 1–82; Adams, "County Agent's Report, 1937," 8; "1938," 45.

40. *Gothenburg Times,* May 11, 1939.

41. U.S. Department of Commerce, Bureau of the Census, *Sixteenth Census of the United States: Population,* II, part 4, 635; Adams, "County Agent's Report, 1939," 43.

42. Dawson County Abstract of Votes, II, 198, 203, 210.

43. *Gothenburg Times,* September 1, 1938; *Lexington Clipper,* September 22, 1938, and July 13, 1939; *Cozad Local,* December 29, 1939.

44. The *Omaha World Herald* was highly critical of the WPA. See especially its editorial of May 6, 1938.

45. *Lexington Clipper*, February 17, 1938, and April 25, 1940.

46. *Gothenburg Times*, August 31, 1939.

47. *Lexington Clipper*, September 5, 1940.

48. *Cozad Local*, April 7, 1939.

49. *Lexington Clipper*, August 1, 15, 1940.

50. This perception of the New Deal was evident well beyond Dawson County. See James T. Patterson, "The New Deal in the West," *Pacific Historical Review*, 38 (August, 1969), 317–27; or Robert S. and Helen M. Lynd, *Middletown in Transition: A Study in Cultural Conflict* (New York: Harcourt, Brace and Company, 1937), 109.

51. *Lexington Clipper*, August 8, 1940. In a series of interviews conducted by the author in 1966, the third-term issue and concerns that Roosevelt had become power-hungry were cited more frequently than any other single factor in explaining the local rejection of Roosevelt in 1940. See also James B. Beddlow, "Midwestern Editorial Response to the New Deal," *South Dakota History*, 4 (winter, 1973), 17.

52. Dawson County Abstract of Votes, II, 230–236; U.S. Department of Commerce, Bureau of the Census, *Fifteenth Census of the United States: Population*, III, part 2, 75, 98–99. For a detailed evaluation of the 1940 German-American vote in eastern Nebraska, see Robert W. Cherny, "Isolationist Voting in 1940: A Statistical Analysis," *Nebraska History*, 52 (Fall, 1971), 293–310.

Selected Bibliography

LOCALITIES — ARTICLES AND CHAPTERS

Argersinger, Jo Ann E., "'Assisting the Loafers': Transient Relief in Baltimore, 1933–1937," *Labor History*, 23 (Spring 1982), 226–245.

Barr, Michael, "A Comparative Examination of Federal Work Relief in Fredericksburg and Gillespie County," *Southwestern Historical Quarterly*, 96 (January 1993), 362–390.

Bauman, John F., "Black Slums/Black Projects: The New Deal and Negro Housing in Philadelphia," *Pennsylvania History*, 41 (1974), 311–338.

——, "Safe and Sanitary Without the Costly Frills: The Evolution of Public Housing in Philadelphia, 1929–1941," *Pennsylvania Magazine of History and Biography*, 101 (January 1977), 114–128.

Biles, Roger, "The New Deal in Dallas," *Southwestern Historical Quarterly*, 95 (July 1941), 1–19.

——, "The Persistence of the Past: Memphis in the Great Depression," *Journal of Southern History*, 52 (May 1986), 183–212.

Bolin, James Duane, "The Human Side: Politics, the Great Depression, and the New Deal in Lexington, Kentucky, 1929–35, *Register of the Kentucky Historical Society*, 90 (Summer 1992), 256–283.

Boulard, Garry, "State of Emergency: Key West in the Great Depression," *Florida Historical Quarterly*, 67 (October 1988), 166–183.

Burran, James A., "The WPA in Nashville, 1935–1943," *Tennessee Historical Quarterly*, 34 (Fall 1975), 293–306.

Buttenwieser, Ann L., "Shelter for What and for Whom? On the Route Toward Vladeck Houses, 1930–1940," *Journal of Urban History*, 12 (August 1986), 391–413.

Chafe, William N., "Flint and the Great Depression," *Michigan History*, 53 (Fall 1969), 225–239.

Colwell, Robert F., "San Angelo, 1933–1936: Drought, Flood, Depression," in Robert C. Cotner, et. al., *Texas Cities in the Great Depression*, Austin: Texas Memorial Museum, 1973, pp. 171–187.

Davies, David L., "Impoverished Politics: The New Deal's Impact on City Government in Providence, Rhode Island," *Rhode Island History*, 42 (August 1983), 86–100.

Dorn, Richard D., "The Civil Works Administration in Toledo, Ohio," *Northwest Ohio Quarterly*, 65/66 (Autumn 1993/Winter 1994), 4–33.

Dorsett, Lyle W., "Kansas City and the New Deal," in John Braeman, Robert W. Bremner, and David Brody, eds., *The New Deal: The State and Local Levels*. Columbus: Ohio State University Press, 1975, pp. 407–419.

Erickson, Herman, "WPA Strike and Trials of 1939," *Minnesota History*, 52 (Summer 1971), 203–214.

Fleming, Douglas L., "The New Deal in Atlanta: A Review of the Major Programs," *Atlanta Historical Journal*, 30 (Spring 1986), 23–45.

Garvey, Timothy, "The Duluth Homesteads: A Successful Experiment in Community Housing," *Minnesota History*, 46 (Spring 1978), 2–16.

Genevro, Rosalie, "Site Selection and the New York City Housing Authority, 1936–1939," *Journal of Urban History*, 12 (August 1986), 334–352.

Grant, H. Roger, and L. Edward Purcell, eds., "A Year of Struggle: Excerpts from a Farmer's Diary, 1936," *Palimpsest*, 57 (January 1976), 14–29.

——, "Implementing the AAA's Corn-Hog Program: An Iowa Farmer's Account," *Annals of Iowa*, 43 (Fall 1976), 430–442.

Greene, Larry A., "Harlem, The Depression Years: Leadership and Social Conditions," *Afro-Americans in New York Life and History*, 17 (July 1993), 33–50.

Hardaway, Roger D., "The New Deal at the Local Level: The Civil Works Administration in Grand Forks County, North Dakota," *North Dakota History*, 58 (Spring 1991), 20–30.

Holland, Reid, "The Civilian Conservation Corps in the City: Tulsa and Oklahoma City in the 1930s," *Chronicles of Oklahoma*, 53 (Fall 1975), 367–375.

Kalmar, Karen L., "Southern Black Elites and the New Deal: A Case Study of Savannah, Georgia," *Georgia Historical Quarterly*, 65 (Winter 1981), 341–355.

Knippa, Lyndon Gayle, "San Antonio II: The Early New Deal," in Cotner, et al., *Texas Cities in the Great Depression*, pp. 69–90.

Koch, Raymond L., "Politics and Relief in Minneapolis During the 1930s," *Minnesota History*, (Winter 1968), 153–170.

Lapping, Mark B., "The Emergence of Federal Public Housing: Atlanta's Techwood Project," *American Journal of Economics and Sociology*, 32 (October 1973), 379–385.

Long, Durward, "Key West and the New Deal, 1934–1936," *Florida Historical Quarterly*, 46 (January 1968), 209–218.

Lowry, Charles B., "The PWA in Tampa: A Case Study," *Florida Historical Quarterly*, 52 (April 1974), 363–380.

Marcuse, Peter, "The Beginnings of Public Housing in New York," *Journal of Urban History*, 12 (August 1986), 353–390.

Moehring, Eugene P., "Public Works and the New Deal in Las Vegas," *Nevada Historical Society Quarterly*, 24 (Summer 1981), 107–129.

Mohl, Raymond A., "Trouble in Paradise: Race and Housing in Miami During the New Deal Era," *Prologue*, 19 (Spring 1987), 7–21.

Morgan, Iwan, "Fort Wayne and the Great Depression: The New Deal Years, 1933–1940," *Indiana Magazine of History*, 80 (December 1984), 348–378.

——, "The Fort Wayne Plan: The FHA and Prefabricated Municipal Housing in the 1930s," *Historian*, 47 (August 1985), 538–559.

Nailos, Heath, "Tarpon Springs and the Great Depression," *Tampa Bay History*, 15 (Spring/Summer 1993), 71–90.

Nelson, Lawrence J., "Oscar Johnson: The New Deal and the Cotton Subsidy Payments Controversy, 1936–1937," *Journal of Southern History*, 40 (1974), 399–416.

Nelson, Clair E., "Remembering the CCC: Buck Meadows, California, 1933–1934," *Journal of Forest History*, 26 (October 1982), 184–191.

Rainard, R. Lyn, "Ready Cash on Easy Terms: Local Responses to the Depression in Lee County," *Florida Historical Quarterly*, 64 (January 1986), 284–300.

Reiman, Richard A., "The New Deal for Youth: A Cincinnati Connection," *Queen City Heritage*, 44 (Fall 1986), 36–48.

Reuchel, Frank, "New Deal Housing, Urban Poverty, and Jim Crow: Techwood and University Homes in Atlanta," *Georgia Historical Quarterly*, 81 (Winter 1997), 915–37.

Rouse, David S., "Pages from My Past: The Civilian Conservation Corps," *Wisconsin Magazine of History*, 71 (Spring 1988), 205–216.

Rynder, Constance B., "Progressive into New Dealer: Amy Maher and the Public Works Administration in Toledo," *Northwest Ohio Quarterly*, 24 (Summer 1981), 3–19.

Salmond, John A., "'The N.Y.A. at the Seaside': A New Deal Episode," *Southern California Quarterly*, 55 (Summer 1973), 209–217.

Sandeen, Eric J., "The Design of Public Housing in the New Deal: Oskar Stonovov and the Carl Mackley Houses," *American Quarterly*, 37 (Winter 1988), 645–667.

Schwartz, Joel, "The Consolidated Tenants League of Harlem: Black Self-Help vs. White Liberal Intervention in Ghetto Housing, 1934–1944," *Afro-Americans in New York Life and History*, 10 (January 1986), 31–51.

——, "Tenant Union in New York City's Low-Rent Housing, 1933–1949," *Journal of Urban History*, 12 (August 1986), 414–443.

Sheridan, Lawrence, "The College Student Employment Project at the University of Kansas, 1934–1943," *Kansas History*, 8 (Winter 1985–1986), 206–216.

Shinn, Paul L. "Eugene in the Depression, 1929–1935," *Oregon Historical Quarterly*, 86 (Winter 1985), 341–369.

Simmons, Jerold, "Dawson County Responds to the New Deal," *Nebraska History*, 62 (Spring 1981), 47–72.

Smith, Douglas L., "Continuity and Change in the Urban South: The New Deal Experience," *Atlanta Historical Journal*, 30 (Spring 1986), 7–22.

Sobczak, John N., "The Politics of Relief: Public Aid in Toledo, 1933–1938," *Northwest Ohio Quarterly*, 48 (Fall 1976), 134–142.

Soden, Dale E., "The New Deal Comes to Shawnee," *Chronicles of Oklahoma*, 43 (Summer 1985), 116–127.

Sparks, Randy J., "'Heavenly Houston' or 'Hellish Houston'?: Black Unemployment and Relief Efforts, 1929–1936," *Southern Studies*, 25 (Winter 1986), 352–366.

Stave, Bruce M., "Pittsburgh and the New Deal," in Braeman, et. al., *The New Deal*, pp. 376–406.

Swanson, Merwin W., "The New Deal in Pocatello," *Idaho Yesterdays*, 23 (Summer 1979), 53–57.

——, "Pocatello's Business Community and the New Deal," *Idaho Yesterdays*, 21 (Fall 1977), 9–18.

Taylor, Brenda Jeanete, "The New Deal and Health: Meeting Farmers' Needs in Ropesville, Texas, 1933–1943," *Journal of the West*, 36 (January 1997), 38–46.

Tidd, James Francis, Jr., "Stitching and Striking: Sewing Rooms and the 1937 Relief Strike in Hillsborough County," *Tampa Bay History*, 11 (Spring/Summer 1989), 5–21.

Tobin, Sidney, "The Early New Deal in Baton Rouge as Viewed by the Daily Press," *Louisiana History*, 10 (Fall 1969), 307–337.

Trout, Charles H., "Reconstructing Boston in the 1930s: The Historian and the City," *Proceedings of the Massachusetts Historical Society*, 90 (1978), 58–74.

Tuman, Judith Jenkins, "Austin and the New Deal," in Cotner, et al., *Texas Cities in the Great Depression*, pp. 189–207.

Vacha, John E., "They Had the Last Laugh: The WPA in Cleveland," *Timeline*, 11 (March–April 1994), 28–41.

Van Sickle, Frederick Mercer, "A Special Place: Lake Forest and the Great Depression, 1929–1940," *Illinois Historical Journal*, 79 (Summer 1988), 113–126.

Wade, Michael G., "'Farm Dorm Boys': The Origins of the NYA Resident Training Program," *Louisiana History*, 27 (Spring 1986), 117–132.

Williams, Bobby Joe, "Let There Be Light: Tennessee Valley Authority Comes to Memphis," *The West Tennessee Historical Society Papers*, 30 (1976), 43–66.

Zelman, Donald L., "Alazan-Apache Courts: A New Deal Response to Mexican-American Housing Conditions in San Antonio," *Southwestern Historical Quarterly*, 87 (October 1983), 123–150.

LOCALITIES — BOOKS

Argersinger, Jo Ann E., *Toward a New Deal in Baltimore: People and Government in the Great Depression*. Chapel Hill: University of North Carolina Press, 1988.

Biles, Roger, *Memphis in the Great Depression*. Knoxville: University of Tennessee Press, 1986.

Blumberg, Barbara, *The New Deal and the Unemployed: The View from New York City*. Lewisburg: Bucknell University Press, 1979.

Bremer, William W., *Depression Winters: New York Social Workers and the New Deal*. Philadelphia: Temple University Press, 1984.

Ford, James, *Slums and Housing, with Special Reference to New York City: History, Conditions, Policy*. New York: Arno Press; reprint of 1936 edition.

Klein, Philip, et al., *A Social Study of Pittsburgh: Community Problems and Social Services of Allegheny County*. New York: Columbia University Press, 1938.

Millet, John David, *The Works Progress Administration in New York City*. New York: Arno Press; 1978 reprint of 1938 edition.

Smith, Douglas L., *The New Deal in the Urban South*. Baton Rouge: Louisiana State University Press, 1983.

Stave, Bruce M., *The New Deal and the Last Hurrah: Pittsburgh Machine Politics*. Pittsburgh: University of Pittsburgh Press, 1970.

Trout, Charles H., *Boston, the Great Depression, and the New Deal*. New York: Oxford University Press, 1977.

LOCALITIES — DISSERTATIONS

Arnold, Joseph L., "The New Deal in the Suburbs: The Greenbelt Town Progam, 1935–1952." Ohio State University, 1968.

Bauman, John F., "The City, the Depression, and Relief: The Philadelphia Experience, 1929–1939," Rutgers University, 1969.

Daoust, Norma Lasalle, "The Perils of Providence: Rhode Island's Capital City During the Depression and New Deal." University of Connecticut, 1982.

Fleming, Douglas Lee, "Atlanta, the Depression and the New Deal." Emory University, 1984.

Fricke, Ernest B., "The Impact of the Depression in Allentown, Pennsylvania, 1930–1940." New York University, 1974.

Jones, Gene, "The Local Significance of New Deal Relief Legislation in Chicago, 1933–1940." Northwestern University, 1970.

Kotlanger, Michael John, "Phoenix, Arizona: 1920–1940," Arizona State University, 1983.

Leader, Leonard, "Los Angeles and the Great Depression," University of California at Los Angeles, 1972.

Lofton, Paul Stroman, Jr., "Social and Economic History of Columbia, South Carolina, During the Great Depression, 1929–1940," University of Texas, 1977.

Matthews, Glenna Christine, "California Middletown: The Social History of San Jose in the Depression," Stanford University, 1977.

Meister, Richard J., "A History of Gary, Indiana, 1930–1940," University of Notre Dame, 1967.

Stellhorn, Paul Anthony, "Depression and Decline: Newark, New Jersey, 1919–1941," Rutgers University, 1982.

Verdiccio, Joseph J., "New Deal Work Relief and New York City, 1933–1938," New York University, 1980.

COUNTIES — ARTICLES

Autobee, Robert, "Rye Patch Dam: A New Deal for the Lower Humboldt," *Nevada Historical Society Quarterly*, 37 (Fall 1994), 200–214.

Brent, Joseph E., "The Civil Works Administration in Western Kentucky: Work Relief's Dress Rehearsal Under Fire," *Filson Club Historical Quarterly*, 67 (April 1993), 259–276.

Hinson, Billy G., "The Civilian Conservation Corps in Mobile County, Alabama," *Alabama Review*, 45 (October 1992), 243–256.

Hurt, R. Douglas, "Gaining Control of the Environment: The Morton County Land Utilization Project in the Kansas Dust Bowl," *Kansas History*, 19 (Summer 1996), 140–153.

Keathley, Clarence R., "Reflections on Public Welfare in Washington County, Missouri, 1919–1941," *Missouri Historical Review*, 82 (October 1987), 51–70.

COUNTY — BOOK

Tweton, D. Jerome, *The New Deal at the Grass Roots: Programs for the People in Otter Tail County, Minnesota*. St. Paul: Minnesota Historical Society Press, 1988.

COUNTY — DISSERTATIONS

Craft, John Taylor, "Depression and New Deal in Pendleton: A History of a West Virginia County from the Great Crash to Pearl Harbor, 1929–1941," Pennsylvania State University, 1980.

Tuttle, Timothy Clarke, "Surviving the Depression: The New Deal Comes to Dutchess County," New York University, 1996.

A NOTE ON THE EDITOR

Bernard Sternsher is Emeritus Professor of History at Bowling Green State University. He grew up in Fall River, Massachusetts, and studied at the University of Alabama and Boston University. He has written *Rexford Tugwell and the New Deal* and *Consensus, Conflict, and American Historians,* and has edited *Hitting Home: The Great Depression in Town and Country; Women of Valor* (with Judith Sealander); *The New Deal: Laissez Faire to Socialism;* and *The Negro in Depression and War.* He lives in Perrysburg, Ohio.